298th Army Band:

A History

Allen R. Lawless

Harry F. Reinert, Editor

DEDICATION

This book is dedicated to the soldier-musicians who served in the 298th Army Band and its various designations—the 108th Cavalry Band, the 156th Infantry Band, the London Base Command Band, the European Theater of Operations (ETO) Band, the 300th Infantry Band, the 298th Infantry Band, the 298th Army Ground Forces (AGF) Band, and the unofficial but popular designation of the Berlin Brigade Band. I am grateful for your service to our country and to the Berliners.

Table of Contents

ACKNOWLEDGMENTS

To Mr. Frank J. Rosato, the first bandmaster of the 156th Infantry Band and eventual first bandmaster of the 298th in the immediate aftermath of World War II, I am humbled by your gracious gift of a text that comprised the bulk of my research of the 298th's early history. This text contained evidence of your tenacious, dogged determination to see the band perform music as its primary mission while in England. Reading Henry Glaviano's book inspired me to write this account of the "rest" of the 298th's history.

To Mr. James Ridolfo, nephew of Frank J. Rosato, thank you for your gracious support. Your prompt and courteous responses to my queries and the surprising and most welcome gift of photographs have helped me portray your uncle's work in a fitting manner. I sincerely hope this effort is worthy of your uncle's contribution in leading the bands under his charge.

To those 298th veterans who have passed on since contributing to this book, including Frank Rosato, Ralph Cuellar, Bill Ervin, Roger Woodrum, Chuck Ramsey, Bob Badgley, Richard Naujoks, R.J. Johnson, Ross Maser and Tom Trimble, thank you for the opportunity to have served with you (in the case of Ralph, Richard, Ross and Tom). Your selfless contributions in relating your stories when your own time here with us was limited reminds me how valuable we are to each other.

Contributors, in thought, word and deed are:

Badgley	Bob (Badge)	Lant	Richard
Bankston	Thomas Jackson	Larson	Jerry
Barboza	David	Lindstrom	Ward
Bardeck	Lothar (Joe)	Loc	Jim
Barnes	Jeff	Long	Billy Jack
Barzal	Steve	Lopez	Angel
Bertel	Markus	Luvaas	Karen
Biring	Larry	Malone	Bruce
Bradford	FL (Brad)	Martin	Joseph
Brett	Don	Mason	John
Brookfield	John	Mastric	Todd
Brown	Lawrence (Fish or Blue)	Mazak	Mark
Bumgarner	Michael	Mitchell	Shawn
Carpenter	Thomas	Mittag	Fred
Chiles	Larry	Mutter	Leonard "Mac"
Claes	Ray	Naujoks	Richard
Consaul	Charles W.T. (Frogg)	Nelson	Al
Conwell	Michael	Olszyk	David
Cordero	Robert	Papa	Sebastian (Sebby)
Cornwall	James	Parmenter	John
Crowder	George	Percoski	Erik
Creighton	Paul	Perry	Dutch
Dodson	Ken	Pickrell	Kevin
Eason	Dan	Pittman	Joe E.
Ellis	Mark "Elmo"	Rabert	David

Entwistle	Kevin	Randolph	Beth
Ervin	William "Bill"	Raschke (Gagnon)	Cindy
Eschenfelder	Chris	Ratliff	David
Evangelista	Paul	Reinert	Harry
Fischer	Dick	Reinhart	David (Skip)
Fleshman	Rick	Ridolfo	Joseph T.
Freeman	Phil	Roncari	Judith
Gainey	Patrick	Ronnbeck	Robert
Garcia	Robert	Rosato	Frank
Garcia	Juan	Rynerson	Robert
Garrett	Horace	Salamone	Paul
Genzel	Achim	Schwanke	Inge
Gerding	John	Scifres	Don
Gerding	Carla	Seals	Mike
Gerry	Sally	Shieff	Rick and Amy
Gleason	Bruce	Silvia	Bob
Gottwig	Jeff	Smith	David M.
Hamilton	Randy	Smith	David A.
Hanson	Johnny	Smurthwaite	Jeff
Harper	Jeff	St. Clair	Vic
Hartney	Tom	Steger	Dan
Hawkins	Bobby	Svoma	Kyle
Healy	Pat	Sweezey	Tom
Hermann	Dan	Tapia	Al
Heron	Carol	Thompson	Allen
Hill	Larry	Todd (Rohrbaugh)	Kim
Hoffmann	Reiner	Tomes	George
Hopkins	John	Tootill	Tom
Hurvitz	Lou	Trimble	Tom and Lesa
Jackson	Bob	Von Bronewski	Reinhard
Johns	Chuck	Von Kamp	Bill
Johnson	Robert J. (R.J.)	Wagner	Chris
Johnston	William	Wagner	Robert
Jorgensen	Mike	Wason	Cheryl
Karpen	Sy	Weems	Billy
Kaufman	Mike	White	James
Keller	David	Wilklow	Harry
Kilmer	Mike	Williams	Larry
Kimata	Norman	Williams	Robert
Kinkennon	John	Wilson	Doug
Pollock	Willie (P.K.)	Woodrum	Roger
Poulin	Alfred J. (Shorty)	Yost	Mike
Pursifull	Monte		

To 298th clarinetist and veteran Harry Reinert, thank you for editing the manuscript and teaching me more than a few things about the skill of writing. Your patience with me, an inexperienced and fledgling beginner, is the sole reason this book is complete. We, working together, completed more in one year than I had in nine.

And to my wife Margaret, whose support and confidence keeps me going, my love and deepest thanks.

INTRODUCTION

The 298th Army Band, operating under several different names throughout its history, was a normal line band of the U.S. Army assigned to the U.S. Sector of Berlin, Germany, immediately following World War II. The word "line" band is used to denote that this band differentiated from the more "premier", "special", or "major command" bands of the U.S. Army that were stationed in Washington, D.C., the U.S. Military Academy at West Point, and even the 33rd Army Band stationed in Germany.

From the time the 298th and 300th Infantry Bands, operating under a single banner as the ETO Band, arrived in Berlin on July 8, 1945 until its deactivation on September 15, 1994, a period of more than 49 years had passed. The band served continually during that period of time, a distinction that resulted in the band's recognition as the longest-serving U.S. military unit in the city. While the names of the band changed slightly throughout this lengthy period of service, notably the London Base Command Band, the 298th Infantry Band, the ETO Band, the 298th Army Ground Forces Band, the 298th Army Band, or the Berlin Brigade Band, the unit was the same. The musical mission of the band also remained the same, namely to provide appropriate musical support to the military command and, when and where appropriate, to the community at large. The band's secondary, non-musical mission varied slightly over the years, however, ranging from providing security to driver support to medical support at the hospital back to security.

This 49-year period encompassed events of extraordinary historical significance including the Potsdam Conference, the Berlin Airlift, and the post-war massive refugee influx from east to west halted only by the erection of the Berlin Wall in August 1961. Other notable events included the American/Soviet standoff at Checkpoint Charlie in October 1961, the Tripartite Agreement with the Soviets in 1971, and the killing of Major Arthur D. Nicholson, an officer assigned to the U.S. Military Liaison Mission, in 1985.

Countless incidents involving Soviet aircraft harassing Allied aircraft in the three air corridors from West Germany to West Berlin and return resulted in a number of deaths. The less dangerous, but otherwise significant intimidation by the Soviets toward the Western Allies extended over into other areas including the interference with rail, truck, and barge transportation, electrical power, and fuel infrastructure. The "hateful Wall," as described by President Clinton in 1994, represented an even deadlier form of threat when East German border guards gunned down over 200 people in their attempts to escape to the West.

The Cold War, a significant political and military struggle between the West and East, simmered throughout this entire period up until November 9,

1989 when the Wall fell. The voice of the East German people broke the shackles that bound them, evidenced by the East German government's announcement on November 9, 1989 that the Wall stood open for all. Unrestricted travel would be permitted to and from East Berlin. This single event reverberated through Europe and the world, not just Germany, and is still being felt today.

During these and other times, the 298th Army Band was there to support military and civilian leadership whenever called upon to do so.

While the band's principal and fundamental mission was to support the U.S. military garrison in Berlin, the band was often called to serve and perform throughout the rest of Europe, the British Isles, and even into Africa. Most of these performances occurred in the latter part of the band's history, however, after the political and military situation had stabilized.

Military bands, including the 298th, are no different than any other military unit. They are manned by men and women from different backgrounds, experiences, and principles. But the discipline and art of music is common to all band musicians. Each was trained in music to one extent or another; many held advanced degrees in music education and music performance. While one can argue that the musical element was stronger during one period as opposed to another, or more inherent to one soldier than in another, the soldiers of the 298th did their duty throughout the entire 49-year period following World War II. There is no question that the 298th Army Band had a significant positive impact to the U.S. military's community relations with the Berliners and to U.S. Army Europe. The expressions of support and friendship expressed by the Berliners are evidence of that. They were an intensely responsive audience whenever and wherever the band performed in the city; they expressed heartfelt loss when the 298th was to be no more.

BEFORE THE WAR

The 298th Army Band traces its lineage to the 156th Infantry Band of the Louisiana National Guard (Glaviano, 1992)[1] The original musicians of the 156th Infantry Band stemmed from the Louisiana National Guard Band, an element of 28 men in the original Table of Organization. Louisiana State University itself featured a robust Reserve Officer's Training Corps (ROTC) program, requiring all first and second year students, with few exceptions, to enroll. LSU Band members also participated in the program.

In a curious mix of civilian/military protocol, the assistant band director of the LSU Band was also the warrant officer of the National Guard Band. Frank Rosato would remain as the bandmaster of this unit throughout its pre-World War II history, throughout the war, and the immediate aftermath. Rosato, son of a university music professor, demonstrated a passion for both music and leadership. He transferred that passion into the leadership—musical and military—throughout his period of service.

The Selective Service Act of 1940, the first peacetime draft enacted by the U.S. Congress in U.S. history, required men between 21 and 36 to register with local draft boards. The period of service was only 12 months and the age range was modest, but as the hostilities in Europe and in the Far East accelerated, these attributes changed in late summer 1941 to require service beyond 12 months.

The Selective Service Act (SSA) of 1940 was doubtlessly enacted as a preparatory measure in response to the escalating war in Europe and the Far East. Nazi Germany's efforts to expand its *"Lebensraum"* and the Empire of Japan's conquests to grab critical raw materials through the 1930s created political instability in the world. While the official policy of the United States during this time was to stay neutral, the United Kingdom's prime minister Winston Churchill's push to involve the United States resulted in a gradual involvement, witnessed by the Lend-Lease Act and other types of direct military aid to the U.K. and the Soviet Union.

The members of the 156th Infantry Band who were eligible to register under the SSA did so in compliance with the law. But in addition to the initial SSA of 1940, President Roosevelt called for mobilization of various units of the National Guard on November 25, 1940. This callup involved the 156th Infantry Band, its parent regiment, the 156th Infantry, and the 61st Brigade of the 31st Infantry (Dixie) Division, among other units. President Roosevelt called for 12 months of continuous active service. Shortly after mobilization, the members of the National Guard band were given the option to discharge or to remain. All but nine members opted to discharge.

156th Infantry Regiment

These nine musicians were then assigned for a paper assignment to the 108th

3

Cavalry Band, which was under the direction of Warrant Officer Frank Rosato. On November 25, 1940, the 108th Cavalry Band was redesignated as the 156th Infantry Band. By late December 1940, the band had fully activated along with the entire 31st Infantry Division and had deployed to Camp Blanding, Florida, for intensive military training.

At this time in the history of Army bands, the Army had no typical or standard mission for regimental bands during wartime. The decision as to what to do with a regimental band was left entirely to its commander. The regimental commander of the 156th Infantry, Colonel James H. Kuttner, decreed that the regimental band would not function as a military band during normal duty hours. The band would function as a military unit. Specifically, the band trained as litter bearers and performed other duties of a supportive nature. While off-duty, however, Glaviano reported that the band frequently rehearsed and performed for themselves and the rest of the regiment. This practice carried through the entire period that the band was assigned to the 156th Infantry Regiment.

Camp Blanding, located southwest of Jacksonville in north-central Florida, was a rustic encampment with few amenities. Glaviano's book displays several photographs that depict dusty roads, tent encampments, and ramshackle buildings that had been hurriedly constructed.

When the band wasn't out marching 20 mile forced marches with full packs and 30 mile road marches with field packs, it marched up the company street playing reveille each morning. The rest of the day was spent in other military training to include first aid and the inevitable KP and other ancillary duties. Nevertheless, Rosato made sure that the band's instruments were nearby, even following the grueling road marches, and ordered the band to play as the rest of the regiment finished the road march. This endeared the band to the rest of the regiment because they saw that the band performed its military mission and took

31st Infantry Division (Dixie)

care of the esprit element as well. Private First Class Oliver East composed the regimental march, entitled *Men of the Hundred and Fifty Sixth*, which quickly became a favorite with the regiment.

The band acquired a fair amount of sheet music throughout this period due to its previous affiliation with the 108th Cavalry Band and through Rosato's father, who was a longtime professor of music at Tulane University.

Glaviano wrote: One evening, drummer Frank Vicari went to Jacksonville, Florida, to listen to any dance bands that happened to be playing in the local nightclubs and hotels. He listened to a "society band" at the George Washington Hotel and met its leader. Frank told him about the Army band and that they would like to form a dance band but had no music. Frank asked the bandleader if he had any old music that he could give him. The bandleader gave Frank about 25 stock arrangements that he was no longer using. A "stock" is a store-bought arrangement of music for use by dance bands as opposed to a special arrangement for a special band. These stocks were just what the Army band needed to start a dance band.

Despite the regimental commander's insistence that the band not function as a musical ensemble while on-duty, the band did find ways to get in rehearsal time. Due to the musicians' close affiliation with New Orleans and that style of jazz, there was intense desire on the part of the musicians to play that music. Using the stock arrangements procured, a dance band was formed and began to play.

Mr. Rosato, who played 1ˢᵗ trumpet in the dance band and led the ensemble, had been promoted to Chief Warrant Officer by this time. He provided enough leadership to have persuaded Sammie Anzelmo and Nick Gagliano (4th tenor and 3rd alto, respectively) to give the dance band a try despite their relative inexperience. They enjoyed the experience, evidently, which was deepened by their listening to New Orleans-based music on the radio at night.

Along with Mr. Rosato's promotion, other changes to the dance band also occurred. Bill Reynolds, bass, stepped down in favor of Joe Labruno, who had played in Louis Prima's band before the army came along. Andrew Wrable replaced Billy Chapelle on second trumpet as well.

Mr. Rosato was able to wangle some daytime rehearsal for the dance band and they took advantage of an extended lunch break to rehearse until about 2:00 P.M. most days. By this time, the band began to play for dances in the division recreation hall and this later expanded to playing for all the USO shows that performed at Camp Blanding while the band was there. An affiliation with the USO came into play later.

The band's first experience in playing for the general public occurred during one week in April 1941, when the band went to Ocala, Silver Springs, and St. Augustine, Florida. In addition to the gigs they played, the band was able to ride glass-bottomed boats in Silver Springs, which evidently was the scene where many of the Tarzan movies were filmed.

The band interrupted its training at Camp Blanding at the end of May 1941 by reporting for additional training in southern Louisiana for the summer months. Following this stint, the band went back to Camp Blanding for an additional two months and then in November 1941, went to North and South Carolina for winter maneuvers, bivouacking near Charleston. Following this series of exercises, the band once again went back to Camp Blanding.

On December 7, 1941, shortly before the band was to have ended its active federal service, events would overtake the men of the 156th Infantry Band in ways they could not have foreseen.

OUTBREAK OF WORLD WAR II

Toward the end of the band's 12-month federal service, the empire of Japan attacked the Hawaiian Islands' naval, air, and ground forces in and near Pearl Harbor. The date is stamped in American history: December 7, 1941. Following President Roosevelt's determined speech to Congress the following day, Congress declared war on Japan. Several days later, Germany declared war on the United States. Suddenly the U.S. was enmeshed in a global war, and while there was some resistance to to it, the country came together like never before. Military forces were organized, trained, and the industrial might of the United States was quickly transformed to a complete and total war effort. Nothing less than unconditional surrender of the Axis powers, which had grown to include Italy, could be considered.

These realities were not lost on the 156th Band. The soldiers of the band, now involved in the war for its duration, continued to train as soldiers during the day and entertained the troops at night. There is no doubt that most of the members, having completed the mandated 12-month period of active federal service, were ready to return home. The attack on Pearl Harbor precluded that, and there was no lack of ill will as to the timing of that event. While no military band is immune from grumbling, the band dug in and under its capable leadership, performed its military duties with the same passion as it performed its unofficial musical duties.

The regiment directed a new mission for the band. There were rumors of possible submarine landings by German U-Boats, so the band and the 156th Infantry Regiment redeployed to Fort Fisher located north of Myrtle Beach, South Carolina. The regiment, with the band, was directed to prevent such landings. While stationed at Fort Fisher, some troops did obtain leave time and this helped morale considerably.

Moving around was getting to be a habit and in mid-March, 1942 the 31st Division was ordered to Camp Bowie, Texas. While on the way, they found occasion to perform impromptu concerts in Savannah, Georgia; Gainesville, Florida; and Natchez, Mississippi. Finally, in Mandeville, Louisiana, the band had an opportunity to visit with family members. The reception was a wonderfully welcome respite.

The tour at Camp Bowie was also short-lived; the band remained there only until September, 1942. Since the purpose of Camp Bowie was a training station for soldiers departing for eventual combat, the 156th Infantry Band was only one of 16 other regimental bands. Yet the band was selected to perform at all the USO shows which were prevalent and popular at the time. One of the main USO performers was actress Carole Landis. The band's relationship and friendship with Ms. Landis would prove to be a valuable

6

experience in the band's later service in London.

The 156th Infantry Regiment was an element of the 61st Brigade of the 31st Infantry (Dixie) Division. This assignment was changed, however, when the Army adopted its "triangular" concept respective to its divisions. An infantry division under the older "square" concept consisted of four infantry regiments. In adopting the triangular concept, the typical infantry division would be comprised of only three infantry regiments. Therefore, in mid-1942, the 156th Infantry Regiment was released from the 31st Infantry Division. The 31st Division ultimately deployed to the Pacific where it served with distinction. The 156th Infantry Regiment with the Regimental Band shipped out to England.

After receiving orders to report to Ft. Dix, New Jersey, and then to New York City for embarkation to England for war service, the band boarded the H.M.S *Orantes Barrow* for transport across the Atlantic. The regimental commander had initially ordered the band to leave its instruments behind and not to have them loaded aboard ship, but Mr. Rosato was able to convince him to rescind that order. At the last minute, the instruments were loaded on board and it would be possible for the band to perform as a band, a subject of great concern to Mr. Rosato.

156th Infantry Band

The voyage itself, while uncomfortable, was uneventful. The band arrived in Liverpool in October, 1942 and traveled further to Broadway on Avon, designated as its next encampment.

The ubiquitous military training continued, but Mr. Rosato showed determination and doggedness to seize every opportunity for the band to perform as musicians. Parades, concerts, dances were supported by the band, and it wasn't long before the band began developing a reputation as a fine musical ensemble. This was not lost on the regimental commander, however, and there was some pressure put on Mr. Rosato to reduce this perceived frivolity. Despite this, Mr. Rosato secured the regimental commander's permission on a number of occasions for the band to travel to London. One such event occurred in November, 1942 for a performance at the Washington Red Cross Club and other locations. A subsequent performance the next day at Kew Barracks was met with wild enthusiasm; and on the day after that, the band performed in front of King Peter of Yugoslavia at the English Speaking Union. Mr. Rosato's determination to have the band perform as a band was beginning to pay off.

After returning to Broadway on Avon following these engagements for more military training, the band returned to London in late November for another series of performances, and the friendships resulting from that experience would benefit the band even more.

The 156th Infantry Regiment already had a connection to London. Company I of the regiment was assigned to guard the London Base Command, which was the U.S. Headquarters. Also, the regimental recreational officer, Captain Citrano, happened to be a good friend of Rosato's. Mr. Rosato learned that Citrano was scheduled to make a trip to London to secure some athletic equipment, and Rosato asked his friend a favor—to ask the U.S. Headquarters for permission for the band to come to London yet again. Citrano agreed to do so.

Quite by coincidence, Carole Landis happened to be in London on a USO tour and was in negotiations with Brigadier General Pleas B. Rogers, the commander of all U.S. troops in London, for eventual USO performances there. After Landis requested the services of an American band and was told that there were no American bands available, Landis informed General Rogers of the 156th Infantry Band while she and her entourage were at Camp Bowie, Texas. She explained that this band was exactly what she needed. In overhearing this conversation, Citrano mentioned that the 156th Infantry Band was in the north of England, only 100 miles away, and could be obtained with the appropriate approvals. General Rogers, seeing the problem essentially solved, quickly agreed and issued the necessary orders.

The 156th made the trip to London on temporary duty and stayed three days, playing a number of shows. Landis, once again being completely happy with the band's performance, suggested to General Rogers that it would be a marvelous idea for a band to be stationed permanently in London. This idea was echoed, of course, by Mr. Rosato and General Rogers began seeing the value in having an asset like the 156th directly in London.

The band again returned to London on temporary duty a number of times, each time incurring more and more resistance from the regimental commander. Finally, the regimental commander received orders from General Rogers to release the 156th Infantry Band to Special Services Headquarters of the London Base Command. Mr. Rosato and the 156th Infantry Band made their last trek to London. CWO Rosato had prevailed – the band would stay a band and not be subjected to a steady diet of military training, above and beyond what was tactically necessary.

DUTY IN LONDON

Transferred to London Base Command, the band took up residence near St. James Place in January 1943. As Glaviano wrote, "this was the first time in their military career of more than two years, except for the brief stay in the warehouse in Broadway on Avon, that the band moved into a real building rather than tents... It was a bare building, but it was home. The band divided itself into small groups of three to five men to share rooms. They used army folding cots, which they carried, as beds. This was January and it was cold at that time in London and there was no heat in the building." Despite these conditions, the band was happy to be where they were.

London Base Command

The band continued to perform, playing dozens of parades, concerts, and dances, and became a unit of Special Services, London Base Command, under the command of General Rogers. At this time, they changed their shoulder patch from the 31st Infantry (Dixie) Division to that of the London Base Command. Consequently, the name of the band changed to that of the London Base Command Band.

London Base Command

The daily routine became more musically oriented. After rising, barracks clean-up and chow in the mess hall located about a block away, physical training was led by an NCO out in the street. This consisted of about 15 minutes of calisthenics. Afterwards, there would be either some kind of military training or—more often—a rehearsal. The building featured a room on the second floor which was large enough to accommodate all 28 musicians.

More USO shows, radio broadcasts, and events with celebrities such as Bob Hope comprised their performances. There were Sunrise services, soccer games at Wembley Stadium, gigs at the Officer's Club and always at the American Red Cross Club. They performed virtually anywhere at any time.

One problem remained. With only 28 men in the band, it was increasingly difficult to respond to the number of requests for band support. Mr. Rosato made a number of requests to expand the authorized number from 28 to 56. His reasoning was simple: a regimental band numbering 28 could readily support a regiment. But a command the size of the London Base Command, with the number of soldiers in the thousands, required a larger band to accommodate all the requests the band received. Many of the British military bands numbered far more than 28 musicians each, and there were many more British bands than American. Despite this rationale, General Rogers was somewhat reluctant to increase the size of the band. Mr. Rosato, however, continued to repeat this request with the general at every opportunity. Meanwhile, the buildup to the eventual invasion of Europe continued. American troop presence in England continued to grow and the opportunities for musical support increased in proportion.

In June 1943, the band moved to new quarters near Hyde Park.

Mr. Rosato wrote, "Once in London, we were so much in demand that General Rogers asked what more did I need to take care of all the work that was being assigned to the band. Things happen fast in the army. So, now we are in London and are known as the London Base Command Band and can now function more efficiently.

We provided the following services:

1. A beautiful fifty-six piece Marching Band,
2. A beautiful fifty-six piece Concert Band
3. Two fifteen piece Dance bands,
4. A Glee Club, and
5. A five piece String Unit for special occasions requested by the General to entertain V.I.P.'s, including Madame Chiang Kai-shek (Rosato, 1992).²"

Mr. Rosato had the general's help in expanding his band. General Rogers had under his command four other bands in addition to the London Base Command Band. He issued a verbal order to Mr. Rosato and to each of the other four bandmasters that Mr. Rosato would visit each of the other bands, audition and select from each band seven musicians who would then be assigned to the London Base Command Band. Assurances were given that this manner of cherry-picking would not devastate any given section within the band. In other words, Mr. Rosato would not bleed any one band dry of premium quality musicians. Mr. Rosato would then have the capability of massing his expanded band or splitting it up for multiple performances at the same time. This plan was executed and Mr. Rosato selected his musicians.

Creation of the 298th and 300th Infantry Bands

General Rogers received from Washington, D.C. the news that he was not authorized to have a 56-man band. After relaying the bad news to Mr. Rosato, the general instructed Rosato to keep his musicians, but to split them up "on paper." One band would become the 300th Infantry Band and the other the 298th Infantry Band. Each band would number the maximum allowable strength of 28. Corporal Jim Abel, who had a master's degree in music, accepted an appointment as Warrant Officer, Junior Grade, and was appointed Warrant Officer bandmaster of the 298th Infantry Band, effective 7 March 1944.

Adjustments were made to both the 298th and 300th bands in terms of instrumentation, staffing and promotions, music preparation and training, and in time, Mr. Rosato was able to field two 16-piece dance bands at the same time. Each of these bands could also field an 8-man combo. Those who didn't perform in dance bands or combos were put to use as well by participation in parades and non-jazz events. This maximized use of the band in as many ways as possible while still providing time for training and maintenance of instruments and equipment.

Both bands were booked six nights per week to perform at dance halls and clubs. In addition to performing, the musicians made sincere efforts to be appropriate ambassadors of good will.

ETO Band

General Dwight Eisenhower arrived in London in December 1943 to command Supreme Headquarters, Allied Expeditionary Forces (SHAEF). His mission was to command the forces that would invade the continent of Europe and defeat the Axis powers. General Eisenhower's presence in commanding SHAEF gradually brought a new designation for the band--the European Theater of Operations (ETO) Band. A new shoulder patch that depicted the breaking the chains that enslaved Europe was designed for the band to wear. Live music was the principal form of entertainment, so the band was in heavy demand. The band found new capabilities within themselves. A men's glee club was formed and also performed. Parades and ceremonies filled out the calendar.

ETO

According to records in the National Archives in College Park, Maryland, the 298th Army Band was activated at London, England, Westminster, per General Order 13, Headquarters Special Troops ETOUSA, effective 20 December 1943. The commanding officer was Captain Sidney F. Birge, Infantry.

London continued to be in the middle of an active war zone as the Germans launched V-1 and V-2 rockets from the Continent. These buzz bombs and rockets landed, exploded, and caused severe damage. The V-2 rockets were especially feared because they traveled at supersonic speeds, exploding without any air raid warning. Sal Anzelmo, saxophone and clarinet player with the band, was the recipient of two Purple Hearts for wounds received from two separate attacks (Roberts, 1985).[3] Despite the ever present danger, the band continued to travel and perform, connecting for brief periods with musicians from Glenn Miller's band and Artie Shaw's band (without Artie, who was still in the States). Glaviano wrote that the musicians rehearsed together and collaborated, sharing their stories and their experiences.

Change to 298th Army Ground Forces Band

Just two days before D-Day, the 298th Army Band on 4 June 1944 was reorganized and redesignated as the 298th Army Ground Forces Band under General Order #18, Headquarters Special Troops, ETOUSA. The order was dated 29 May 1944; the initial station was London, England. The commanding officer was identified as WOJG James W. Abel.

In February 1945, the band supported a "Celebrity Cavalcade" at the Royal Albert Hall. This was a fund raiser and the program featured many distinguished artists and bands, including 12-year-old Petula Clark, who grew up to become a star known for many popular songs in the 1960s. Glaviano wrote that after this very lengthy show, which went into the early hours of the morning, Petula and her father missed the last subway train back home and were stranded. Mr. Rosato agreed to transport the young girl and her father home on the band's bus. While on the late-night trip to the girl's home, a trip that took about an hour, the young girl sang on the bus accompanied by a few acoustic instruments. On later occasions, Petula made a few rehearsals with the band and performed on several occasions as well, as often as her father could accompany her. The entire family became close to the band.

VICTORY IN EUROPE

The European war came to a close on May 8, 1945 with the German surrender in Reims, France. The political decisions that had taken place prior to Germany's surrender initially divided up the country into three zones of occupation. Berlin, the capital of the defeated country, would also be divided into three zones of occupation. The Soviet Union, the United Kingdom and the United States took initial steps toward occupying their respective zones. Within a short time, France was added as a Western Ally and she received a portion of territory in the southwestern part of Germany along with a section of northwestern Berlin.

Germany lay in ruins. In particular, her larger cities were devastated. The center of Berlin was almost completely destroyed, and what was left of the city was being systematically ransacked by the Soviets, who had taken the city in April after a monumental battle. The Soviets were removing equipment and infrastructure in the name of "war reparations." They were also committing horrendous crimes against the Berliners, including robbery, rape, and murder.

It was also not in the best interest of the Soviet Union to permit the Western Allies to take possession of their respective occupation sectors of Berlin, so the Soviets employed delaying tactics to keep the Western Allies out throughout May and June. Finally, after the Allies retreated from the Elbe River and returned to their zones of occupation, the Soviets permitted the Americans, British, and eventually the French, to take possession of their assigned sectors in Berlin.

Back in London, General Rogers called Mr. Rosato in for a talk. Now that the European war was over and the band had been on continuous active duty since November 1940, the musicians in the band were anxious to return home to their families. Knowing this, the general hesitated before he told Mr. Rosato that he would like to have the band support President Truman at the Potsdam Conference. Potsdam had been selected as the venue for the last Allied Conference of the war. Only the Big Three—the U.S., the U.K., and the Soviet Union—would attend. France was not invited and would not take part. This Conference, General Rogers explained, was extremely important politically and performance by the band at the meeting would provide the proper character and dignity expected of such an event. The downside of this request was that the Conference was scheduled to begin on July 17, more than two months after the German surrender and long after the band members had expected to return home. General Rogers also said that he would prefer for the band to perform at the formal ceremony that raised the U.S. colors at the American Headquarters in Berlin. This event would also take place in mid-July. The general was careful to present this not as an order, neither written nor verbal, but rather as a request.

After the initial shock and the inevitable complaining, the essence of the request became clear. It was an opportunity to be a part of history and to contribute to the post-war effort. Mr. Rosato wanted to take vehicles to Berlin rather than fly; he felt that he and the band should see the physical condition of the Continent as a result of the all-encompassing war. General Rogers concurred and signed off on the necessary travel orders. The general told Mr. Rosato that the band would travel as the 300th Infantry Band and the 298th Infantry Band, purely for logistical reasons. General Rogers assured Mr. Rosato that the band was essentially one unit, but it was necessary that the band travel as two elements.

The last performance of the ETO Band in London occurred on June 6, 1945. Afterwards, band members packed their equipment and their personal belongings into appropriate vehicles and set off on June 8 for Southampton and the ferry to the Continent. The men spent the night on board the ferry just off Le Havre, France, and disembarked the next day. Since the harbor was full of sunken vessels as a result of the furious fighting which had occurred there during the war, it was difficult to navigate safely through the debris. Their next stop was Etretat, a small village north of Le Havre, where they spent the night of June 9.

Gasoline was a problem. Their vehicles—a curious assortment of reconnaissance vehicles, trailer trucks for equipment, at least one bus and other trucks for the musicians—all needed fuel. They were traveling on verbal orders only and had no written justification for fuel. But they were able to get the needed gas and rations and they set off again.

Both elements, traveling separately, made their way to and through Paris, again receiving gas and rations along the way. The 300th traveled a northerly route through Belgium and into Aachen, Germany. The 298th, traveling in two trucks only, passed through Paris and proceeded on through Belgium as well. Both units passed through Duren, Köln, Düsseldorf, Essen, and Dortmund. The devastation was everywhere. Dead animals and decomposing bodies lay rotting in the open.

In preparing for Berlin, decision makers in the Western Zone of Germany ordered the 2nd Armored Division to Berlin to assume initial occupation duties.

The division established a staging area for the Berlin occupation troops near Bienrode (Braunschweig). Facilities were established along what would become the Helmstedt autobahn to accommodate up to 5,000 soldiers who were to make the overland march to Berlin. Finally, Company B of the 208th Engineer Battalion and two officers and men from the Reconnaissance Detachment, HQ, 2nd Armored Division, were alerted and moved to Babelsberg on 29 June 1945. Babelsberg was a central, Soviet-controlled staging area for the Western Allies. According to Colonel Frank Howley in his book *Berlin Command*, this area just outside Potsdam, southwest of Berlin, was guarded by Soviet sentries. Once admitted, even the Western Allies could not leave without Soviet permission. This proved to be a source of genuine frustration and irritation for Howley and is well documented in his book.

Once the Soviets finally ceased their delaying tactics, these 2nd Armored Division elements were placed on special duty with the Berlin District Headquarters.

The ceremony that officially changed over the U.S.-assigned sector from the Soviets to the Americans took place on Andrews Barracks on 4 July 1945. A photo from this ceremony depicting the 2nd Armored Division Band in the foreground documents this ceremony.

2nd AD Band, Andrews, 4 Jul 45

Following the ceremony and toward the end of the duty day, the 2nd Armored Division Band set up a bivouac in the Grunewald, along with many other combat units.

Howley documented another ceremony which was held on what would become "4.Juli.Platz", otherwise known as the "Four-Ring". The Four-Ring, a large, paved area approximately two city blocks long and one city block wide, was conveniently located parallel to and alongside the Telefunken Research Complex, an area of Lichterfelde that would be a focal point for U.S. troops in Berlin for the next 49 years.

All of this preceded the actual arrival of the 298th and 300th Bands out of London. While the 2nd Armored Division was entering the city, the 298th and 300th Bands were preparing for their own march to Berlin for eventual support of the Potsdam Conference. Leaving Hoechst, near Frankfurt, both bands made the final push to Berlin, arriving in the U.S. Sector in the late afternoon of 8 July 1945.

Glaviano wrote that he and Mr. Rosato took residence in private homes, presumably undamaged by the more recent artillery shelling by the Soviets and bombing during the war by the Americans and British air forces. The rest of the band billeted in private homes as well. These were temporary arrangements, and the band soon set up in the old Telefunken complex, which very quickly became known as McNair Barracks.

The Potsdam Conference began on July 16, 1945 and ran until August 2, 1945. Held at the Cecilienhof estate in Potsdam, a large and beautifully manicured villa, the setting was idyllic and peaceful, in stark contrast to the war that only recently had ended. President Truman and the bulk of his entourage stayed at a villa that the media dubbed "The Little White House." Located at Kaiserstrasse 2 in Babelsberg, this villa formed the backdrop for the band's performances nearly every day, generally in the late afternoon. A large lawn in the rear of the villa provided space for the band, which set up just in front of the veranda.

President Truman's aide, Charlie Ross, called Mr. Rosato and informed him of the guest list for the afternoon's entertainment. Mr. Rosato would then prepare a program and rehearse the band. Regardless what Mr. Rosato programmed, the president often had a request. Favoring the Missouri Waltz, the band played that piece on numerous occasions. President Truman always acknowledged the piece with a smile and a wave to the band. On occasion, the president would sit at the piano and play a little. Mr. Rosato observed that he always seemed to have a great time.

The band played a mixture of marches, overtures, waltzes and popular songs of the day including "Peg O' My Heart," "By the Light of the Silvery Moon," and "The White Cliffs of Dover."

Just prior to one performance, Mr. Rosato recalled Premier Stalin's arrival at "The Little White House." Beginning with a cavalcade of motorcycles ridden by tall, angular, and unsmiling Soviet sentries armed with submachine guns, they parked their vehicles and silently took their position at port arms. Only when they were positioned did Stalin exit his limousine. Mr. Rosato had just started playing at that point and found the entire procession unsettling. He later said, "I had never performed under such tense conditions before. Never ever. Buzz bombs in London were an everyday occurrence. This was supposed to be a friendly thing. It brought home the element of danger." (Mullener, 1995)[4]

POST-WAR BERLIN

Soviet forces that took Berlin in the final days of the war systematically destroyed much of the city through constant, horrific artillery bombardments and direct fire. Much of what wasn't destroyed in this fashion had already been destroyed through Allied bombing campaigns. Twelve percent of all buildings had been razed to the ground; 76 percent were in ruins; 8,500 hospital beds remained from the previous 35,000; 128 of the 150 bridges were destroyed. There was no public transport, no gas or electricity, no water supply. The sewage system didn't work and dysentery and typhus had reached epidemic proportions. (Tusa, 1997)[5]

The Soviets, having actually taken Berlin in vicious fighting throughout April, spared no quarter. From the time the surrender was signed in early May through early July, Soviet soldiers brutalized the Berlin population by countless rapes, murders, and robberies. Howley describes the orders given to U.S. forces conducting occupation duties to use lethal force, if necessary, to prevent anyone from committing these crimes. The 2nd Armored Division Letter of Instruction (LOI) #80, dated 15 July 1945, states, in part: "All guards, security detachments, security patrols, etc., will be immediately instructed to use whatever force is necessary, including use of firearms, to enforce all orders; to apprehend any individuals, allied military or civilian, who jeopardize the performance of the mission in any way; and to stop and apprehend any personnel found looting, robbing, raping, or otherwise creating disturbance in the American Sector of Berlin."[6]

These actions were needed to address the "nightmare of debauchery, looting and havoc which followed once the guns were silent. Little girls, young women, grandmothers were raped. Hundreds died of wounds because there were no hospitals to treat them or of venereal diseases for which there was no penicillin. Watches were snatched from their owners or hacked off with the hand if resistance was offered. Day and night, carpets, china and glass were looted; furniture and paintings were smashed or burned by drunken soldiers."[7]

The Soviets intended to settle accounts. Their country had been systematically sacked and brutalized in much the same manner in which they were engaging the Berliners. Red Army authorities made no attempts to discipline their brutal hordes.[8] Beyond the mayhem directed toward the Berliners themselves, the Soviets were dismantling infrastructure, manufacturing capability, and machinery that could be moved – but even then it couldn't be moved very far as the Soviet apparatus failed to consider the differences in the rail gauge between the two countries. For years, overland travelers to Moscow would encounter mountains of German industrial equipment, crumpled and rusting by the wayside.[9]

Howley also described several encounters with drunken Soviets accosting Berliners in attempts to rob them. One incident in particular resulted in several Soviet deaths, a circumstance that the Soviets protested. Howley wrote that the Russians complained that a dozen of their men had been shot by American patrols. One was a Russian officer, caught robbing a German home. He had pulled a gun on the American MP, who had surprised him as he started looting, and the MP promptly poured eight slugs from a tommy gun into the Russian's stomach. The officer was in the hospital a long time, but miraculously, he lived.

Colonel General Boris Gorbatov, the Soviet commander in Berlin, protested strongly against this shooting. Howley responded with the facts – the Soviet officer had pulled a gun on the American, who responded in accordance with his training and his instructions. Gorbatov contended that one bullet would have been sufficient, but eight bullets constituted "aggression." (Howley, 1950)[10]

American and British soldiers created problems as well. The fact that the war was all but over and that the Allies were victorious led some into less-than-disciplined behavior and excessive alcohol use. Dr. William Stivers of the Center of Military History, Ft. Leavenworth, in an unfinished discussion paper dated August 5, 2003, notes the following: "Instead of ensuring public safety, many of these soldiers, including officers, devoted themselves to enjoying the victors' spoils. Freed from the deadly seriousness of combat, they indulged in acts of indiscipline and outlawry ranging from currency fraud, black marketing, and theft of requisitioned goods to violent drunkenness, rape, assault, and robbery…According [to] a July 1946 intelligence report sent to the head of U.S. military government for Germany, Lt. Gen. Lucius Clay, the U.S. troop crime rate in Berlin was nearly thirteen times the rate for the Military District of Washington (Stivers, 2003)."

Despite genuine efforts to maintain order and discipline and to protect the populace, many women deliberately made attempts to dress as men in an effort to disguise themselves and prevent possible attack.

Harry Reinert, in his personal memoirs, described the carnage:

> My first indication of the level of destruction in Germany resulting from the massive bombing in World War II was what I saw in Frankfurt. But even that could not prepare me for the sights in Berlin. I had of course seen photographs of the bombed out buildings and piles of rubble, but no mere photograph could have the impact of viewing the destruction in person.
>
> The neighborhood where we were billeted was relatively unscathed by the Battle for Berlin which came at the end of the war. The first Saturday after I arrived in Berlin, I took the U-bahn into the center of the city. I got off the subway at

Friedrichstrasse and walked up the stairs to come out at the Brandenburg Gate. During the war, I had read everything I could find about Berlin, so I had some concept of what the center of the city had once been. On the west side of the Brandenburg Gate, Unter den Linden boulevard cuts through the middle of the Tiergarten, an enormous park. When I gazed out from the Brandenburg gate in mid-April 1947, the Tiergarten had the look of a moonscape.

Siegesallee in the Tiergarten

Where lush gardens had once stood, the ground was scraped bare. On my right was the burned out hulk of the old Reichstag, the torching of which in 1933 had given Hitler an excuse to take total control of the country. In front of it was the Soviet war memorial. Perhaps a quarter mile down the wide boulevard stood the Siegessäule, the Victory Column raised to celebrate the Prussian victory in the Franco-Prussian War in 1867. The ultimate irony was the French flag flying on the column.

Giving the whole scene a surrealistic feeling like something from a Salvador Dali painting was a row of statues standing isolated and alone toward one edge of the Tiergarten. These were statues of great historical figures, ranging from Frederick the Great to Bismarck to Wagner, lining what was called Siegesallee (Victory Boulevard). Within a couple months after I took my pictures, the statues were removed and buried in the grounds of Schloss Bellevue. As I ambled across the barren land toward the statues, I came across an old man standing waist deep in a hole he was digging. I asked him what he was doing, and he explained that he was digging for tree roots to use for fuel.

On the other side of the Brandenburg Gate, scarcely a wall was standing; all one saw was block after block of piles of rubble. This had been the cultural and fashion center of Berlin, here had stood the Adlon Hotel of Vicki Baum's novels Grand Hotel and Hotel Berlin '43 and nothing was left but a mountain of rubble, punctuated occasionally by a plumbing pipe sticking out grotesquely 50 feet above the ground. The overall effect was sobering, for the area was so vast and I was so small standing in the midst of it. (Reinert H. , 2005)[11]

The Soviets were anxious to create, establish, and maintain a communist political and social order within the former German capital. To accomplish this, the Americans, British, and the French, who by now were also granted an occupation zone in Germany and in Berlin, would have to abandon Berlin. Howley worked tirelessly, and not without frustration, to work within the framework given to him by the American Sector Berlin military governor, Major General Floyd Parks, to keep the U.S. in the city.

The Telefunken Complex was a communications research and development and manufacturing site for the German company during the war. The company itself was fairly successful and enjoyed producing a number of technological communication advances throughout its existence, beginning in the early part of the 20th century. At the end of the war, the U.S. military confiscated properties and buildings in the less damaged part of the city (chiefly Dahlem, Zehlendorf, and Lichterfelde) for housing officers and soldiers. The Telefunken complex was one of these confiscated.

The many villas in Dahlem and along the Schlachtensee in Zehlendorf were popular for the officers. These homes, grand in architectural style, had been owned by many affluent Berliners, some of whom, but not all, were ardent Nazis. These homes were confiscated without a backward glance. Other areas in South Lichterfelde, located not far from the former barracks of the SS Leibstandarte Adolf Hitler (his personal bodyguard regiment) were also confiscated. For a city that was decimated by war and had few precious resources, including suitable housing, the confiscation of properties by the Allies was an added hardship for the Berliners. This was one area in which no discussion was entertained.

The central focus of the post-war military government in Berlin was to de-Nazify the city, obtain and keep control, and then to restore Berlin to a civilized city. Virtually all infrastructure had been destroyed, including subways, railways, bridges, and most buildings. Electrical power stations were operating at a fraction of their pre-war capacity. Coal, the principal fuel, was in short supply and winter was fast approaching. People were starving; there simply wasn't enough food in the city for everybody.

While the military government issued "scrip", a form of currency to be used by soldiers, the city's own currency was undergoing substantial changes. This chaotic, unpredictable situation led to the formation of illegal black markets. Black markets, while technically illegal, were openly supported by the Soviets. The Americans recognized the black markets as existing, but took efforts to control them by implementing a Currency Control Book, as outlined in appropriate military messages, circulars, and other directives. (Smith, 1945)[12]

Throngs of people descended on the hub at Potsdamer Platz, south of the Brandenburg Gate and near the destroyed remnants of the Reich Chancellery. This area was historically a focal point of the city itself in better times, evidenced by streetcar, rail, and subway stops, and during these turbulent times also served in the same capacity. Potsdam itself, located 10 miles west of downtown Berlin, was also a mecca for black marketing activities. Cigarettes and bottles of alcohol were traded for goods and services. "Mickey Mouse" watches were also a favorite of the Soviets; they would pay astronomical sums for these simple wristwatches.

Black marketing was such a huge part of life in Berlin that the U.S. soldiers stationed there in 1945-46 sent more money back to the States than they earned! While the Berlin black markets flourished during the early years of the occupation, the German currency reform of 1948 effectively ended it by the creation of the West German Deutsche mark. Other commodities such as hard liquor, cigarettes, and coffee/tea on the German economy remained highly taxed and therefore expensive. This made equivalent American products which were not taxed highly desired and thus, a secondary black market associated with these commodities took place. Controls in reducing this black market took the form of rationing these items.

The 298th/300th band remained in the former Telefunken complex for only four days. Internal historical documentation refers to this area as a "Master Work Camp." On 13 July 1945, the band moved its operations and billets to the Onkel Toms Hütte area of Zehlendorf, which was within one subway stop from the newly adopted U.S. Headquarters, Berlin District, known as OMGUS.

The Onkel Toms Hütte neighborhood, named for a former rest stop in the Grunewald forest and located on the way from eastern Berlin to Potsdam, featured a subway stop, opened in 1929, by the same name. This working-class neighborhood at the southern edge of the Grunewald forest featured about 1,100 apartments and about 800 single-family homes. It was spared significant bomb damage during the war, presumably because the Americans had planned to use this area in Zehlendorf as a billeting site for occupation troops. These apartments in which the band took residence were originally built for working-class families. They were modest in size and construction, containing two or three bedrooms, a kitchen, a single bathroom, and typically a narrow balcony. These same apartments became the new home for the band and they remained there for the next three years.

Reinhard von Bronewski, retired Berlin police officer who later worked with American military police, shared that the U.S. quartermasters evicted his mother and other family members from their home. They weren't even entitled to keep their furniture. They were instructed to pack only their personal items, leaving all apartment belongings behind. Bronewski said that he understood that the GI's did as they were instructed, but it was still very new and frightening from the vantage point of the vanquished. From the vantage point of the victors, finding a measure of sympathy for the families of the German soldiers that had been killing and maiming those who had been lost on the long road to Berlin was unthinkable.

Harry Reinert wrote about his experiences in Onkel Toms Hütte:

We were billeted in a group of four-plex apartments located near Onkel Toms Hütte arcade and subway station. I have identified the address of my unit as Wilskistrasse 29. When my sons Harry and Ted and I went to Berlin 25 years later, I was finally able to find the buildings which we had called home. Living conditions for the troops in Berlin were very good: we had four men in each three bedroom apartment and our mess hall was the dining room in the building that was formerly Hermann Goering's headquarters (von Bronewski).[13] We

OMGUS mess hall

could reach the dining hall by riding the subway to the next stop (occupation forces, of course, could ride the subway free of charge). At tables seating only six to eight men each, waitresses gave us a printed menu of what was available for that meal and we would mark our selections which were then served a short time later.

Rather than ride the subway, whenever possible we would hail a jeep with a German driver and have him drive us back to our billets. After lunch one day, three of us were walking along the sidewalk hoping to hail a ride when a staff car pulled up to the curb and a general sitting in the back seat opened the door and offered us a ride. For a buck private who was still somewhat awed by a captain, this was quite an experience. The general chatted with us very genially and insisted on delivering us right to the gate of our compound. The Berlin *Observer*, the local Army newspaper, a few weeks later carried a feature story about this same general—Brigadier General Robert A. McClure--as he was preparing to head back to the States. Apparently he was famous around Berlin for exactly the sort of hospitality he had shown us. I realized then that he could be friendly with the troops because he felt secure in his own position—he did not have to prove anything to anyone. This observation later carried over into civilian life as well, e.g. when I was active in regional and national foreign language organizations, occasionally I would meet someone who insisted on being addressed as "Doctor So-and-so," whereas most of my colleagues—at least, the ones who knew their stuff and knew they knew it—were totally unconcerned with their titles.

Mom Neubauer

For each four-plex, the army hired a *Putzfrau*, a cleaning lady, whose job it was to keep the places clean. But we were told that we were responsible for cleaning our own gear, including the white scarves which became soiled very quickly. The Putzfrau in our unit was Frau Ella Neubauer, whom we all called "Mom." She was a short, wiry woman in her 50s with a marvelous sense of humor. Mom knew only two words of English, which she had undoubtedly learned from the American GIs—"shit" and "OK." She would tease the men by doing such things as switching off the bathroom light while someone was shaving, then stand in hallway laughing as her victim came storming out of the bathroom swearing fiercely. In spite of her orders to the contrary, she would insist on washing our white scarves for us, undoubtedly believing that we would not be able to do an adequate job ourselves.

Mom knew I was trying very hard to improve my German

and she would help me by correcting my pronunciation and grammar and feeding me new vocabulary...On my 18th birthday, I had a dental appointment in the morning and when I returned to the billet I complained to Mom that this was a lousy way to spend a birthday. She suggested I should just go lie in the sun and forget rehearsal that day...as though I had a choice. When I got back to my room after breakfast the next morning, there was a bouquet of flowers in a vase on my desk. "Where did the flowers come from, Mom?" I asked. "They are for your birthday, for your mother in America," she explained.

Perhaps it should be explained that the German custom of expressing birthday greetings, paying for the cost of cakes and desserts, and other niceties was typically done by the birthday boy himself!

A NEW MISSION

The mass exodus of the original musicians of the 300th/298th following the Potsdam Conference and the official flag-raising ceremony at the Group Control Council led to real problems. While the 2nd Armored Division Band had certainly been in Berlin since arrival in early July 1945, there is mention of only a ceremony at Andrews Barracks on July 4, 1945 by the 2AD Band and the official flag raising ceremony at what was to become the Allied Kommandatura on July 22, 1945 by the 300th/298th Band. The Group Control Council managed to organize and publish a newspaper while the council was still in Höchst, near Frankfurt, and then moved its operations to Berlin in time to publish within weeks of arriving in Berlin, on July 28, 1945. This newspaper, called appropriately enough The *Grooper*, reported only a few performances by unofficial and pickup groups in the Berlin Command's from its first issue through December 1945.

The turbulence continued with the 2nd Armored Division's relief by the 82nd Airborne Division in August. In turn, the 82nd Airborne was relieved by the 78th Infantry Division in December. Newspaper reporting continued through this time with the *Grooper* and also by a newcomer, the Berlin *Sentinel*, but only scant mention was made of any band performances. It is certain, however, that a steady troupe of VIPs made its way to Berlin Tempelhof, with the appropriate honor guard in place to greet them.

The three major combat units, the 2AD, 82nd Airborne, and 78th Infantry, all had their own bands throughout the war. The 2nd Armored Division, at least for a portion of its wartime service, had bands in each of its Combat Commands A and B. Since the focus of the *Grooper's* news and commentary for the first few months of publication was chiefly redeployments, billets and transportation mention of band performances or even of the bands themselves wasn't a high priority.

The bands were manned by musicians whose high wartime point total meant being sent home as quickly as humanly possible. The sheer numbers of musicians being sent home clearly had an impact to the bands within Berlin. This was partially addressed by recruiting of soldiers within the rest of the command who had a musical background.

Despite these issues, the newspapers made determined efforts to report and publish their findings. They too struggled through power blackouts, staff redeployments, and even shortages of newsprint, to find newsworthy items and report them. In fact, just as the immediate post-war bands scrambled to find replacement musicians, so too did the Grooper, even after the newspaper had changed its name to the Berlin Observer.

Harry Reinert, clarinetist with the 298th Army Ground Forces Band from

February – August 1947, sought an opportunity to gain experience as a journalist. Harry reported that in June 1947, a memo was circulated through the Berlin command seeking those soldiers with journalistic experience. Harry had worked for a time for a small newspaper in Arkansas and as his ambition was less toward music and more toward journalism, he jumped at the opportunity. At the conclusion of the interview process, he was selected for the Staff of the *Observer*. The second anniversary of the Berlin *Observer*, published on July 28, 1947, contained several photos of Harry and his associates while performing their tasks. Harry reported that he had continued to live in the band billets at the Onkel Toms Hütte compound, but he was released from duty with the 298th and worked at the *Observer*, a curious example of how replacements in and out of Berlin meant some creative thinking to fill needed positions irrespective of training or job title.

No significant mention of the 2nd Armored Division Band, 82nd Airborne Division Band, or the 78th Infantry Division Band was reported in the Berlin Military District's various newspapers. Neither the *Grooper* nor the *Observer* nor the *Sentinel* contained appreciable information. With none of these bands making any documented appearances, only the 298th—the assigned Berlin Military District Band—was left to support a series of celebrations, parades, and similar events held in the city following Japan's capitulation in September 1945. Had the invasion of the home islands of Japan moved forward as planned in Operation Downfall, projected American casualties approached 1.2 million. (Editor, Operation Downfall, 2011)[14]

While the 298th was busy getting settled and trying to stay sane in an incredibly chaotic situation, the Potsdam Conference began. The "Big Three"—Truman, Stalin, and Churchill (later replaced by Attlee, after Churchill's party lost the election)—met to decide the fate of post-war Germany and to plan on an occupation strategy. Glaviano wrote that supporting this Conference was one of the two most inspiring events for the ETO Band. Band internal historical

President Truman thanks the band

27

documentation states, "On 16 July 1945, the 298th Army Ground Forces Band played a concert for President Truman from 1900 to 2000 hours." These concerts continued on a daily basis for those interested in attending, but were not necessarily attended by the heads of state. The band also supported the official flag-raising ceremony at the U.S. Allied Control Council in Berlin on July 20th and a more meaningful flag-raising ceremony on July 22nd. Glaviano further added that General Lucius Clay, the military governor of Germany and later to become the hero of the Berlin Airlift, stated that the flag raised over the U.S. Headquarters on that day had been the same flag that flew over the U.S. Capitol on December 7, 1941, the same flag that was raised over Rome when that city capitulated, and would then be sent to General MacArthur to be raised over Tokyo upon final victory in the Pacific. This ceremony, simple and short, was attended by President Truman, Secretaries Byrnes and Stimson, and Generals Eisenhower, Bradley, Patton, and Clay.

Thus, the 298th Army Band completed its mission as requested by Brigadier General Pleas D. Rogers in London. The band members were understandably more and more anxious to return home, but until orders were received to do so, Mr. Rosato kept the band busy with performances wherever and whenever possible. Bob Hope and his sidekick Jerry Colona visited Berlin and indicated surprise at seeing the band, thinking that the musicians had gone home long before. Jack Benny also visited Berlin and the band supported his act for the USO. Other celebrities, including Ingrid Bergman and Martha Tilton, also came to Berlin during those tumultuous early post-war months.

In August and September, morale in the band continued to plummet. Mr. Rosato conferred with Major General Floyd Parks, the commanding general of the U.S. sector of Berlin, and explained that the band had served faithfully and honorably and wished to go home. General Parks expressed regret, but stated that the band's presence was essential to the morale of the entire command. Therefore, the band members could not be considered for rotation back to the States. This was a bitter disappointment to the musicians, but plans were made to grant some of them leave to a much-needed break.

Glaviano stated that the 300th Dance Band continued to play, but the 298th Dance Band did not. Despite this, a Red Cross club opened and the 300th Dance Band frequently played there.

Totally frustrated, Corporal Ernest J. Tassin wrote a respectful, but still fuming, letter to Brigadier General George S. Eyster, the Deputy G-3 for the U.S. Forces, European Theater (USFET) in Paris, complaining bitterly about not being permitted to rotate back to the States. Tassin explained that while he was required to wait while other soldiers with more "points" rotated home, he had now amassed a total of 86 points and was being forced to wait while others in the Allied Control Council with fewer points were being sent home ahead of him.

Tassin received no response to his letter. Thoroughly embittered, he telephoned the commanding general in Berlin and discussed the letter with him. After listening, the general put Tassin on a three-way phone conversation with him and General Eyster in Paris. After suitable pleasantries and discussion, Eyster was ordered to put the entire band on the next ship returning to the States. While this didn't quite happen either, the entire incident forced the issue to be settled more quickly than if Tassin had not written the letter at all.

By mid-November, Mr. Rosato and all band members were issued honorable discharges and were back in Louisiana or their home state. The former members of the 156th Infantry Band all made it safely home. Rosato himself was the last to leave of the original musicians, which was in keeping with his leadership style. He felt his job was done, his soldiers had served their nation with dignity and honorable service, and it was time to go home. And here, the record mentions only the 298th without explanation as to why the "298th" designation and not the "300th" was selected for the band's numerical name. A decision had been made to deactivate the 300th, but record of that decision has not been located.

While Mr. Rosato completed his active Army duties, by no means did he intend to stop making music. Upon his return to the New Orleans area following his wartime service, Frank Rosato became involved with the American Legion Metairie Post 175. The New Orleans Times-Picayune, in an article dated Thursday, August 26, 2004 published the following story:

> For almost six decades, Frank Rosato has directed the American Legion Metairie Post 175 band. Last week, its 45 members decided it was time to show their appreciation.
>
> Eighty-one people gathered Aug. 18 at Barreca's Restaurant in Metairie for a surprise appreciation dinner for Rosato, 89, band director since 1945.
>
> "Mr. Rosato has dedicated his life to music, and this is a way for us to pay tribute to him," said Harold Pecunia of Slidell, event organizer.
>
> Rosato, of Metairie, was accompanied to the dinner by his wife, Selema, and their two sons Frank and John.
>
> "When we left the house, they told me we were going for a ride," Rosato said. "This is definitely a surprise. And I feel very honored to be recognized this way."
>
> Rosato grew up in New Orleans where his father, a music teacher, began teaching him how to play the piano, cornet, and saxophone before he was 10 years old. He graduated from Tulane University with a degree in civil engineering.
>
> "My father wanted me to go to Tulane," Rosato said. "He said he would teach me all the music that I needed to know."
>
> When World War II began, Rosato was leading the 156th

Infantry National Guard band at Jackson Barracks, which was deployed to England. The band served as goodwill ambassadors for the United States and played at Buckingham Palace as well as several USO shows with Bob Hope.

The band also played at the Potsdam Conference near Berlin following Germany's defeat in 1945. President Harry Truman, Prime Minister Winston Churchill of Great Britain and Russian leader Joseph Stalin were at the conference. Truman personally congratulated Rosato and his band for their performance.

"It was exciting to shake hands with the president and to have him personally congratulate you on your band's performance," Rosato said.

As the American Legion Metairie Post 175 band's longtime director, Rosato has earned the admiration and respect of members.

"Frank Rosato has accomplished so much and touched so many lives," said tuba player John Maggiore, of River Ridge. "People all over the city know and respect him for what he has done."

For band member Jerry Semerad of Algiers, Rosato's leadership ability is what sets him apart.

"He (Rosato) knows how to lead," Semerad said. "He knows how to handle a band and bring them together."

And, for Rosato, who also plays the bass horn in the Ira Milan Polka Band, that is what being a bandleader is all about.

"It is a wonderful thing when you can take so many different instruments and put them together and make beautiful music," Rosato said.

Frank Rosato died in his sleep on March 27, 2006, at the age of 91.

While the original musicians of the 298th/300th bands had finally departed for greener pastures back home in the States, the band itself remained in the city. The band was manned with only a few musicians, one of them being Seymour (Sy) Karpen.

Sy, who had moved over to the 298th from his impromptu job as an MP in Berlin, had been a radio operator with the 70th Infantry Division and had served in Italy, France, and Germany. He saw a lot of combat before suffering a shrapnel wound near Saarbrücken in February 1945. Sy received treatment in an Army hospital. When he was released from the hospital and therapy in June 1945, the war was over. But rather than returning home with about 40 other combat soldiers who had also suffered wounds and had recovered, Sy was assigned without training to military police duty. Sy remarked in his memoirs,

"They decided to make us military policemen. They disregarded the fact that half of our group had severe mental problems, were unstable, and were not to be given any weapons. We were immediately issued .45 cal. pistols and other MP paraphernalia."

Sy and his group were then trucked first to Frankfurt and then on to Berlin, where he and his contingent were one of the first U.S. groups to access the city in late June 1945. One of Sy's initial duties as an *ad hoc* military policeman in mid-July 1945 was to forcibly evict the Berliners who were living in the Onkel Toms Hütte area for use by U.S. soldiers as billets.

The dearth of musicians in the 298th led to the command searching its

Sy Karpen and friends, Onkel Toms Hütte

own resources within Berlin for replacements. Sy wrote: "Soldiers were being sent home according to a point system based on length of time in service, medals, etc. It seemed that musicians in the 298th Army Ground Forces Band were being sent home and they needed musicians. Luckily, I had listed on my record that I played clarinet and saxophone. They asked if I would like to transfer to the army band. I was out of being an MP within 24 hours and with a great sense of relief I went to where the band was housed and got a clarinet. I proceeded to practice for 16 hours a day since I hadn't played in two years and was very rusty. The guys thought I was nuts. The fingering and tone came back very quickly. I guess it was like riding a bike. Once you learn how, you never forget. I was buddy with another sax and clarinet player, Sol Cohen. We were in the same house together and played next to each other in the band. Sol

31

remained a musician after he was discharged and even played at our wedding. His professional name was Sol Consor."

Sy continued, "The band had mostly new players so we practiced quite a bit to get used to each other. We ended up playing every night at a nightclub called Club 48. This was dance music for the enlisted men and women. I remember liquor was served for 10 cents a drink. Each soldier was issued a case of beer per week and a fifth of whiskey every month, if they wanted it. There was so much drinking at that time that I can't remember what went on between Christmas 1945 and New Year's of 1946. I do recall a huge New Year's party that we played at that was arranged by the allied powers. It was held in some mansion that had a tremendous ballroom. Each country supplied native food, liquor and wine. In addition, each country provided entertainment. Our band was the entertainment for the United States. I recall drinking with the Irish guard soldiers which was Great Britain's entertainment. They all wore kilts and paraded with drums and bagpipes. I found out what they wore under their kilts. NOTHING! We ate caviar, lobster, all kinds of sausages from each country, beautiful cakes and foods that I have no idea what they were. We drank the finest cognac, vodkas and wines from each country. It was an unbelievable shindig with more important people that I could name under the same roof. It was after this party that Sol and I decided that we were drinking too much and gave away our ration of liquor to the other guys in the band.

"There were some wonderful musicians in our band. The leader was an accordionist who wrote music and also had perfect pitch. If we were out of tune he went crazy. We had a tenor sax player that was fantastic and would have been famous if he wasn't a drunkard. He got drunk almost every night. We had a jazz guitarist that wrote wonderful jazz music for a trio we created with piano, guitar, and tenor saxophone.

"I played alto sax, baritone sax, and clarinet. In the marching band, I played B-flat and E-flat clarinets. The E-flat clarinet was for the solo in Stars and Stripes Forever because we didn't have a piccolo player.

"We got time off and I traveled to Switzerland for a week in Geneva and Davos where I almost broke my neck trying to learn how to ski. We visited Heidelberg and Marburg, Germany. The days went by just waiting to be sent home.

"There was one major incident that occurred in which I was almost put before a court martial. Time went on and the fraternization laws were suspended. We were told to be friendly with the Germans. I couldn't do it. One day we were told that we were to play for a show that consisted of German singers and dancers. I refused to play for any Germans. The Captain ordered me to play and I refused. He was furious and told me that I was disobeying an order and could be court martialed. I then told him I would play but if any German entertainer criticized me or the way I was playing, I would kill or cripple that person. He saw that I meant it and excused me from playing in that show. The other guys in the band understood and respected my feelings (they were not former infantrymen).

"We played for the Saturday parades and the nightclub dances in Club 48. I was promoted to Tech 5 (corporal) and at the end of May 1946 I was told to get ready to be sent home. We boarded a Liberty ship and sailed for the United States. It was a terrible trip home as every time the ship hit a wave, it shook all over. I was afraid that I wouldn't make it home, but I did. A lot of us cried when we saw the Statue of Liberty. When we were lining up to disembark, my name and others were called out to get off the ship before anyone else. I went down the gangplank with my duffel bag and there was my mother and my father waiting for me. We hugged and kissed and cried together. I won't even try to describe the emotions we felt. I went on to Ft. Dix, New Jersey and got discharged on June 10, 1946. Two and one-half years had gone by. I was 20 years old but felt like I was twice that age and still not old enough to vote. I had spent my crucial teenage years in the service of my country and could never retrieve them. Do I have any regrets? I have some but realize that there was a great evil in the world that had to be destroyed. Hitler and Nazi Germany showed what results when bigotry and racism are ignored. We must make sure it never happens again."

Unit historical documentation refers to WOJG James Abel as the original commanding officer of the 298th. As previously stated, this was a paper assignment inasmuch as Mr. Rosato insisted on running both the 298th and 300th Bands, at least from a commander's perspective. Glaviano, a set drummer, ran the 298th Dance Band when it performed. With WOJG James Abel's departure from Berlin in early October 1945, the 298th entered an extraordinary time by having a Women's Army Corps (WAC) lieutenant as a commanding officer. Sy remembers First Lieutenant Rosalyn W. Hershenson with affection: "She was extremely kind to us all—but not very military-minded. This was a blessing, because for those of us who had seen combat (there were a few of us left), we simply didn't care too much for a lot of military-type harassment. We were content to rehearse, do our jobs, and maintain ourselves and our areas, but we certainly didn't need some officer to come in and throw his weight around. Hershenson didn't do that to us. Perhaps she instinctively understood. In any event, she did care enough for us to actually pass out birthday cards to us on our birthdays! We were allowed to rehearse without all the formal tie-tying stuff. She allowed the noncoms to run the band, especially for the musical part of things. She knew what she could do and what she couldn't do, so she did the right thing by deferring to the noncom musicians."

Sy recalled a different WAC lieutenant: "Can't remember her name, but she was a pain in the ass as she required us to rehearse in full uniform, with ties, etc. She had no musical background. She and other GIs loved that Cole

Porter tune, 'Don't Fence Me In.' The band hated it. The tenor sax player burned his sheet music on the dance floor one night in protest. We thought it was hilarious and never played it again. We may have been a few sheets to the wind."

Lieutenant Hershenson served as commanding officer of the band until she was relieved by First Lieutenant Harry A. Buzzett in April 1946.

Speaking of the WACs, Sy and Sebby Papa both mentioned that they were ordered to guard the WAC building. This building, also located in the Onkel Toms Hütte area, was a favorite hangout of GIs and required a certain measure of security. While the number of WAC soldiers certainly numbered a few, in comparison to the rest of the American soldier presence in Berlin, it wasn't uncommon for there to be conjugal visits between WACs/GIs.

The 298th played five or six nights a week at Club 48, the enlisted club located on the corner of Kronprinzenallee and Saargemünderstr. After Alaska and Hawaii joined the United States in the late 1950s, Club 48 was redesignated Club 50. Still later this structure would be renovated to become the Checkpoint NCO Club. Club 48 was a nicely built club, very ornate in comparison to many other enlisted clubs, and featured a full restaurant, dance floor, cola and ice cream bar, in addition to the regular fare. In the main ballroom, the tables were bedecked with the name and other information from each of the 48 United States. The Berlin command was, in fact, so proud of this club that they published hardcover books full of photographs depicting the club. These were given away to GIs as souvenirs. Sy Karpen still has his copy, though it is very fragile.

Entertainment in Berlin was scant, since there was no television and limited radio, so Club 48 was just about the only place in town where one could unwind. The September 25, 1945 issue of the *Sentinel* makes mention of the 82nd "All American" Club on Grunewaldstrasse (Low, 1945). This new club, recently opened, featured music rooms for jazz and classical music, sandwich and ice cream stations, along with offerings of a professional photographer, sculptor and even the occasional Armed Forces Network (AFN) broadcast. Entertainment was apparently also on tap, but no specific mention of a particular artist or group; neither was there mention of alcoholic beverages. That made Club 48 very popular for the occupation soldiers in Berlin, as long as attendees had a pass. The band was featured on a regular basis – sometimes several nights a week – and as long as the girls came to dance, most of the soldiers frequented Club 48 when permitted to do so.

AFN radio sent its first broadcast over the airwaves on August 4, 1945 via a wire strung between two trees in a bombed-out building on Podbielskiallee. This herculean effort resulted in AFN-Berlin with its first programming day being 20 hours long (Editor, AFN Berlin Celebrates 25th Anniversary, 2009).[15] To combat Soviet propaganda aimed at Berliners, the U.S. government authorized DIAS (Wire Broadcasting in the American Sector) later to become RIAS (Radio im amerikanischen Sektor). This German-language radio station began broadcasting on February 7, 1946 (Editor, Chronology: RIAS-Berlin and the RIAS Berlin Commission, 2014).[16]

As Berlin slowly recovered from its wartime wounds, the occupying forces adjusted and settled in. In May 1946, the 78th Infantry Division was deactivated. Replacing the division, which was largely a regiment at this point due to redeployments and departures, was the 3rd Infantry Regiment which took its station in Berlin from West Germany.

Out with the old and in with the new. The combat soldiers were largely gone, their mission complete. Replacing them were their younger brothers and they arrived in force ready to take their place in occupation of Berlin. Two of these, destined for the 298th Army Ground Forces Band, which numbered about 28 musicians in mid-1946, were Sebby Papa and Harry Reinert.

INITIAL OCCUPATION DUTY

When Mr. Rosato and the other veterans of the wartime 298th/300th bands headed home for discharge, the 298th was again a regimental band, authorized for only 28 men plus one warrant officer. But there was a problem finding enough replacements in Berlin even to meet that quota.

Changing Times

The sudden surrender of Japan only three months after VE Day created momentous and unexpected political, economic and social changes both at home and abroad. Within the year after VJ Day in August 1945, around 80% of the men in the Army were released from active duty. This was a manpower drop of around seven million men, leaving the Army with only around 1.4 million personnel in uniform. The 298th, as well as every other military organization, suffered major cuts in manpower. The situation was so critical that when Mr. Rosato asked Major General Floyd Parks, the commanding general of the U.S. sector of Berlin, to release the original members of the 298th band so they could rotate home, Gen. Parks said the 298th—apparently the only remaining military band in the city—was too valuable to be rotated out of Berlin at that time.

Commanders in the field were passing the word on to Washington, D.C. that this massive exodus of veteran troops was creating a great hardship on all units in the Army. In a matter of only a few months, the Army launched a high-powered recruiting campaign with the slogan, "40,000 Good Jobs a Month." There was no longer a draft, so the Army needed to recruit volunteers. This campaign targeted specifically young men in the 17-19 year old category, and the youngest veterans being discharged. The manpower ratio both in the Army and in civilian life had been turned upside down with the seven million veterans suddenly swarming into civilian life. Most of the veterans who had been drafted or had volunteered when they joined up were promised their old jobs back upon their return. For three and a half years the United States had enjoyed full employment, but most of these workers were women and boys who were filling in for the men who had gone to fight. "Rosie the Riveter" became a popular patriotic symbol. Boys eight and nine years old were handling paper routes with 200 customers. Harry Reinert, who joined the Army in 1946, carried mail holiday seasons in 1943 and 1944 and all summer in 1945, the summer he had just turned 16. Three months after VJ Day, when very few of the veterans had returned home yet, he had a full-time evening job as a reporter for his hometown daily newspaper during his senior year in high school.

In the months when the seven million veterans returned home and reclaimed their jobs, this meant that the workers who had held those jobs for the past three years suddenly became unemployed. In many cases Rosie the Riveter resented being cast out of her job, for she had come to enjoy the personal freedom and income that came with it. The government even produced a short video shown in movie theaters with a kindly middle aged man speaking on behalf of the government and thanking all the housewives who had pitched in to help during the war. Now that the war was over, he said, it was wonderful that women could go back to their kitchens and cook and clean and take care of their families and not be concerned with a career or with making a living. The flood of returning vets also meant very few jobs were available for those young men just coming out of high school, or even for the younger veterans who had gone into the service directly from high school and therefore had no job to return to.

With the sudden job shortage at home, the Army's offer of "40,000 Good Jobs a Month" was very persuasive and the campaign was successful. Army camps around the country were teeming with recruits being trained to replace some of the veterans who had returned home.

Ever since the Revolutionary War, programs had been set up from time to time to train military band leaders, but until World War II, no programs were developed for bandsmen. In 1943, a training program for bandsmen was established at the Quartermaster Replacement Training Center, Camp Lee (later to become Fort Lee), Virginia. This training was intended only to orient qualified draftees on the mission and operation of an Army band. It did not include any courses designed to increase the individual's instrumental proficiency. In 1946 the program had expanded into the Army Band School, which provided an intensive eight-week course in all aspects of music for new bandsmen.

Recruiters had been alerted to be looking for potential band personnel. Sebby Papa said that when asked by the recruiter if he played any musical instrument, he answered, "trumpet." The recruiter stamped Sebby's paperwork with the annotation "Critically Needed Specialist," and he was on his way to either Camp Lee, Virginia or Camp Crowder, Missouri, along with all the other new recruits from around the country who had been identified by their recruiters as potential bandsmen. After the traditional eight-week basic training course, the recruits went into the eight-week Army Band School training program, which was organized around eight bands, one new band with 65-70 members being organized with incoming recruits each week.

At the end of their eight weeks of training, the new bandsmen were given a short delay en route to go home and then reported in to Camp Kilmer, New Jersey, to await orders to ship out. All of the men who were transported to Germany in the early months of 1947 reported similar experiences. For ten days, they were ferried across the stormy north Atlantic in a troop transport ship that was designed to carry more than 3100 troops. Since most of the band contingents had no more than 500-600 men, the ship was so light, it bounced like a cork on the waves, and seasickness was widespread. These ships were also scheduled to be filled with combat veterans on their way home.

Once they were ashore in Germany, the groups spent a day or two in Marburg, located north of Frankfurt, then went down to either Aßmannshausen am Rhein, a picturesque village which had been a resort in the wine-growing region, or in Sonthofen, a German village close to the Swiss border. For the recruits, Aßmannshausen was far removed from the usual Army life. They lived in hotel rooms, took their meals at a hotel dining room with linen tablecloths and napkins and were served by formally dressed waiters. While he was on site in either location, each man was auditioned and assigned to a band in the United States Zone of Germany. After a week or ten days, the first contingent of replacement bandsmen boarded the train heading to Berlin.

After the original 298th band finally had rotated back to the States and been discharged, the band had embarked on an 18-month period of trials while they waited for replacements to arrive. From the time Mr. Rosato left in 1945, the 298th, now a small "pick-up band," struggled along with no consistent guidance or direction. The few remaining members rehearsed regularly under direction of an NCO musician who acted as director, and they still participated in military ceremonies, but the position of bandmaster changed every month or two. WOJG Abel was followed by WAC 1st Lieutenant Rosalyn W. Hershenson, and she in turn was replaced by 1st Lieutenant Harry A. Buzzett, who was replaced by Captain Gorden J. Hartzier in June, 1946. The procession of officer non-musicians continued until the assignment of WOJG Peter Berg in December, 1946. His assignment was brief, however. He was relieved in January, 1947 by 2nd Lieutenant Lawrence J. Gallagher. After a two-month stint, Lt. Gallagher was relieved in March 1947 by CWO Louis Ferraro, a fully-qualified bandmaster, and the band finally began to travel on a steady course.

Replacements Arrive

A photograph of the 298th Band marching in the Army Day parade on April 9, 1947, just a few weeks after Mr. Ferraro's arrival, appears to have only 26 men in the group. A contingent of 15-20 new recruits fresh from the Army Band School arrived in Berlin on April 7. These new recruits were generally very young and thus—unlike many combat veterans—had no deep seated animosity toward the Germans. Therefore, they were better able to carry out the new mission of American troops: to hold back the Soviets and to win the hearts and minds of the German people.

Three days later, on April 12 the expanded 298th represented the United States at a four-power concert commemorating the second anniversary of the death of President Roosevelt. Each occupying power sent a music representative. The French provided a small chamber music ensemble to play a couple of numbers, the British brought on stage a soprano and piano accompanist, and the U.S. had the 298th Army Band play the national anthems of the four occupation powers. Then the Soviets brought on the Russian Army Chorus, about 70 men strong. In one of their numbers, the chorus was singing at full volume when suddenly a tenor standing in the center of the front row began to sing a obbligato above the entire chorus. It was a thrilling performance.

General Lucius Clay assumed duties as Military Governor of occupied Germany and chief of OMGUS, relieving Gen. Eisenhower in March 1947. Gen. Clay had his headquarters in Berlin. The Berlin *Observer* reported that on his birthday on April 23, 1947 the band, "numbering around 65 members," formed in the yard outside his residence around 6:30 a.m. and played a group of numbers, mostly Southern tunes, since Gen. Clay originally hailed from Georgia. Some of the men felt this was a terrible thing to do to a general, but he came out onto the porch in his robe and pajamas and waved to the assembled musicians.

About noon that day, the general's staff car pulled up at the band orderly room and a sergeant began carrying a cardboard box filled with various liquors inside. Mr. Ferraro spotted this and challenged the sergeant, "Sergeant, where are you going with that whisky?"

"Into the orderly room, sir," the sergeant replied.

"Who told you to do that?" Mr. Ferraro demanded.

"General Clay, sir," said the sergeant.

"Well, get on with it then, man," countered Mr. Ferraro.

In appreciation for the early morning serenade, Gen. Clay had sent over a rather sizable collection of various liquors for members of the band. The booty was divided evenly among the band members, averaging about one fifth of booze for every three men.

Even in its shattered state, Berlin was a popular tourist destination for celebrities, footloose politicians, and even high Army officials. Wallace Beery, silent and talkie character actor, for example, visited Berlin in late 1945. The band greeted him at Tempelhof Airfield in an honor guard ceremony. Many other celebrities would soon follow. Members of Congress came to get a peek into the Soviet sector through the "peephole in the Iron Curtain." Ceremonies greeting these arriving VIPs were held usually at Tempelhof Airfield or the U.S. Headquarters, Berlin District (OMGUS). On occasion, the ceremony would take place at the Rail Transportation Office (RTO) in Lichterfelde. When word came that a notable was expected to arrive in Berlin, the band loaded on 2.5 ton 6x6 trucks well in advance of the plane's ETA and went to Tempelhof for the greeting ceremony. After waiting for an hour for the visitor to arrive and playing for maybe three minutes, the band then climbed back into the trucks and headed back to Onkel Toms Hütte for a practice session. The worst part about most ceremonies was the number of insufferable dry runs. Waiting for the VIP to arrive was especially difficult in cold, wet, rainy weather.

In his book *As Though I Had Wings*, trumpeter Chet Baker commented that during the period he was in Berlin, the band would make the trip out to Tempelhof Airfield several times each week and regardless of bad weather conditions, the ceremony would take place. Chet remarks that in freezing weather, he'd have to keep his trumpet mouthpiece in his mouth to keep it from freezing to his lips[17] (Baker, 1997). In freezing weather, valved brass instruments froze solid while trombone players had to contend with freezing slides.

Building a Bigger and Better Berlin Band

When Mr. Ferraro took over the 298th on March 5, 1947, it had only 21 men on its roster. When the first wave of replacement musicians arrived a month later, the word was already out that the Army had big plans for the 298th—it was going to become the equivalent in Berlin of the Army Band in Washington, D.C. The first step was to increase its size, and by May, the band roster contained 65 names. As part of this upgrading of the band, each band member had a uniform tailored specifically for him. Along with that tailored uniform, each band member received a white silk scarf to be worn around the neck, white gloves, a white Sam Brown belt, a white helmet liner, and paratrooper boots. Mr. Ferraro oversaw implementation of these changes as well as orienting the new arrivals to the band and getting them settled. And all this was in addition to a very busy schedule. The 298th was the only Army band in Berlin, so as other units also had increases in their ranks, there was a growing list of requests for the band to support various military ceremonies. This also meant taking the long ride out to Tempelhof several times each week.

At the beginning of May, the band started preparing special music for weekly lawn concerts every Sunday afternoon. In effect, the band had a six and a half day work week. Harry Reinert wrote home in early June: "Today has really been a popper. We started off by going out to the 16th Infantry and playing while they had drill, and then ran through tomorrow's retreat parade three times. Then we went out to Tempelhof and met Under Secretary of War Peterson. Now we have to go back at 4 to meet some other joker. And we were supposed to have gotten off after the inspections this morning. That's the way it goes."

Mr. Ferraro was relieved by CWO Marion E. Durbin on May 12, 1947. The 298th had not actually functioned as a military unit in garrison in almost two years. Mr. Durbin set his goal to bring up the military character of the band to a level in accordance with its size and mission. Being a skilled musician, he could deal with the soldiers of the band as a musician in addition as an officer. He set about to assess the band's strengths and weaknesses; he began highlighting those strengths and began correcting the weaknesses. He was determined to provide stability and leadership to the band. To improve the military aspect of the band, he began by imposing practices and procedures which the band members had not seen since basic training. Several of the men groused about the new rules, but Sebby Papa had a more generous impression—when he had surgery on his nose in June, Sebby said, Mr. Durbin came to see him in the hospital, which Sebby thought was "very nice of him." Sebby worked in the office for several weeks after his hospital stay, and he found Mr. Durbin a good and caring man.

Sebby recalls that Mr. Durbin conducted the band for a significant ceremony in Belgium in October, 1947. The band went on temporary duty to Antwerp, one of the very few times the band in its early history did so, to take part in the return to the United States of the remains of World War II dead. This was a high-profile ceremony, one in which Sebby was proud to have participated. It was a somber ceremony, dignified and fitting to commemorate the sacrifice of many tens of thousands of American soldiers during the war.

Talented Musicians

The new recruits were not involved in the Army Day parade on April 9, but later that day, Mr. Ferraro assembled the enlarged band for an initial rehearsal. He passed out a piece of music for the men to sight-read. Harry Reinert, one of the newly arrived recruits, sat in the second clarinet section. His commented that the music had so much black ink on the page, he wondered if perhaps the printer had simply printed the music on black paper and stuck in a few white spots. He said the tempo was so fast he could scarcely keep track of where he was, much less play the notes. Sitting on solo first stand in the section was a man older than most of the other band members. Reportedly he was a music professor at Duke University. Sitting next to him was a young recruit who had just arrived in Berlin. When the band had finished the piece, the older man said to the younger, "That A back there is a sharp," to which the new arrival answered, "Yeah, I know. I noticed that too late."

When Sebby Papa was assigned to the 298th Army Ground Forces Band, he roomed in a two-man apartment on Wilskistrasse with trombonist Robert Badgely, who also fronted the 298th Dance Band. They quickly became good friends. Sebby also recalls sitting alongside a very young Chet Baker in rehearsals, dance band jobs, and performing ceremonies and parades. Chet started his Army career as an underage 16-year-old who had lied his way into the Army. Discovered during his training at Ft. Lewis, Washington, Chet was given the option to take a discharge or to stay in. He chose to stay in and found himself on the way to Germany as a clerk, assigned to Berlin. Shortly after his arrival in the war-torn city, Chet heard the 298th rehearsing in the Onkel Toms Hütte area. He made his way over to the band's orderly room and found himself talking about his ability to play trumpet to a rather imposing master sergeant, who told Chet to return the next morning and talk to the first trumpeter, Paul Martin. Sebby remembers Martin as a top-notch lead trumpet player from Michigan. After listening for a few minutes, Martin told Chet to report to the master sergeant so that transfer paperwork could be drawn up to transfer Chet to the band.

Chet Baker

In these years, Chet wrote that he knew very little about jazz. While in Berlin, however, he began listening to such artists as Stan Kenton and other big bands. He was ecstatic to discover big band jazz and other forms of jazz including bebop. He spent a lot of off-duty time crafting his art. It didn't take long for Chet to become the regular trumpet soloist or "ride man" for the 298th Dance Band. Sebby remembers Chet having a phenomenal ear. As a poor music reader, however, Chet would pretend to play the first time reading down a chart, but the second time through, Chet could play every note. He continued building on that skill.

Chet preferred understatement in his highly creative melodic interpretations. Interacting with and complementing him were rhythm players of varying skill. Three years after his discharge from the Army, Chet's interpretations in a series of recordings accompanied the work of several great "cool jazz" innovators of the 1950's, including Gerry Mulligan, Stan Getz and others. Even 25 years after his death, Chet's recordings are a staple on the NPR jazz station in Tacoma, Washington.

Sebby learned a great deal from Chet as well, and used that experience when he fronted his own big band for some 35 years.

A German Officer's View of the Army

Harry Reinert saw in June a memo circulated through the Berlin command seeking soldiers with journalistic experience. Since he had decided on a career in journalism, he applied for a position on the staff of the Berlin *Observer*. (The second anniversary issue of the Berlin *Observer*, published on July 28, 1947 contained several photos of Harry and his associates performing their tasks.) Harry continued to live in the band billets at the Onkel Toms Hütte, but he was released from duty with the 298th.

At that time, all jeeps in the American sector of Berlin had German drivers. The paper had a jeep and driver assigned to it. While Harry rode down to the print shop for the paper one day, the driver, a man probably in his early forties, asked Harry how he liked his Army experience thus far. Harry responded that he didn't like it at all. He complained about the demands of the job and, in particular, about the unreasonable demands by a rigid and intolerant bandmaster. The driver's response surprised Harry, for he said that he had been an officer in the German Army and liked it. He felt that the Army taught a young man what he needed to learn in order to be successful in any field: he learned self-restraint, ability to work cooperatively with others, tolerance, patience, discipline, and a sense of belonging to a cause greater than himself. The entire experience with the jeep driver, as brief as it had been, stuck with Harry over the years. While he had no intention of staying in the Army, he recognized the value of the experience.

Politics in a Political City

As events in Berlin in the first few years after the ending of World War II unfolded, the rift between the Western Allies and the Soviets became increasingly wider. Colonel Frank Howley recorded in his book *Berlin Command* that meeting after meeting of the Kommandatura (the collective military commanders of each Berlin sector) was characterized by stonewalling, delaying tactics, and other attempts by the Soviets to disrupt the proceedings and to niggle at virtually every point of discussion. Of particular interest to the Soviets were the upcoming elections—they wanted to be absolutely certain that the SED (communist) party won these elections in October 1946, and subsequent elections. The Soviets' clear, unmistakable objective to Col. Howley was to make it so difficult for the Western Allies that they would leave the city—an opportunity that would rid Berlin of the Allies and remove the proverbial thorn in their side. Despite the blatant interference of the Soviets with the election process, the SPD (Social Democrats) won 48.7 percent of the vote. While not a clear majority, the SED party finished far behind with 19.8 percent of the vote. Even in the Soviet sector of Berlin, the SED amassed only 21 percent of the vote.[18]

These issues didn't necessarily concern the 298th, because the Berlin command continued to morph. The 298th Army Band needed a larger battalion-sized element for appropriate administrative, quarters, rations, and military justice support, and thus was assigned to the 7782nd Special Troops

Battalion.

The Berlin Blockade – A Political Background

Colonel Frank Howley recorded that the working relationship between the Soviets and the Western Allies continued to degrade through 1947. The Allied Kommandatura meetings more often than not were contentious and bitter with distrust. Col. Howley recorded the bulk of the issues while dealing with them in his official capacity as Director of OMGUS, but communicated these issues to General Clay as necessary. The problems had a central theme— the Soviets were not the friends that they and the various World War II conferences represented themselves to be. The faux protests registered by the Soviets and communicated to General Clay had a telling effect on Gen. Clay, however, despite Howley's efforts. Col. Howley wrote, "During the months of September and October, 1947, I had a series of five conferences with General Clay. While the conferences probably seemed unimportant to him as commanding general, they reaffirmed my own feeling that my thinking was in complete disagreement with American policy in Berlin and, logically, I could expect no personal advancement [in rank]."[19] Those five "conferences" functioned more as being called to task for decisions Col. Howley had made, but he remained committed to his decisions and found himself more and more at odds with Gen. Clay. After two and one-half years of dealing with the Soviets, Col. Howley was convinced that the Soviets could not be trusted and certainly could not be relied upon in reporting the facts on any given issue. Gen. Clay, while he indicated respect and admiration for his subordinate, did not see what Col. Howley had seen on a daily basis. Clearly, Gen. Clay saw things in a different light in his position as Military Governor. But Col. Howley was fed up and in another conference with Gen. Clay, he announced his desire to return home to Philadelphia "to learn more about our democracy at its historic source."[20]

Two days before Col. Howley's departure, however, Gen. Clay called him in and, after some small talk during which he seemed as if he had a larger issue to discuss, suddenly blurted, "Frank, how would you like to come back on active duty as Commandant?" Col. Howley agreed to do so, but nonetheless returned home to Philadelphia for a three-week visit, then came back to Berlin on December 1, 1947, to assume his duties as Commandant, American Sector, Berlin, and to receive the single star of a Brigadier General.

Despite Gen. Howley's experience and knowledge of the Soviets and their tricks, the political situation between the Soviets and Western Allies continued to deteriorate. Finally, on June 16, 1948, the Soviets walked out of the Kommandatura. The Soviets had already begun the harassment and interdiction techniques of rail, road and barge transportation to and from Berlin. They knew, as Gen. Howley knew, that prohibiting road and waterborne transportation to and from the city would cripple Berlin in a matter of weeks.

On June 24, 1948, the Soviets imposed the Blockade. All road, barge, and rail traffic was halted. Stores of food and fuel in Berlin were minimal, and since virtually all food and fuel had to be brought to the city, there was not much in reserve. In response, the Americans implemented Operation Vittles, the resupply of Berlin by air through the three air corridors that remained open by international agreement and would continue to remain open. The British instituted a similar plan, but cooperated with the Americans fully. The French took no part in any of this, but did agree to allocate land in the French sector to begin the construction of another airfield. Several thousand German workers labored aggressively under Allied engineers and completed the work within two months. This airfield ultimately became Tegel Airport.

Währungsreform (Currency Reform)

The capitulation of Germany on May 8, 1945 not only affected the political structure, but the economic structure as well. Initially, a barter economy quickly changed into an active Black Market, responsible for at least half of all commercial transactions. During the first three years of occupation of Germany, the U.K. and U.S. vigorously pursued a military disarmament program in Germany, partly by removal of military equipment but mainly through an import embargo on raw materials—part of the Morgenthau Plan approved by President Franklin D. Roosevelt.

Former U.S. President Herbert Hoover, in one of his reports from Germany in March 1947, however, argued for a change in U.S. occupation policy: "There is the illusion that the New Germany left after the annexations can be reduced to a 'pastoral state' (Morgenthau's vision). It cannot be done unless we exterminate or move 25,000,000 people out of it."[21] Hoover further noted that, "We can keep Germany in these economic chains but it will also keep Europe in rags." (Reinert E. a., 2008)[22]

Reflecting the changing view in Washington, Secretary of State George C. Marshall in a commencement address at Harvard University on June 5, 1947 first called for American assistance in restoring the economic infrastructure of Europe. His short speech introduced what became the Marshall Plan and a distinct reversal in policy from the Morgenthau Plan.

With its unstable economy, the BRD (Bundesrepublik Deutschland)—the West German democracy created by the three Western Allies—would be unable to benefit from the $1.4 billion in Marshall Plan money coming in from the United States. Currency reform (die Währungsreform) was essential to stabilize the economy and simultaneously destroy the Black Market.

On Sunday, June 20, 1948, Ludwig Erhard introduced the Deutsche Mark (DM) as the legal currency replacing the old Reichsmark (RM), in use since

1933. That Sunday, every man, woman, and child in West Germany received 40 DM, and another 20 DM was circulated later.

The new currency was exchanged at a rate of DM 1 = RM 1 for the essential currency such as wages, payment of rents, etc. Other privately held Reichmarks, e.g. accumulated from Black Market sales, could be exchanged at a rate of DM 1 = RM 10.

Die Währungsreform also marked the beginning of the West German reconstruction, labeled the Wirtschaftswunder (economic miracle).

The actions that Sunday so outraged the Soviets that they imposed the Berlin Blockade on the following day. The Soviets intended to starve the Berliners to the point that the Western Allies would leave their assigned sectors. The Soviets didn't believe that the Western Allies could supply the city with fuel, food, medicine, and essentials to sustain life: but they didn't count on the three air corridors that, by international agreement, stayed open providing air access to and from Berlin.

The Berlin Airlift

The Berlin Airlift was a political more than a military confrontation. Nevertheless, discussion ensued about forcing the issue by sending one or more combat divisions through the Soviet zone of occupation to enforce the delivery of food, fuel, and critical supplies that the city needed. This would have been seen as overly provocative, the decision-makers said. Implementing an airlift was seen as a viable option. The transportation experts weren't so confident, however. There weren't the aircraft available, and those aircraft, mostly old and well-worn C-47 "Goonybirds, " could handle only a little over four tons per haul. The vaunted C-54 aircraft became the workhorse, replacing the Goonybird. The C-82 "Flying Boxcar" handled larger equipment, even automobiles, having a carrying capacity of 7.5 tons. As the Airlift proceeded, streamlining efforts both in the air and on the ground resulted in a staggering 4,688 tons over the period April 15-16, 1949. This meant that a plane landed at the three landing zones within Berlin (Tempelhof, Gatow, and Tegel) every 1.5 minutes. Realistic scenes of the movie "The Big Lift" were shot in Berlin after the Blockade was lifted. This film starring Montgomery Clift and Paul Douglas as the only Hollywood actors. The film garnered no awards for drama, but it is filled with incredible shots of war-torn Berlin and Tempelhof Airfield in 1948-49 and live shots of the German crews loading and unloading the planes.

All this effort was not without sacrifice. Electricity was restricted to four hours per day. Fresh fruit and vegetables were a thing of the past, dried potatoes being a staple in a diet of only 1,500 calories per day. Winter proved to be less severe than in recent years, yet some still died of exposure.

The unbridled success of the Airlift spelled political and social doom for the Soviets. They had gambled that the Western Allies would not be able to supply the city with even minimal quantities of food and fuel. They lost that gamble and the aftermath of the Berlin Airlift not only disassociated the Soviets even further from the Berliners in the East of the city, but also spelled a change on the Western side.

The Berlin Airlift, as difficult as it was and for the many restrictions it meant over the course of the operation, endeared the Western Allies to the Berliners, who began to see the Allies, particularly the Americans, not as conquerors but as protectors. Indeed, the policy of the United States in keeping a foothold in Berlin was solidified with the Airlift and continued until the political changes associated with the Wall's demise in 1989 spelled an end to the occupation of Berlin by all Four Powers.

The Band Played On

Throughout all of this, the 298th Army Band (redesignated from the previous "298th Army Ground Forces Band" effective June 1, 1947) (Durbin, Unit History, 298th Army Ground Forces Band, 1 Jan-31 Dec 47, 1948)[23] continued in its mission of providing musical support in honor guards and official military settings, in addition to more relaxed and less formal gatherings. Even during the beginning months of the Airlift, from June through December 1948, not less than six honor guard ceremonies were held at Tempelhof or OMGUS. (Durbin, Unit History, 298th Army Band, 1 Jan-31 Dec 48, 1949)[24] Tempelhof was favored due to the attractive, weather-protective overhead roof that permitted aircraft to taxi directly underneath, but OMGUS was also a receiving point.

The rebuilding of the city following the war had slowed due to the more immediate need of feeding and fueling the city throughout the Blockade and Airlift, but upon the Blockade's lifting, those efforts resumed. As in any conflict, whether military or political, the biggest victims were the children. Trumpeter Ward Lindstrom recalls playing for children's orphanages and for the handicapped. A special program called Operation Cheer was instituted during the Berlin Airlift and the band was integral in supporting this program. Ward provided a copy of a barracks-made newsletter that illustrates the creativity (or perhaps boredom) of at least a few bandsmen during his tour. Fully tongue-in-cheek by the newspaper's name *The Drag*, this newsletter heralds the duty and the good fortune to have been trained as a musician, then to find oneself in Berlin.

The Drag does provide a measure of respect that at least most of the band had toward Master Sergeant Matlock, a flute and piccolo player and usual rehearsal conductor. Ward remembers him being competent and capable of rehearsing the band efficiently and responsibly.

Master Sergeant Matlock was a clear opposite to his predecessor Master Sergeant Richard C. Hawkins, who was undoubtedly the NCO referred to by nervous trumpeter and gig-seeker Chet Baker as "unsmiling, leathery face[d]—he was about forty-five or fifty years old— sat at a desk in the corner with a four-foot brass-ended red, white, and blue-tasseled baton propped up behind him." Baker went on, "He looked up and I started talking. I didn't stop speaking until I heard 'Come around in the morning and you can talk to our first trumpet player.'"

Ward recalls Hawkins as being a combat veteran whose sharp jaw had been broken in North Africa by a rifle butt in hand-to-hand fighting. Despite this rather courageous service, Hawkins was known to sneak out of the compound after hours without a pass, accompanied by several of his entourage. He further decided he'd rather just not bother coming to work and went AWOL. He was found shacked up downtown. He was reduced in rank to private and sent back to the States. Ward later heard that Hawkins got all his stripes back. Clarinetist Roger Woodrum (1949-54), agreed, "Hawkins was old school. He believed in working hard and playing hard. While his antics cost him his stripes, he did get them all back some years later while back in the States." Snare drummer Bill Ervin (1949-55) also concurred with that statement.

The Airlift had no appreciable impact on the band, save for rolling blackouts. Life continued as it had, with and without Richard C. Hawkins. Hawkins' antics no doubt provided an example—not necessarily a good one—to Ward and his four of his buddies. They'd been uptown on the Ku-Damm having a good time when they realized they needed to get back to the barracks. Five of them climbed aboard his 200 cc motorcycle and miraculously made it back to Onkel Toms Hütte without crashing and killing everybody.

Another distinction that Ward recalls is his role as Physical Training Instructor and as Troop Information Education Instructor. These duties became associated with a more organized and regimented unit and were reflective of the 298th's maturation as not only a band, but as a military unit. For example, Ward recalls setting up, organizing, and going out to the Grunewald twice yearly with M1 carbines and instruments. (The band would play during chow.) The band's support of the troops while in the field was a visible sign of not just community relations and political support in the conduct of honor guard ceremonies, but also of the band's willingness to roll up its collective sleeves and entertain under less formal conditions.

Most GIs appreciate meeting a good woman while they serve and Ward was no exception. Ward met Elizabeth Wolter, the woman who was to become his wife, in Berlin. He recalls getting married in New York on his way home from Berlin; getting married in Berlin in those days was somewhat problematical. While Elizabeth, as a teen girl, was sent to Czechoslovakia in early 1945 for safety, her father, an architect involved with the reconstruction of the Hauptkadettenanstalt (Central Cadet Training Facility) in Lichterfelde (later to become Andrews Barracks), made the grievous error of referring to

Hermann Göring as a "pig". He was arrested and sent to prison until Hitler released all prisoners so they could become martyrs in defending the city during the last days of the war.

With the Soviets embarrassed and their influence somewhat reduced within Berlin, the citizens of Berlin continued to rebuild with a new currency that seemed to finally shed its Nazi cloak and looked forward to better times.

AFTER THE AIRLIFT

Despite the Blockade and Airlift, the status of Berlin stayed the same. The city remained under occupation by the Four Powers and would continue to remain under occupation until the Four Powers agreed to end it. While West Berlin retained a connection to the "temporary" new West German capitol in Bonn and East Berlin became the illegal capitol of the German Democratic Republic, the Berlin delegates to the government in Bonn had no vote. To have permitted the Berlin representatives to have a vote would have called into question the entire status of Berlin. The Western Allies were adamant about this political reality, and while the United States formally recognized the Federal Republic of Germany in 1955, the two Germanys did not even recognize each other until Willy Brandt's *Ostpolitik* policies in 1972 diplomatically confronted the reality of East Germany. The Western Allies, however, did not recognize East Germany until 1974.

The Soviet Union saw the presence of the Western Allies in Berlin as a thorn in their side. Nikita Khrushchev, in his meeting with U.S. President Kennedy in Vienna in June 1961, would famously say, "The U.S. is unwilling to normalize the situation in the most dangerous spot in the world,. The USSR wants to perform an operation on this sore spot—to eliminate this thorn, this ulcer—without prejudicing the interests of any side, but rather to the satisfaction of all peoples of the world" (Kempe, 2011).[25]

The Soviets used all manner of harassment including intimidation, delay, and aggression to impede the Western Allies' access to and presence in Berlin. The Soviet Union wanted the entire city under her sphere and the Allies out. These policies did not come to pass, but it wasn't for lack of trying. More deliberate and blatant harassment techniques still cropped up, even to the point of loss of life. In particular, MIG fighter aircraft buzzing Allied aircraft through the air corridors occurred with increasing frequency. Duty train and other rail transits were suddenly and mysteriously halted due to "technical difficulties." None of this had the same impact as the Berlin Blockade, but for the man on the ground not only were these harassment techniques a nuisance, they were sometimes deadly.

Until the Wall was erected in August 1961, Berlin was still, for all practical purposes, an open city. There were no tangible barriers between the different

Refugee concert, with young conductor

sectors and people moved freely in and out, some living in the East and working in the West, and vice-versa. The freedoms enjoyed in the West were not reciprocated in the East and this meant the advent of refugees from the East coming to West. Refugee centers began popping up in West Berlin, one of the better known located in Marienfelde, a subdistrict in the southern part of the American sector. This center opened in 1953 and was one of several refugee centers supported by the 298th Army Band during the immediate post-war era.

CWO Marion E. Durbin had indeed stayed on longer than any of his predecessors, except for CWO Frank Rosato. Mr. Durbin remained in Berlin until his replacement arrived in early 1950. The year 1948 had seen several noteworthy changes in the 298th. For example, one warrant officer and 38 enlisted men were attached to the band from Headquarters and Headquarters Company, 7782nd Special Troops Battalion. These men were to serve with the band as the 7753rd Augmentation Detachment, created in May 1948, an action that in essence doubled the 298th roster (Grummish, 1948).[26] The purpose of this decision, according to CWO Carroll H. Grummish who had transferred from the Special Troops battalion with the rest of the men and who commanded the Augmentation Unit, was to bolster the band and give it the strength of a division band. But that wasn't all. In July 1948, the 7868th Fife and Drum Unit was also attached to the band as a Field Music Corps and continued to function with the band throughout the remainder of the year. At one time, according to Bill Ervin, the 298th Army Band, 7753rd Augmentation Unit, and the 7868th Fife and Drum Corps consisted of about 100 musicians.

The 298th was eventually reorganized as a band with an authorized strength of 56 men and two warrant officers. With Mr. Durbin commanding the band and WOJG Gordon Booth (also a trained bandmaster) assisting him, this made the 7753rd Augmentation Detachment superfluous, so it was deactivated (Moore, 1949).[27] Mr. Grummish and 19 men were transferred directly to the 298th Army Band.

Roger Woodrum recalls Mr. Grummish as "Mr. No." "Since he ran the supply room and that was the place where you went when you needed reeds or other materials to do your job, he was famous for telling us 'No' for the simplest, most routine requests. Brass players couldn't get valve oil. We reed players couldn't get reeds. Grummish was not very cooperative with us, and we learned to go around him and get the things we needed, or to make do with what we had."

Mr. Grummish had served as a bandmaster in the 8th Armored Division during World War II. After having been assigned to the 298th as its commander for a little over one month—from February 15 to March 26, 1950—Mr. Grummish returned to his former command.

The historical reports from Mr. Durbin made frequent mention of the difficulties in receiving "qualified" musicians from the Army's personnel replacement system. The large, 100-man 298th, along with the white and colored Honor Guards (the Army was still very much segregated despite President Truman's January 1948 executive order to de-segregate the armed services) and the Horse Platoon of the 16th Constabulary all served to provide expected and customary ceremonial duties within the city of Berlin. The Horse Platoon also had a more tactical mission in providing overwatch in the East, but its 34 men and 31 horses also spent time in ceremonial garb. In time, the white and colored Honor Guards merged to become the Berlin Drill Team, and the Horse Platoon was deactivated in 1958.

According to Reinhard von Bronewski, retired Berlin police officer, the Onkel Toms Hütte complex was returned to the original owners on September 6, 1947. Perhaps the former WAC living quarters of this neighborhood were returned, as von Bronewski claims, but Mr. Durbin's annual report of 1949 states the 298th had remained in their Onkel Toms Hütte apartments until June 1949, at which time they moved to the former Telefunken Research Complex, now called McNair Barracks.

After several years of living apartment-style, two or three men to an apartment, band members reverted to living barracks-style at McNair. Ervin remembered the band facility being just inside the Goerzallee main gate, and to the right. He remembered it being suitable, but not remarkable. Roger Woodrum provided a little more detail: "We had the whole lower floor of the first building as you came in the gate. The white honor guard had the second floor. Yes, we had two honor guards there, white and black. Both were outstanding at silent drill. Also, there was a horse platoon and at all honor guard ceremonies, the band, the white honor guard, the black honor guard, the color guard (which consisted of four black members of the black honor guard), and the fife and drum unit were all there. Those units greeted all the high brass that came to Berlin and there were a ton of them."

The move to McNair lasted until July 1950. Most likely to move and consolidate the combat troops into McNair from Oliver Barracks in Lankwitz (a smaller U.S. Kaserne that housed the 16th Constabulary Squadron), the band left McNair and moved to Building 2, Roosevelt Barracks in Lichterfelde.

In the early 1950s, the bloated band gradually lost personnel through attrition and the band then settled into an authorized strength of about 40, a number that remained more or less constant through the rest of the band's existence. One warrant officer bandmaster and one enlisted bandleader comprised the senior leadership, with three sergeants first class assisting the enlisted bandleader in actual running of the band.

Roosevelt Barracks, while small, also has a significant history.[28] Roger Woodrum recalls, "We had a three-story barracks. The basement was the supply room. A Corporal Rose was the supply sergeant and he drank like a fish, but was one of the best men there. He was an old combat veteran. The second floor was offices, two rehearsal halls, and rooms for the NCOs. The third floor had rooms for the other EM. Wilmont Trumbull was the CO there at Roosevelt. As we made the move from McNair to Roosevelt, he had taken over from Marion Durbin at McNair."

Most German "Kasernen" featured a large grassy area in the center of buildings that ringed it. Roosevelt Barracks was no exception. The 298th frequently used this large grassy area to conduct drill band rehearsals and ceremonies.

This arrangement at Roosevelt Barracks also didn't last long, Beginning in 1951, Roosevelt Barracks became the home of the 6941st Guard Battalion, a unit of German nationals whose mission it was to guard the various U.S. complexes in Berlin.

In 1951, the band made its next-to-last move to Building 909, Andrews Barracks. Formerly the Hauptkadettenanstalt, i.e., the Prussian "West Point," it morphed into a "Gymnasium" or training center of a political bent during the Weimar Republic following World War I, and then became the headquarters of the SS Leibstandarte Adolf Hitler (Hitler's personal body guard regiment) during World War II. This small but picturesque installation in the south of Lichterfelde became the home of the 298th Army Band for the next 43 years.

Andrews Barracks

When the Treaty of Versailles after World War I essentially disabled the German military machine, the Hauptkadettenanstalt was closed in 1920, followed by the Gymnasium until 1933. The Third Reich's expanding militarism required that the facility be converted for German troops. Over the next few years, the troops occupying the Kaserne varied but principally housed and trained Hitler's personal bodyguard regiment.

Review of the original layout of the Kaserne during the academy days reveals substantial changes. For example, three of the four large barracks blocks, each shaped like a central hallway with wings extending toward the center of the arrangement, no longer exist. The original entrance to the Kaserne was on Altdorferstrasse; this central area was demolished during the 1930s to upgrade for the Nazi military units which were to occupy the Kaserne.

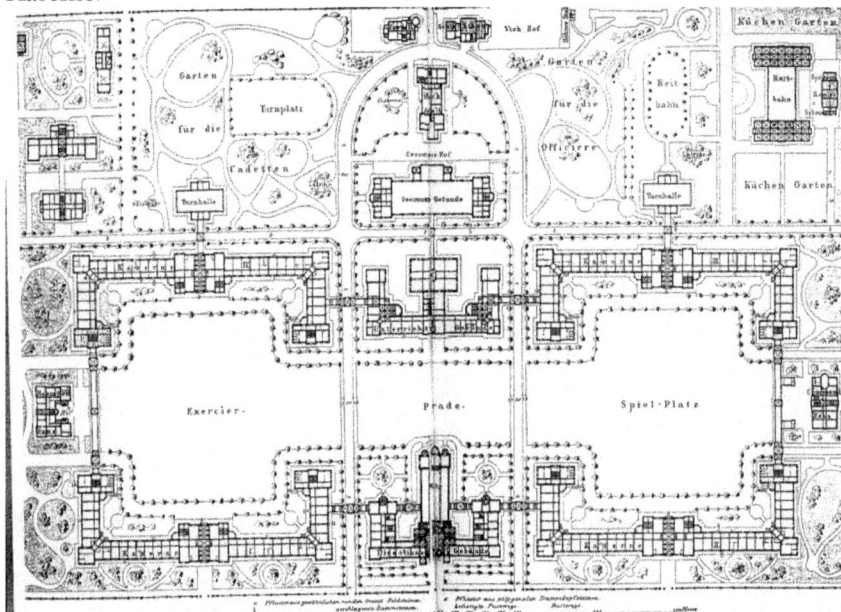

Hauptkadettenanstalt, before WWI

The Kaserne was also expanded toward the south and incorporated numerous vehicle maintenance facilities and parking, all of which was used by the Americans following the war. New buildings were erected and still others were torn down. The Maintenance Facility used by the Berlin command was depot-level and employed hundreds of Berlin workers over the years. The southern expansion of the Kaserne also included the sports field affectionately referred to as "Yankee Stadium" after the American takeover. The entire addition to the Kaserne more than doubled the original size.

The central square of the Kaserne featured a small building in the center of it; this was torn down in the 1930s. The indoor swimming pool was also built in the 1930s and was used as a training pool for the swimmers in preparation for the 1936 Summer Olympics, which were held in Berlin.

Night of the Long Knives

The rise of the Nazi party during the early 1930s and the ascension of Adolf Hitler to ultimate power in January 1933 resulted in an internal squabble within the party. The Nazi Party's "Sturmabteilung" (SA), otherwise known as the "Brownshirts" or "Stormtroopers", was one of two para-military wings of the party. The other was the Schutzstaffel, or "SS", which was subordinate to the SA. The SA was led by Ernst Röhm, a personal friend of Hitler's from the early Beer Hall Putsch days in Munich.

The SA formed as a force to both protect the party's leaders and to engage in street fighting and beer hall brawling to eliminate political opposition. In time, the SA grew in size to dwarf the German Army which was limited to 100,000 men as a condition of the Treaty of Versailles following World War I. When Röhm, a mere captain, was elevated to cabinet rank and actually advocated that the German Army (Reichswehr) be incorporated into the SA, Göring and Himmler feared that Röhm and the SA were too powerful. They convinced Hitler that the SA should be purged of its more strident members. Hitler ordered Himmler's SS to seek out and murder those who had been listed and over a 72-hour period from June 29 to July 1, 1934, hundreds of SA members, including Röhm, were rounded up and executed.

One of the execution sites was the small courtyard at the northwest corner of the *Hauptkadettenanstalt*, which lay just to the north of the Kaserne's hospital. By this time, the entire Kaserne had become the home of the SS Leibstandarte Adolf Hitler (LAH), a select group of soldiers who were reliable, trustworthy, and who fit certain height and weight requirements. LAH soldiers weren't necessarily Nazis, but they represented the finest soldiers Germany could offer. Fewer than 3% of those who applied were selected for service. The others were sent to lesser units.

After arrest and transport to the LAH Kaserne in Lichterfelde, the victims' identities were confirmed in the Kaserne's administration building. A detail of LAH soldiers comprised the firing squad which was augmented by a drummer. After being escorted to the execution site, a few words were spoken to condemn the SA's actions and to justify what was about to take place, and then the order was given to fire.

Executions occurred throughout the day until late at night. The shots and cries of "Heil Hitler!" from those who did not understand why they were arrested much less being executed, rang out every 20 minutes. The tension is so unbearable for the families of officers living in the barracks that many leave their apartments to take refuge elsewhere in the city (Gallo, 1997)[29]. The coup de grâce came after a short silence. Trucks arrived and the blood-drenched bodies were loaded onto the truckbeds. The trucks then were driven off to a crematorium for disposal.

The exact number of those executed in the entire purge will never be known. The SS destroyed its official documents relating to the purge. Other historical documents put the number executed at the SS LAH Kaserne at approximately 15 (Unknown, 2004).[30]

Some years later, 298th Army bandsmen on CQ duty encountered odd noises where none should have occurred. Scraping sounds and strange lights appeared late at night during all-night tours of duty. Herman the Ghost became an occasional, if unwelcome visitor to building 909, and his presence was acknowledged both as a humorous, but still spooky, part of the building's lore. Following Building 909's complete interior renovation in 1985/86, trombonist Dan Hermann obtained a modest concrete slab in the shape of a headstone, painted Herman's (no relation to Dan) name on it, and complete with a mini-ceremony, planted the headstone just outside the south entrance to the building. Perhaps with this special place and ceremony, Herman would be finally at rest. It is unknown if Herman was one of the SA leaders who was executed during the SA purge so long ago, or if he was a student of the Hauptkadettenanstalt who died for another reason.

Building 909

Located on the northeast corner of Andrews Barracks, at the intersection of Baselerstraße and Finkensteinallee, this building enjoyed a quiet corner of the Kaserne. The building itself dates from the Hauptkadettenanstalt days and served as the Kaserne's hospital. The first floor had contained the surgical suites and examination rooms, while the second and third floors featured hospital rooms and ancillary medical facilities.

Those ancillary facilities included two smaller neighboring buildings that formed a small enclave within the Kaserne itself. The smaller, single-story building located at right angles to the band building was used for various purposes during the U.S. Army's occupation. It was a headquarters for various Special Troop units or battalion staff and after the building was renovated in the mid-1980s, it became the Berlin Command's Dental Clinic. During the academy days and for an undetermined period afterwards up till the U.S. occupation of the Kaserne, the building that became the dental clinic was known as the "Isolierbaracke." This small building was used to keep patients in isolation.

Still another very tiny structure was actually a bunker. This bunker ran parallel to Baselerstraße on the inside of the fence and was known as the

"Leichenhalle" or morgue. This bunker remains to this day, though it remained locked and only seldom used as an outdoor storage facility.

The building located just to the south of the band building was known in one sketch of the Kadettenanstalt as the Beamtenhaus (Administration Building) and in another as the Lazarett (essentially a separate medical facility where especially sick patients were quarantined). This building served multiple purposes. It contained a pharmacy and doctors' quarters, in addition to serving an administrative function and a facility where especially sick patients were cared for. This building was so severely damaged during World War II that it was never repaired; the local fire department used it to practice putting out fires that were purposely set in the building. Allen Thompson said. "We had always thought of that building as being a sort of 'sister building' to ours. Not much of it was left and what little there was wasn't tenable for anything except scorching once in a while."

The Beamtenhaus/Lazarett, or rather the shell of this building, was razed in the early 1960s, according to John Parmenter, who served as part of the Long Thrust augmentation effort in 1963. John asserted that the bomb-

Building 909, South entrance

damaged "sister building" was still standing in 1963. The infantrymen stationed on Andrews at the time used it for ammunition storage. The structure was eventually torn down and the Andrews Barracks outer fence was erected in that location.

Building 909 had three stories and a basement. Approximately 80 yards long and 30 yards wide, construction and renovation efforts occurred in the early days of the American occupation to convert the operating rooms into offices, the supply room, and the arms room. On the second and third floors, hospital rooms were converted to barracks rooms. A curious feature of some rooms was the presence of an ordinary sink. Some of these had been removed, but others remained. For those lucky occupants whose rooms still had a sink, that made the trek to the latrine for shaving or oral hygiene less of a chore.

The basement had storage facilities and, it was said, even a morgue. The band used the morgue to store stocks of beverages which were given to the band and picnic supplies left over from parties.

All of this historical discussion about a relatively simple building may not make a lot of sense to the casual reader. But to those who lived and worked within Building 909, the building meant a great deal. It was a home; it was refuge. It was a familiar set of surroundings to young men and women who were perhaps in a foreign country for the first time in their young lives. The strangeness of the language spoken outside the gate, the condition of the rest of the city, particularly in the years just after the war, and the brashness of the Berliners themselves were elements that one faced. For many, known in some circles as "barracks rats," it was the only place to be even after duty hours. Dealing with the U-Bahn, the S-Bahn, and the bus system was too much hassle. Foreign money in the form of Reichsmarks, then military scrip, and then after 1948 the Deutsche mark was too much to worry about. Staying in the building, in one's room, perhaps with a good book or AFN radio or even in later years with a record on the stereo, to say nothing of practicing, was all some bandsmen needed.

About two-thirds of the way down the first floor hallway hall and prior to the sorely-needed major renovation in 1985-86 which gutted the building, an interior wall separated the band's area on the first floor from Headquarters and Headquarters Detachment. HHD was another unit whose function was not quite understood, according to Master Sergeant Lou Hurvitz, Enlisted Bandleader of the 298th from 1981 to 1984. This wall was not part of the original construction and was erected during the Fifties to provide a separate office area from the rest of the band.

Lou tells the story:

"It seems as if there was a silver Chevy that was always parked on the north side of the band building (toward the back). As I recall, this Chevy was a sporty-looking job that boasted twin (front to back, I believe) racing stripes. Again, my memory is clouded by 21-plus years of minutiae, but I think these stripes ran not on the sides of the car, but over the top and the trunk (again, I could be wrong).

"This NCOIC of this little detachment did not appreciate someone from the band parking in HIS designated parking spot. (It was NOT his parking spot; it was unmarked.) But, he thought that he would have some fun with the band's NCOIC and came in to complain about a soldier from the band parking in that spot. Oh, by the way, need I mention that the offending vehicle was the Chevy described in the preceding paragraph? Well, this NCOIC came in and complained vigorously, demanding that I have my soldier move his car.

"I jumped to my feet and slammed my fist on the desk so hard I thought that the vibration could be felt through the entire band building. I walked around the desk and got in this soldier's face (maybe about two inches from him). I locked his heels at attention! I then told him not to f*!k (pardon the language, but that's the word I used) with my troops and that Building 909 was MINE and I decided who parked where (which was BS, but it sounded good). I also told him if he EVER came in to the band area again, he'd have serious problems. I gave him 10 seconds to get his sorry ass (oops, there I go again!) out of my building. He protested, saying that nobody had ever talked to him like that. I told him to get used to it and to get the hell out of my building!"

A large, wooded area with many mature trees separated the band building from the Olympic-sized pool to the east. This pool, built as a training pool for the 1936 Olympics, was popular as a venue for physical training. It featured not just a 50-meter long pool, but also a 10 meter diving platform and shorter diving boards.

Mature trees shed their leaves every fall and a project undertaken by the band every year involved leaf-raking. Everybody took part in this activity, done in civilian clothes. Raking leaves into huge piles and having the "suck truck" come by to vacuum them up wasn't fun, but it had to be done prior to the obligatory inspection.

The basement of the building was also divided in half. During the early 1980s, the Berlin Brigade Commo Platoon inhabited half of the basement. The other half was allocated for the band's use. This area was mostly designated as a dayroom, complete with pool table, foosball table, and a home-built bar, along with the aforementioned storage rooms.

The second and third floors of the building were designated as barracks space, with some areas designated for the music library, drug and alcohol coordinator's office, instrument repair, and in later years, a TV room/reading room. Some rooms, especially on the third floor, were huge—easily 20 by 20 feet. Other rooms were known, not so affectionately, as "bowling alleys" due to their narrow width and lengthy depth. Of course, latrines and laundry rooms complemented each floor.

As the years went by, the building began showing its age. Since the building was first constructed in the early years of the military academy (1870 – 1880) with renovations in the mid-1930's to accommodate the Nazi Army units assigned to the Kaserne, gradual deterioration of the basic sewage, heating, plumbing, and electrical systems ensued. By the early 1980s, that manifested itself as errant wiring that dangled from the high ceilings and a particularly bad odor emanating from the 1st floor male latrine's sewage piping. Paint and plaster had begun falling from the walls and ceiling.

"The building was a great facility, but it clearly needed major repair," said Lou Hurvitz. "We did make it clear to the Directorate of Engineering and

Housing that the facility should be planned for extensive renovation in the next few years. It was becoming not such a great facility due to the natural deterioration."

Lou's comments did not go unheeded. By the time 1985 arrived, building 909 was to receive a complete renovation. This work, costing over 5 million Deutsche marks, would take more than a year to complete. The entire building would be gutted—floors, interior walls, electrical, heating, plumbing—and complete rebuilt.

To prepare for the move, the 298th had to move everything out. All belongings, equipment, music library, weapons, basic load of ammunition, field gear, all had to go. The band worked laboriously to take everything just a short distance away over to building 904, the western portion of which was empty. The band set up shop there and within a week or so in early 1985, was back in business.

The renovation took approximately a year. After it was finished, Building 909 was a showcase in band halls. Rehearsal rooms of various sizes were finished and treated with sound absorption panels. A sound room was designed in the middle of a circle of rehearsal rooms to service all of them for recordings or sound enhancement. Practice modules were procured and outfitted upstairs for personal and small ensemble practice. These could be used in off-hours to reduce disruption of others. Offices were configured with specific functions in mind rather than piecemeal, set-up-where-you-can arrangements. Barracks rooms were outfitted with new furniture, large wall lockers, better bunks, even small refrigerators. Personnel living off-post had a room in which to store their gear, including uniform items and instruments. The music library now had ample room for the huge collection of sheet music that the band had accumulated over the years. Perhaps the most amazing thing was the new telephone system. Rather than only three telephone numbers for the entire band, each office had its own number. Sharing phones became a thing of the past and the anomaly known as "Hitler's revenge" (the inefficient and ineffective telephone system that was so archaic that shouting on the telephone to another facility was the only way to be heard) also died with the old structure.

THE 1950s AND BEYOND

The Selective Service Act of 1948 reinstated the peacetime draft, which required men between the ages of 18 to 26 to register. The onset of the Korean War in June 1950 took advantage of the draft accordingly. The 298th received its allocation of musicians through a personnel system that first sent men to Germany, then evaluated them at one of two audition centers – one at Aßmannshausen am Rhein and another in southern Bavaria in Sonthofen. Some of these musicians were sent for additional training to Eastman Barracks, located next to the former concentration camp at Dachau, before reporting for duty in a theater that contained up to 21 Army bands, including the 298th.

CWO Marion Durbin yielded command of the 298th Army Band to CWO Wilmont Trumbull in February 1950, with Mr. Booth continuing to serve as junior bandmaster. Bill Ervin, who arrived in Berlin in December 1949, and Ward Lindstrom, who left Berlin in August 1952, both remember CWO William Hershenow, an older officer long past normal retirement age. Apart from mention in a barracks-generated newsletter in June 1952 which memorialized Hershenow's service and his apparent "passing," Internet research indicates that Bandleader Hershenow received reassignment orders from the 7th Field Artillery to the 26th Infantry as far back as 1922 and spent the war years as bandmaster of the 439th ASF Band at Ft. McQuaide, California.

The Era of the Draft Continues

Many of these men of this era were draftees who were exemplary players and some were less skilled. Still others had enlisted rather than be drafted, and whether deliberately or through other means, found themselves as Army musicians.

The draft created two different types of Army musician. The career musician usually had seen combat and the problems associated with it. The career musician, senior in grade and rank, had seen peacetime and the bureaucracies that came along with that. Some career musicians were better instrumentalists than others and some lacked in that area. But the career musician saw to it that the band functioned as a band and as a military unit. Above all, the career musician who could carry his own musical load and perform the leadership and training that was needed for the younger musician carried significant respect. The example that they set often inspired the younger soldiers to perform beyond themselves.

Those same career soldiers, along with their drafted or volunteer younger comrades, were now confronted with yet another war. A new war in Korea saw bitter fighting in horrific conditions. Some of those in the 298th wondered if their assignment in Berlin would end with orders to be deployed to Korea.

The second type of musician with the draft was the skilled instrumentalist. Highly intelligent and extremely capable, most draftees had no interest in Army music but had resigned themselves to serving their hitch—whether at 18 months or two years, depending on the program at the time—and then getting leaving the Army. Many of these players were extraordinarily gifted and had played in and for big-named ensembles. Their playing did their speaking.

Regardless of niche, all of these musicians picked up their instruments and fell into ranks when it was time for a ceremony or honor guard. Not too many bandmasters tolerated reduced numbers of available musicians from commitments, even with a larger band like the 298th in the early 1950s.

Guns and Gambling—A Dangerous Mix

Weapons qualification is a standard soldier-related duty. The band's assigned weaponry in the late 1940s and up until the advent of the M14 rifle in the early 1960s was the M1 carbine. This was a lighter weapon firing a .30 caliber cartridge, which was not necessarily intended largely for straight-line infantry; for the more combat-oriented soldiers of the day, the M1 Garand was the normal rifle. The M1 carbine, plus an M1911 .45 pistol or two in addition to basic loads of ammunition to be used only when and if ordered, comprised the band's armory.

In 1951, not long after the 298th made the move to Andrews, snare drummer Bill Ervin (1949-1955) recalls an incident that was far from ceremonial, but had everything to do with a .45 M1911 pistol. One of the members of the 298th, known as Smitty, was known as a gambler and a loan shark. After one particular payday, Smitty had made the rounds of the band members who gambled, took their winnings, and went over to the black honor guard's barracks on Andrews to continue his winning ways. Smitty continued to win and completely cleaned out a young fellow who had recently reenlisted. Not only had this fellow lost the bulk of his pay for that month, but he also lost his reenlistment bonus. Bill said both Smitty and the fellow who had lost his reenlistment bonus wound up in Smitty's car. The loser pulled out a loaded .45 and put a slug in Smitty's neck. The car remained running with the lights on while the loser fled. Smitty died of his wound before the MPs came by to investigate. Bill said he was pretty sure this story wasn't invented by the anti-gambling lobby.

According to Roger Woodrum, the shooter was caught, tried and sentenced to 10 years in prison. When he got out of prison in the early 1960s, he was found dead, floating face down in a river. Woodrum said he was certain that Smitty's family had something to do with the shooter's death, particularly since Smitty's father was an influential politician in his home state.

Large Bands, New Friends, and New Music

Ervin said that problems existed in the command, even though he wasn't assigned to the band in 1948. Turnover during the first part of the year was almost one hundred percent. Ervin knew that replacing virtually everybody without having that "institutional memory" made for turbulence.

Ervin liked working in the 7868th Fife and Drum Corps. First of all, he was a snare drummer and really enjoyed that type of percussion work. He wasn't really a drum set man—he knew his limitations and since the draft was still in effect, there were plenty of very good set men in the band. So he was happy playing the snare drum and the rudiments that go with it.

Ervin and Arthur (Hap) Honaker became good friends. They were such good friends that they sometimes got into trouble together. They both made and lost rank pretty much simultaneously. Ervin says that Hap was one of those natural musicians who could pick up an instrument, figure it out, and play it very well within days. Hap Honaker made the Army a career and finished as the Sergeant Major of the Army Element of the Naval School of Music (SOM), located at the Naval Amphibious Base in Little Creek, Virginia, retiring in the late 1970s.

Ervin was the type of GI who liked to move around in the city. First, he bought a motorcycle but wound up injuring himself on it. He then bought a 1934 Opel, which ran its course, and then he and Hap had joint ownership of a 1939 Volxhall. Bill wound up becoming sole owner of the Volxhall and then later sold it to Sergeant Tuttle of the band, who later totaled it.

All of this traveling around was clearly the result of everyone in the band having a Class A or unrestricted pass. Possession of a suitable pass was a requirement in those days to leave the compound. Bill says that the Class A pass was changed to a Class B pass during his assignment. Apparently, the senior chaplain learned of the band having the Class A pass, expressed dissatisfaction with it, and convinced the command to revoke it and substitute the less-desired Class B pass. The Class B pass was often called a "Cinderella" pass, for it required the holder to return to the billets by midnight. The Charge of Quarters (CQ) had to conduct bed checks to ensure that the Cinderella pass holders had returned to the barracks on time.

Ervin reports that duty with the band was about what one could expect. Band soldiers wore fatigues during the duty day, beginning occasionally with a march-around the McNair/Roosevelt/Andrews quadrangle when the rest of the troops were out doing PT at 6 a.m. This was supposed to motivate the troops, but Bill said he was pretty sure it just irritated them. Next, the band would have section rehearsal at 8:30 a.m., followed by full band rehearsal at 9:30 a.m. Sectionals were typically run by NCO section leaders and were designed to iron out any musical difficulties with technique, execution, balance, intonation, and other musical nuances. The full band rehearsal, usually run by the warrant officer, would then focus on the ensemble's sound.

The band's frequent performances at ceremonies, honor guards, and other marching-type jobs were assigned by G-3 Operations, typically with just a phone call. The particulars would be gathered over the phone and the band would train for the event, time allowing, then board a bus and go to the Berlin Military Post Headquarters on Kronprinzenallee (renamed Clayallee on June 1, 1949 in honor of General Lucius Clay), the Four Ring, Tempelhof Airfield, or another appropriate site for the ceremony.

On Sundays the band would head over to Truman Hall, essentially a dining facility/club/cafeteria located on the corner of Hüttenweg and Clayallee, directly across the street from U.S. Army Berlin Headquarters. (OMGUS had ended on September 1, 1949) and perform lawn concerts.

It didn't take long for the Berlin command to call on the band to perform duties of a non-musical nature, besides that of truck or bus-driving. Ervin recalls that the band would go out to the Grunewald or other tactical training area and pull guard duty. Sometimes the band would go out and perform for the troops during chowtime.

Army bandmasters had training and skills in conducting larger ensembles. The conductor holds the ensemble together with rhythm, balance, style, and volume. The advent of rock 'n roll and its smaller ensembles revealed to bandmasters some difficulty in concert programming. Instead of the troops showing appreciation for dance bands that numbered approximately 18 musicians and perhaps even a few others indicating approval for contemporary concert band literature, the troops were responding more toward the newer music that was played by fewer musicians. Elvis Presley and his pompadour and Chuck Berry with a hollow-body guitar were becoming more popular than Benny Goodman and Gene Krupa.

Young soldiers wanted to hear smaller combos, rock quartets, a different sound with a driving pulse. They didn't necessarily want to hear the dance bands of a fading era.

Between the changing times, the styles of music that were becoming popular, and the bandmasters who were in charge, there was yet another problem regarding troop support—electricity. Electric guitars needed amplifiers. Amplifiers needed electricity. Since rock 'n roll singing wasn't founded on opera, singers needed amplification, too. Those amplifiers and sound systems needed electricity as well.

To address this problem and to build efficiency in performance, a great many performances were played by sending out acoustic instruments, mostly wind and percussion, armed with march-sized short arrangements of some popular tunes which, quite strangely, also belonged to an earlier era. "Come Home, Bill Bailey," "Muskrat Ramble," "South Rampart Street Parade," and similar Dixieland-flavored tunes were playable by the trumpets, saxes, drums, clarinets, and flutes which comprised the band. A little later on, some swing and rock charts in this wind ensemble format came along, allowing the band to play more contemporary pieces like "Rock Around the Clock," "St. Louis Blues" (for the 1950s), and even some tunes by Spyro Gyra ("Morning Dance" and "Catching the Sun"), and Chase ("Get it On") in the 1970s. These little tunes, playable in just a couple of minutes of minimal setup, often provided the best option for bandmasters for performance in areas where facilities couldn't provide electricity.

This technique worked in other ways as well. While the 298th played its share of honor guard ceremonies in a city that attracted VIPs and celebrities of all types, there were times when performing was not judged by how military the band looked. In direct contrast to the British, whose gala uniforms, leather paraphernalia and even mascots that were live and smelled like goats (probably because they were) never failed to impress the onlooker with their impeccable playing and martial spirit, American bands tended to portray a more relaxed image.

In such performance situations most bandmasters, recognizing the value of this more relaxed style, encouraged the band to relax and play. This meant largely ignoring the Manual of Instruments, the procedure by which a military band brings instruments up to the playing position and down to the ready position in a military manner. It also meant giving a clear downbeat and letting the music and the musicians take their course. In the mid-Seventies when women joined the 298th—depending on the level of frivolity permitted— members of the band would even dance with each other or with members of the audience. The American bands quickly learned that interaction with the audience was a large part of entertainment and success in performance and this transcended the written note or the correct marching maneuver.

Desegregation in the Military

President Truman signed Executive Order 9981 in July, 1948 to end segregation in the armed forces. This order wasn't uniformly embraced by the Army brass. Summary documents from the Truman Library indicate some Army staff officers stated anonymously to the press that Truman's Executive Order did not specifically forbid segregation in the Army. And Army Chief of Staff General Omar Bradley stated that desegregation would come to the Army only when it became a fact in the rest of American society. Even the Secretary of the Army Kenneth Royall was reported in the press to have admitted that "segregation in the Army must go," but not immediately (Editor, Desegregation of the Armed Forces).[31]

In response, President Truman announced the names of five members of the President's Committee on Equality of Treatment and Opportunity in the Armed Services, commonly called the Fahy Committee, after its chairman, Charles Fahy. This committee of five active members also included two black

Americans. The integration process proceeded very slowly, especially in the Army and Marine Corps. The Army instituted several "test runs" and drafted many "integration plans," but no real progress was made until June 1950, when the Army unofficially decided to integrate basic training. The Korean War had an impact on that decision, since combat losses in Korea necessitated replacing white soldiers with black soldiers.

Richard N. Saddler arrived in Berlin for the first time in December 1952. Having just completed the Band Training Unit (BTU) training at the 101st Airborne Division, young Private Saddler, a black American, had thought that the Army was still segregated. He said, "To my surprise, I found my first unit (the 298th Army Band) fully integrated. I was treated like all assigned privates. No different." At this time of transition for the Army, a certain amount of dissonance could have been expected. But Saddler is quick to point out, "The NCOs were really great. Believe it or not, there were very few real racial problems. Most of the assigned soldier/musicians wanted integration to succeed."

Bill Ervin pointed out that there were two bands in West Germany that had been deactivated in the early 1950s. These were "colored bands." The musicians were sent to the rest of the bands throughout Germany and the 298th received two or three. They were treated just like everybody else, Ervin said, and they along with their counterparts had to endure the formations, the reveille, the roll calls, the inspections, the barracks cleanups and even the shortarm inspections. The whole situation was fair across the board.

Dick Saddler is an institution and an inspiration to the Army Band program. He spent some 44 years in uniform, his career lustrous with success. Finally retiring as a Chief Warrant Officer 4 and having been bandmaster/commander of many bands, including the 298th between 1975 and 1977, Mr. Saddler does not hesitate to point out that the principal reason for the 298th's success in Berlin was the very real and palpable relationship the band had with the people of the city. It became even more obvious to the Berlin command that the band was a very valuable community relation asset and the band became more and more available to civilian requestors of band support.

Mr. Saddler was well-liked and well-respected by his peers and subordinates alike. Hornist/trumpeter and instrument repair technician Bob Frushour (1982-85) said that while he didn't serve with Mr. Saddler in Berlin, rather at Ft. Lee, he could see that Mr. Saddler appreciated the musicians under his command and avoided much of the nonsense that seemed to characterize a lot of bands. Bob said that the band rehearsed and performed, which made it an ideal assignment and that he missed Ft. Lee when he left there.

More Replacements

By this time, CWO Wilmont Trumbull was replaced by CWO Wilbur J Moyer. Roger Woodrum recalls that Mr. Moyer departed rather suddenly. "I was supposed to play softball up in Bremerhaven, representing the Berlin command on an ass-kicking team. We were good and we knew it. But because there was some kind of a gig coming up and because Moyer didn't particularly like me, he ordered me not to get on the duty train. So I complied with his order, but before the train left, I called the 7780th Special Troops Battalion's CO and I told him I'd been ordered to stay off the train. As I understand it, the battalion commander called Moyer and they had words. A couple days later, Moyer was gone."

The next CO of the band was CWO Thomas Greening, who was a former glider pilot during World War II. Greening, or perhaps Greene—there is some disagreement about the correct name of this warrant officer—arrived in late 1953 and continued serving until 1956 when he was replaced by CWO Robert C. Lewis.

Allen Thompson arrived in Berlin in 1954 as a euphonium player, having discovered that his college career thus far was less than remarkable. Rather than continue down that path, he opted for a tour in the U.S. Army band program. Allen, originally from New York state, was excited to be in Berlin and completely overjoyed to be able to take conducting and instrumental lessons for a financial pittance. He focused on his playing and his conducting, both skills that served him well after his time in the Army. Allen also took conducting lessons from Hans Doms of the Berlin Philharmonic Orchestra for what amounted to 42 cents per lesson. The British took care of the balance. This kind of education was priceless, despite the low cost. He eventually left Berlin in the spring of 1956 and returned to his studies. He became a music teacher and was appreciated in his community as a dedicated, knowledgeable, and personable music professional.

Allen said that the duty was terrific. The band rehearsed in the mornings and often smaller ensembles or the stage band rehearsed in the afternoons. Allen said he served as the band librarian and took great pride in organizing, cataloging, and documenting the types of music the library had. He said he remembered very well the march-sized arrangements that had "108th Cavalry Band" and "156th Infantry Band" stamped on them and the sheer number of stock stage band charts left over from the early days of the band's existence. The band library was catalogued and filed into more than 25 file cabinets. Mr. Lewis would give Allen a list of the pieces to pull and he'd have them ready to go for the next rehearsal, putting away the pieces that had been turned in.

Allen said, "But that job was taken away from me, presumably because there was an NCO in the band who didn't have an extra job. Even though I was doing well with the library, the band leadership thought the other fellow should have it. I didn't like that very much because I felt I did well, but evidently others believed a more senior member should have the extra responsibility. That's just the way it goes sometimes."

Regardless of what transpired with the librarian job, Allen spoke well and kindly of bandmaster Robert Lewis. "The band was a working band, but there was time for personal activities and interests."

Allen still has the 3-valve Besson euphonium he'd played when he was in Berlin and while his playing has slowed down of late, he is still very proud of his service and his time in Berlin. He is a regular participant in the Berlin U.S. Military Veterans Association reunions.

Euphoniumist Donald Scifres (1957-59) provided a perspective of the band's activities in the late 1950s. Don's roommates were John J. Yeager, a clarinet player from Boston, and Dwight Roper, a tuba player from Missouri. Don recalls Dwight being somewhat obsessive about saving money—he never went anywhere, never spent a cent he didn't have to, and was usually in his rack by 5:30 p.m., following the evening meal.

As far as performances went, Donald remembers playing the refugee camps on Wednesday afternoons. These refugee camps were all over Berlin and the band would make the rounds of them. On the bus to and from the job, Donald remembers the bandmaster, Mr. Serafin. "We had a phrase that we used all the time – 'Re-up and be in "Shook Shook", which was a term we gave to Mr. Serafin. We weren't very kind to him. He was kind of nervous all the time and we capitalized on that." Donald often would pull CQ for others—for a price. He'd assume the duty for $20. On those evenings, Donald would go eat chow, then come back and pull the duty. There was a cot set up in the office and he would sleep on the cot, located next to the phone if it rang.

Richard Lant was first and foremost an infantryman. He loved the infantry and the idea of basic small weaponry. But after some months of working at McNair for one of the infantry battalions, Richard learned that the band was looking for trumpet players. It had been some time since he'd played and he didn't consider himself to be a world-class player, but Richard thought that becoming a trumpeter in the 298th would be a great experience. He arrived in the 298th in June 1960, and after he made the move from McNair to Andrews, he settled in and began working on his trumpet skills. He also spent a considerable amount of time with photography. He took pictures all over Berlin, including the mysterious bunker located just north of the band building, which was, in fact, the Leichenhalle or morgue from the early days of the Hauptkadettenanstalt's hospital.

Richard wrote, "I didn't drink so I was able to do most of the driving and take pictures… Some of us were required to be trained on all weapons from the .45 ACP to the 3.5 inch rocket launcher, all of which I really enjoyed. The band was required also to have five drivers licensed on 2.5 ton trucks, at least one licensed driver on the 5-ton wrecker and drivers also for the 37-passenger Mercedes bus. The band on alerts had a second job, which was guard duty at Berlin Brigade Headquarters."

Richard said that the band had cash paydays in those days. Each soldier had to report to the officer to get paid. He remembered the team effort that was needed to keep the place up and the NCOs with whom he worked: Sergeants Simon, who was an infantryman in Korea; Munar, Lyman, and especially Master Sergeant Riddick. He talked about the leaf-raking that had to be done each fall and that everybody jumped in to get that job done since there was so many trees shedding millions of leaves to clean up. Richard recalled his roommate, Robert Artest, with whom he got along terrifically and then most especially he remembers his marriage to Regina, formerly of East Germany. At that point he left the barracks. Richard and his wife got an apartment just off Hüttenweg near BB.

Richard then spoke of riding the trucks through the East until they got to West Germany and he mentioned taking the duty train to Frankfurt where the band supported a couple of football games. In those days the 298th didn't travel much, so each occasion was memorable.

When prompted about the typical duty day Richard responded that the band got up at 6:30 a.m. and had roll call. After that the band got chow and then at 8:00 a.m. they had their first formation. NCOs announced the training schedule which usually involved concert band rehearsal, drill band at the 4-Ring, and usually individual practice. At lunchtime, more opportunity for chow and then the afternoon was filled with rehearsals of various types led by MSG Riddick or individual practice for those not involved in those ensembles. The duty day ended at 4 p.m. When the band had physical training, it was just calisthenics. The band never did any running or jogging.

Trombonist Paul Creighton arrived the first time in Berlin in January, 1960, a very young 19-year-old just out of basic training. Paul prides himself that he never went to any type of military music school. He maintains it never hurt him in completing a 20-year Army career as a trombonist and scoffs at the idea that any version of a military school of music was necessary in furthering a career. Of the estimated 2,000 musicians who served in the 298th, Paul is one of only two (the other is Vic St. Clair) who served in Berlin with the 298th on three different tours. His first assignment lasted until January 1963, after which departed for other assignments. He returned to Berlin for his second tour in January 1969, but struggled with the band leadership to the point that he found it necessary to curtail his tour. He left for a combat tour in Vietnam in March 1970, but then returned to Berlin for his third tour in March 1971. He said that things had evened out by that time and he stayed in Berlin on that tour until 1977 during which time he met his wife Erena.

Paul remembered going over to Wolfgang and Crystal's (otherwise known as the Märkischer Hof, a local bar and restaurant) with Vic St. Clair during rehearsal break and they'd get themselves a Brötchen. They hadn't had time to eat breakfast when they got up because they'd often been out fairly late the night before. Sometimes a bit of the hair of the dog was needed, which got them through the rest of the rehearsal.

Paul remembers that Mr. Serafin did his best to put on a good show. Mr. Serafin got his chance with the newly-created German/American Volksfest, which got its start in the summer of 1961 and ran each year. All manner of musical support was provided for the Volksfest, including a concert band, a stage band, and smaller ensembles.

Paul also recalls CWO Cortese, Mr. Serafin's replacement who arrived in August 1962, as having a German shepherd named "Tempo". Paul wasn't so sure about the dog's ability to keep time, but Mr. Cortese was fond enough of the dog to bring him around on occasion.

Paul Creighton eventually retired from the Army and continued his career. In the mid-Eighties, Paul became Secretary/Treasurer of the Association of Retired Military Musicians and as a charter member of the organization, was instrumental in forming and developing the administrative and financial aspects of ARMM.

MUSICAL TRAINING

Virtually all U.S. Army musicians had some musical training before entering military service. This training ranged from private lessons to public school music programs to the highest levels of formal training in conservatories and universities.

Formal education within a military setting for 20th century Army musicians began early in the century with Dr. Frank Damrosch of the Institute of Musical Arts (later to merge with the Juilliard Graduate School to become the Juilliard School of Music[32] (Editor, A Brief History)), who recognized that the level of musical knowledge within the Army needed to improve. Although reasonably competent on their instruments, many Army musicians didn't understand fundamentals of theory and harmony, and lacked ear training. He created a program for bandmasters based on the training concepts of the British Army and began training a limited number of students at Ft. Jay, New York, graduating only about five students in 1911. The facility grew through World War I, and in 1920, the school was moved to the Army War College in Washington, D.C.. There the school was designated a Special Services School and counted a yearly load of 215 students (Editor, The Armed Forces School of Music, 2002).[33]

Later into World War II, the need to train large numbers of musicians in a post-World War II Army, resulted in forming Band Training Units (BTU) at Camp Crowder, Missouri, and Camp Lee, Virginia. Located in the southwest corner of Missouri near Neosho, Camp Crowder was established in 1941 as an Army Signal Corps training center, but then also contained a prisoner of war camp for German POWs captured in the fighting in North Africa along with the BTU. A relatively large camp during the war containing some 45,000 soldiers at various levels of training, Camp Crowder declined in use following World War II and was eventually deactivated. The land returned to either original owners or to the state of Missouri following the war (Editor, Area History - Camp Crowder)[34]

Camp Lee, located east of Petersburg, Virginia, was established in 1917 and served to prepare for World War I. Returning to Virginia's control after World War I, the War Department reclaimed the post at the onset of World War II and it eventually became the Army's center for the Quartermaster Corps. The BTU at Camp Lee was an ancillary or "tenant" unit, meaning it had no outward affiliation with the Quartermaster Corps. The Department of the Army renamed Camp Lee as Ft. Lee in 1950 and the post has remained in the Army's organization ever since (Editor, The History of Fort Lee, Virginia).[35]

Army musicians slated for occupation duty following World War II were auditioned either in Aßmannshausen am Rhein, located west of Wiesbaden, or in Sonthofen, a small Bavarian town on the Swiss border. Each site took the newly-arrived soldier through auditions, rehearsals, and other assessments to evaluate his qualifications and to determine his assignment. As many as 21 Army bands were active in the American Occupation Zones of Germany and Austria, and with a relatively high turnover rate due to short service terms associated with the draft, keeping a flow of qualified replacements assigned to the bands was a priority.

Auditions were not automatic tickets to those bands, however. Jack Schneider, who was eventually assigned to the 31st Army Band in Würzburg, wrote that when he arrived in Sonthofen he failed another audition and was sent for further music training at the European Band School in Dachau.

William Grimes and buddies at the Dachau Music School

Musically, he said, "this was the best thing that happened to me, for the instruction lasted four months; the students had some of the best German instructors who were mostly professors [teaching] music theory and composition, lessons, and concerts by the staff..." He added, "The concerts were always followed with student assignments of analyzing and writing on the orchestral performances" (Koefod, 2013).[36]

In his 1949 annual report, CWO Marion Durbin, bandmaster of the

298th, complained that replacement problems continued throughout the year. He wrote that a partial solution was found by training suitable personnel from within Berlin Military Post, but this resulted "in some inferior musicians being assigned to the band at times." Relief came during the last quarter of the year with arrival of replacements from the Zone of Interior (American Zone of occupation), which brought the actual strength up to TO&E authorizations (Durbin, 298th Army Band Annual Report, 1949, 1950).[37] Replacement problems "because of the lack of qualified musicians being shipped overseas" still headed Mr. Durbin's 1950 report. He added, though, that "an adequate number of potentials were assigned to keep the operation and strength at a fairly high level, although the strength was still lower than authorized (Durbin, 298th Army Band Annual Report, 1950, 1951)."[38]

Musical training shifted to the Naval School of Music, located at the Anacostia Naval Receiving Station in Washington, D.C. The Army reached an agreement with the Navy to train soldiers in Anacostia, with the first class beginning in January 1951. This arrangement held until August 1964 when the Naval School of Music moved from Anacostia to the Naval Amphibious Base (NAB) Little Creek, located east of Norfolk, Virginia. At this juncture, the Navy, Marine Corps and the Army conducted musical training jointly. The Air Force and Coast Guard maintained their own training system.

This training arrangement and relationship continued for the next four decades, although at various times the Army considered reviving its own training program for various administrative reasons, chiefly expense. Since the Army sent a larger number of students to the School of Music in comparison to the number sent by the Navy and an even smaller number by the Marine Corps, a considerable amount of money was spent for longer-term training cycles, such as that mandated by the Navy. Another area of concern involved personnel management in assigning those newly-graduated Army musicians to their first band nine months after beginning basic combat training.

Courses of instruction included individual lessons, theory, harmony, ear training, and ensemble rehearsals of various types. Drill band was an essential element, as were the weekly "field nights," which had nothing to do with music and everything to do with cleaning of the School of Music building and barracks/office facilities. Basic music students were expected to practice their instrumental specialty a minimum of 20 hours weekly. Failure to adhere to this standard could and sometimes did lead to administrative repercussions for the student up to and including expulsion from the school, although the defining result was evident at the time of audition. The student was also expected to maintain his instrument and to participate in at least three auditions.

Auditions were conducted using the standard Navy format for testing, namely a numeric scale from 0.0 to 4.0, zero being the lowest possible score and 4.0 being a perfect score. The first audition, known as the Incoming audition, simply measured basic skill levels. Instructors took into account that usually the student had been off the instrument for an extended period of time. The second audition, done generally in the middle of the six-month course, was called the F1 audition. The student was expected to meet a minimum score, typically a 2.5. At the end of the course, the student played his F2 audition. The student successfully passed the basic music course with a score of 2.7. If a student failed to achieve minimum scores at any audition point save the incoming audition, reclassification or reassignment to another job within the Army could result. Reclassifications or reassignments were done "for the good of the service."

While reclassifications and reassignments did occur, they did not occur frequently. A student was given sufficient opportunity for development, particularly in skills that take longer periods of time to develop, such as music reading. An otherwise superb instrumentalist, often on a rhythm instrument such as guitar, piano, or percussion could find himself under consideration for reclassification into another job if reading of basic music notation could not develop to a reasonable standard. As all Army bands find themselves in situations where sightreading of music is a necessary skill, so too must the individual be able to sightread music to a basic level.

The Navy offered several advanced courses, beginning with the F2 course. Also six months in duration, this course trained students in advanced theory, harmony, ear training, arranging techniques, chord progression, basic conducting, and drum majoring, along with maintaining instrumental proficiency. Army students attended a faster version of this course (only four months in duration, the limit of temporary duty). The next advanced course became known to the Army as the enlisted bandleader or "E8" course. This 6-month course took the F2 skill sets and further developed them, with emphasis on conducting and leadership. And finally, the bandmaster course brought warrant officer candidates and commissioned officers seeking this level of training through yet another six month course which was designed to train the student in leadership and advanced conducting skills, along with other pertinent skills in managing band administration, training, operations, supply, and other ancillary functions associated with most bands.

As the Naval School of Music (SOM) was a Navy school administered by the Navy, the Army's presence there—while superior in numbers of students—was as a "guest" or tenant unit. Thus, the Army called itself the Army *Element* (italics added) to the Navy School of Music. The Army Element was led by a Commandant, generally an officer in the rank of Major or Lieutenant Colonel. A Sergeant Major served as senior enlisted. The Sergeant Major had additional responsibilities associated with the Army Band's NCO Academy and as the overall (Proponent) Sergeant Major for Army Bands. The Secretary (generally a senior noncommissioned officer) managed the administration unit. A captain commanded the staff and faculty company and another captain commanded the student company itself. Both companies had first sergeants as senior enlisted.

The Army Element also had support elements in doctrine, training, supply and services, administration, and similar functions. These positions were all filled by Army personnel.

Throughout this period, the Army band program was still largely patterned after the large ensemble, or concert band/marching band, with typical smaller ensembles including a big band of anywhere from 10-18 musicians performing all manner of contemporary or swing charts; a smaller jazz-oriented combo that provided music for more intimate settings; a brass quintet; and perhaps even a woodwind quintet. There were variations of the smaller ensembles, including rock bands, country bands, bluegrass bands, any type of ensemble that would represent the skills of the musicians in that band at that time. All bandmasters were trained to conduct the larger ensembles and this they did to great effect throughout the years. But as times and events changed musical tastes of the general populace, the typical Army band was confronted with finding ways to present more popular and contemporary music to its audience, all while employing all of the musicians in the band. A frequent problem developed in overcommitting rhythm players, who formed the basis for combos and smaller ensembles, in comparison to the lesser-committed oboe or bassoon player, who performed chiefly with the concert band. Bandmasters had to find ways to involve everybody.

Beginning in the 1980s, the Army initiated its own series of advanced courses apart from the Navy. As part of the larger non-commissioned officer education system (NCOES), the advanced courses for bandsmen began with a Primary Leadership Course (later amended to Primary Leadership Development Course) for Soldiers who showed drive and leadership potential. This course involved no musical aspects and targeted young leaders in developing rudimentary skills in leading teams and squads. Decentralized, this course was taught all over the Army and ran about four weeks in length.

For junior NCOs, the Basic Noncommissioned Officer's Course (BNCOC, pronounced "bee-knock") was developed by the SOM. Consisting of a common core of leadership topics common to all junior NCOs irrespective of job code, and then augmented by a technical or "music" track for bandsmen, this course ran approximately three months long. This course focused on leadership principles, drum majoring, section rehearsals, basic conducting, and arranging/chord progression principles.

For senior NCOs, the Advanced Noncommissioned Officer's Course (ANCOC, pronounced "a-knock") was also developed. This took the BNCOC course to a higher level with more conducting and larger ensembles. Drum majoring was not a part of ANCOC.

For first sergeants and sergeants major, the final two courses were taught at the Sergeants Major Academy at Ft. Bliss, Texas. These courses were structured specifically for those positions and did not feature musical training.

All Army courses feature physical fitness tests at the beginning of the course and following the course, along with the required weigh-in. Passing the course requires passing the PT test and weigh-ins. All Army courses also feature a tactical or field exercise.

Today, some 20 years after the 298th was deactivated, the Army trains its own musicians. In October 2010, the Army ended its 60-year relationship with the Navy's programs of instruction and implemented its own series of programs. Following the 1990/91 Persian Gulf War, collapse of the Soviet Union, and subsequent end of the Cold War, the Army began implementing a series of downsizing and force reduction mandates. The Army systematically deactivated bands (including the 298th) and needed fewer musicians, which meant recruiting with a focus on better trained and skilled musicians from the outset. Adhering to the Navy's 6-month basic instrumentalist course for musicians who were already skilled in theory, harmony, ear training and instrumental skills could not be justified.

The new Army programs of instruction were launched and instead of the F1 course of six months, the new basic course ran 10 weeks. These new musicians still needed to learn Army methodologies of marching, the manual of instruments, and other service-specific facets of military musicianship, but they also spent time actively learning how to entertain audiences, a facet of training and education that previously had not been systematically studied. Smaller ensembles and high-energy bands all have a need to project that energy toward the audience; therefore the standard concert band with narrator, while still effective in the right setting, was just an option rather than the only option—particularly for deployed, younger soldiers.

UNIFORMS

The U.S. Army changes its uniforms from time to time. The official claim is that the Army responds to better clothing and equipment technology and implements that technology in the form of better fitting, better looking, and better-functioning uniforms.

World War II era uniforms, worn until the major uniform changes of the mid-1950s, were relatively simple. They consisted of an OD uniform, which featured a full jacket, belted at the waist, and the popular "Ike" jacket, which was a hip-length jacket. The Ike jacket was patterned originally after the British model, which Eisenhower had admired and worn. The garment was popular because it was more comfortable but was modified at least twice, eliminating some bulkiness each time.

ETO Band in OD uniform   **Sebby Papa and friends in Ike jackets**

Soldiers of the 298th wore the OD uniform with the required shirt and four-in-hand tie. Jacket sleeves sported sewn-on rank insignia. The lapel featured distinctive unit insignia. Designers modified the OD service jacket In 1950, providing a fitted waist and narrower sleeves.

Throughout post-World War II, the Army struggled to adopt a long-range policy with respect to uniforms. Uniform and material shortages during World War II had led to a preponderance of differing styles and types of uniforms. The desired policy would specify identical uniforms for officers and enlisted, with the exception of rank insignia. For example, officers who owned and wore the "pinks and greens" uniform did so, unless they were in formation with troops. Enlisted soldiers were not authorized and did not possess that uniform. The "pinks and greens" uniform for officers consisted of an OD jacket with contrasting-colored trousers.

The Army leadership appointed a Uniform Board in February 1949. The Army developed uniforms that were specific to their need—combat uniforms would be separate from semi-formal or garrison uniforms. Despite the progress made by the uniform board and the various experts in selecting a new uniform color and style, the Army dropped plans to implement the changes in 1952. The rationale held that costs could be held down by adopting a "pinks and greens" style uniform for both officers and enlisted. Other considerations kept the original idea from moving forward. But in 1954, the uniform board realized that a change was essential to provide the long-reaching standard that was envisioned in the late 1940's. Therefore, a new uniform color in gray-green was selected to be phased in as stocks of the OD and "pinks and greens" uniforms were depleted.

Proposed ceremonial uniforms

Proposed uniform styles specific for Army bands, developed by the Army Quartermaster Corps in 1953 are shown (photo from the National Archives). The development process resulted in the ceremonial blues uniform that was issued to bandsmen in 1956.

The winter-weight Army green uniform became available in September 1956; recruits received this uniform a year later. The Army green uniform became mandatory semi-dress attire in September 1961. The summer-weight green uniform was developed and adopted in July 1964.

The uniform went through several minor changes, mostly involving gold-to-black bands on officer trousers, along with accompanying width changes, and service cap visor color changes from russet (reddish brown) to black. A light tan shirt was also worn, along with the requisite tie which also changed color from dark green to black. The long-sleeve khaki shirt was dropped, and a wool overcoat was adopted in 1967.

The Berlin command decided to make several local decisions regarding

uniforms and developed the patches seen here (photo courtesy of trumpeter Sebby Papa (1947-48)) and the distinctive unit insignia seen below.

Blazer pin re-drawn by Bobby Hawkins

Civilian attire—"civvies"--was not authorized for wear off-post in Berlin until about 1954. At that point, soldiers having the prescribed pass and wishing to leave the compound could do so only while wearing civilian sport coat and tie, or standard OD uniform. Paul Creighton and Chuck Ramsey both remember having to get into coat and tie to leave Andrews Barracks. "Yeah, we were instantly recognizable as being American military, due to the haircut and the coat and tie. Your average Berliner didn't look like we did." Chuck leaned forward and said, "But we all looked pretty good. Scrubbed, well-washed, and clean. Not too many looked shabby when they went out the gate. And I think it meant something to the Berliners to see us dressed like that. They knew that we had standards to maintain."

Army leadership in Berlin dropped the requirement to wear coat and tie was dropped in the late 1960s, likely in response to the cultural changes associated with that decade.

Now that the Army green service uniform issue was settled, it was time to take a look at adopting an attractive formal dress uniform. Since 1938, the idea had held to keep to a blue uniform for semi-dress and dress needs. Apart from the special dress uniform that had been developed for the 298th in the 1940s, the 298th eventually adopted the ceremonial blue uniform for bands and honor guards, as standardized by the Army. This uniform, often referred to as "ceremonial blues" was adopted in 1956 and is depicted here. It was the favored uniform for many bandmasters after its adoption and was worn quite often for performances which were perhaps not quite as formal as the uniform was supposed to represent. Many bandmasters preferred this uniform for their bands because it was distinctive—most enlisted personnel did not own a dress blue uniform of any type. Furthermore, the band or supply organization issued the ceremonial blues uniform to the soldier. The soldier kept this uniform as long as he was assigned to the unit, turning it in upon departure. Thus, the band stood out when the ceremonial blue uniform was worn.

The standard Army blue uniform was available for purchase. Many career enlisted soldiers purchased this uniform. It itself is distinctive with the prescribed rank insignia on the upper sleeve and large-format service stripes on the lower sleeve.

The decision to wear the dress blue uniform, ceremonial or standard, was also done for practical reasons. Dave Ratliff, commander of the 298th from 1980 to 1984, said that the Berlin Brigade adopted the "Spandau Green" uniform for many ceremonial events. This uniform was an adaptation of the Army green service uniform, incorporating a gloss black helmet liner with appropriate decals and hat brass (enlisted) or rank insignia (officer) on the front; white pistol belt with large brass buckle; bloused and blocked spit-shined boots; branch-specific throat scarf (the band wore a white neck scarf with the Berlin patch sewn on); and white gloves. In the early 1980s, before wearing combat uniforms for semi-formal occasions became fashionable, Spandau Greens were indicated for wear for Allied Forces Day. Since the Berlin command wanted a complete Army band march in front of each of the three infantry battalions, additional band support was needed from US Army Europe. Therefore, as many as three additional bands from West Germany were assigned temporary duty to Berlin to support the rehearsals and the parade. Since these visiting bands were not outfitted with Spandau Greens, the decision was made for all bands to wear the standard dress blue uniform, since all bands were authorized two sets per band member.

Despite the ceremonial blue uniform's popularity with bandmasters, it wasn't favored among the enlisted. As depicted in the many photographs by the band in the 1960s and into the 1970s, this ceremonial dress uniform appeared over-the-top. Festooned with various ropes and dangling aiguillete cords that served no purpose other than to get in the way of the performance of a musical instrument, this uniform was reminiscent of a posh hotel's doorman. Frilly shoulder marks in lieu of the more standard shoulder loops, the lack of rank insignia for enlisted personnel other than NCOs, and the piping on the crown of the blue service cap made the band soldier look decidedly non-military.

Most Army separate and division bands, the 298th included, dropped the ceremonial blue uniform and adopted the standard dress blue uniform in the early 1980s commensurate with the change to the unit's authorization documents (MTOE). The standard dress blue uniform dropped the shoulder marks, piping on the blue service cap, and adopted the blue rank insignia and service stripes for lower enlisted personnel and NCO alike. Additionally, the gold stripe on the outside of the standard dress blues trousers leg looked more like a dress uniform than the two gold pinstripes down the outside of the ceremonial blue trousers.

The leather music pouch also formed a part of the uniform. This photo of the 298th, courtesy of Robert Jones, shows the band wearing the black leather pouch. The pouch held march-sized sheet music that could be instantly called up and played. In later years, the band ordered and received black leather pouches through normal Army supply channels.

In 1984, the 298th also received authorization to issue the wool dress blue overcoat, an overcoat typically worn by the Third Infantry Regiment "Old Guard" in Washington, D.C. This overcoat featured a double-breasted style trench coat in heavy wool. The blue ceremonial belt was also issued. Shiny brass, pin-on rank insignia was worn at the lapel points. This was a very distinguished-looking coat to be worn over the dress blue uniform and was very popular. The heavy coat, along with the prescribed white scarf, protected the band from the elements, apart from rain which has a profound impact on wool, and was comfortable to wear. David M. Smith, commander of the 298th from 1984-88, provides a unique insight into the procurement of the dress blue overcoat:

"Did you know that there is a Dress Blue Winter Overcoat? I didn't until I landed in Berlin...it was only authorized in two US Army Commands: Military District Washington (MDW) and US Army Berlin Brigade.

"A senior officer returned from a trip to DC and had the idea that the Berlin Brigade Band would just look special and shimmer in these blue horse blankets with their contrasting winter-white silk neck scarves and, since the government of the Federal Republic was picking up the tab rather than Uncle, he directed us to order 60 or so of them.

"Did I mention that they were only authorized in just two commands? That meant that they were not a normal supply chain item with thousands of copies of them sitting in a really big warehouse somewhere...they had to be locally-procured...which meant that they had to be locally tailored...which meant that we took about a $40k divot out of the FRG at approximately $600-$700 per copy...times 60 coats or so.

"And right after we took receipt of them, the PERFECT gig came up. Secretary of State Schultz was to fly into a tiny little airfield somewhere out in the Zone and we were tagged to provide arrival music and honors for his visit...blue suits and MDW [Military District of Washington] overcoats...hey, he'd feel right at home.

"So we were wanded by Department of State Security and formed up on the taxiway of this small airbase. It was about 28 degrees Fahrenheit, but we were toasty in our spiffy new duds...and Schultz was imminently due...any minute now...am I telegraphing what's coming...

"There had been a delay...but he was due to arrive presently...and besides, it was warming up a bit, wasn't it? As a matter of fact, the mercury had shot up over the last hour to about 35-36 degrees...as a warm front passed through...which caused the skies to open up with a driving rain that fell at a tropical rate...still no Schultz.

["Damn, these coats get heavy when they're wet...can't go inside and break the security perimeter that had been set up...just had to stand in the rain and take it...Schultz was due to arrive momentarily...]

"I had begun to wonder if anyone else heard this really high-pitched squealing sound...like a platoon of lobsters that had just been thrown into a large pot of boiling water...I guess I never thought that you could actually HEAR wool shrinking...but if you get enough wool wet enough, it almost makes a noise as, little-by-little, just a bit more cuff is shown at the sleeve, the waist and hip measurements tightens a bit and what was an army greatcoat in worsted wool slowly becomes more flannel-like and more stadiumcoat-length.

..."We got past the shrinkage by re-issuing the beasts based upon their new, smaller shapes rather than the size tag in the collar...oh, Schultz never showed up...his plane was diverted to another site."

When Vice President George H. W. Bush visited Berlin in February 1983, the band was directed to wear the dress blue uniform at the honor guard ceremony up at Tegel Airport. The weather was horrific. Alternately raining, sleeting, or snowing, the band withstood the ubiquitous dry run and then the actual arrival of the vice president, without benefit of the dress blue overcoat which was to follow. That blue overcoat would have been handy at that time.

The parade uniform changed throughout the years, as can be seen in the various photographs. From the early OD service uniform to the Army green uniform, these uniforms were augmented by all sorts of accoutrements. These ranged from physical wear of the leather music pouch (seen in many photographs of band members in the late 1940s) to the wearing of white spats/leggings to white helmet liners with white Sam Browne belts to bloused boots. Before the Army completely lost its sense of pageantry in the early 1990s by resorting to the wearing of combat uniforms for all ceremonies, the "Spandau Green" uniform was also worn, as previously described.

Dick Naujoks in Spandau Greens

Ceremonial blues

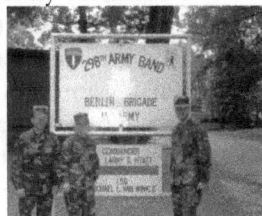

BDU Uniform, 1994

The principal duty uniform in the early years was either plain cotton fatigues of various types and styles, to permanent press fatigues which made their debut in the mid-1970s, to the Battle Dress Uniform (BDU) in 1982. The fatigue uniform changed in style and accoutrements throughout the years, incorporating block-style caps and white name tapes to green, embroidered name tapes and baseball-style caps in the 1970s. When camouflage appeared in

1982, at least two sets of BDUs with the accompanying soft cap were required. Camouflage field jackets were not required for purchase until later but each soldier was required to own two of them.

The invasion of Grenada in 1983 by U.S. forces revealed that the winter-weight BDU uniform was inappropriate for tropical climates. The Army responded by offering a summer-weight version of the BDU uniform, in addition to the winter weight. Other minor stylistic changes were also incorporated, including lengthening the sleeves and reducing the size of the lapel.

For soldiers who had long arms to begin with, the first BDUs supplied a rather comical image. Colonel Frank Adams, Deputy Brigade Commander of the Berlin Brigade from 1982 to 1984, was a tall, rangy man who suffered from Lengthy Arm Syndrome (LAS). The sleeves on his BDUs were easily 10 to 12 inches too short. As a result, he looked like a refugee from an Army-Navy store. The revised BDU design helped him considerably.

Cotton lends itself well to starch. Starched uniforms look snappy and crisp – for about 20 minutes after putting them on. Bandsmen were told not to starch the BDU uniform since an "anti-chemical warfare" compound within the fabric would be destroyed by the starch. Bandsmen ignored the warning and instructed their laundry services to impregnate their BDUs with "heavy starch."

A semi-formal summer uniform was popular in the 1950s and was issued to soldiers up until the early 1980s. The khaki uniform originally consisted of both a long-sleeved and a short-sleeved shirt, but the long-sleeved version (with accompanying tie which was tucked into the shirt between the second and third buttons) was dropped. The khaki uniform also lent itself well to starching. But a wash-and-wear type of khaki uniform, also known as Tropical Worsted or shortened to TWs, was popular in bands. With as many summertime performances as there were, TWs were preferred in lieu of the Army green uniform with poplin/tan shirt and four-in-hand tie. TWs featured the same accoutrements as did the green uniform. Brass, ribbons, unit crests and name tag were all part of the uniform. Fancy aiguilletes were not, however. Some photographs of the TW uniform depicted the distinctive unit insignia (shoulder patch), but this was dropped.

The advent of the "gray-green shirt" in 1980, replacing the tan-colored poplin shirt, also was available in short sleeve and long sleeve versions. Initially, the shirt was worn with brass-colored enlisted rank insignia pinned onto the collar points. (Commissioned and warrant officers had green-tinged shoulder marks indicating rank. These shoulder marks were cloth "sleeves" that were slipped onto the shoulder loops of the shirt.) The Army almost immediately revised the regulation to include black shoulder marks for NCOs and Specialist 5's. Lower enlisted soldiers Specialist 4 and below continued to wear the brass-colored rank insignia pinned to the collar points.

The short-sleeve gray-green shirt could be worn open-collar, with name tag, or a black four-in-hand tie could be worn with the shirt with the collar buttoned. The long-sleeve shirt was required to be worn with the collar buttoned and a four-in-hand tie. The name tag was also required. In subsequent years, the addition of ribbons, regimental affiliation insignia (Adjutant General for bandsmen), and other badges were authorized for wear on both long-sleeve and short-sleeve gray-green shirts. The gray-green shirt was worn with the same Army green uniform trousers. This effectively replaced an entire style and expense of uniform, the khaki/TW, and was more comfortable.

Infantry units dominated the Berlin command, and the 6th Infantry regiment in particular had a long history within the city. This translated over into uniform wear for a short period in 1983, in which the 298th was ordered to wear the 6th Infantry Distinctive Unit Insignia (unit crest) on shoulder loops and shoulder marks. This did not sit well with the band since the 298th was not a part of that regiment, indeed had no regimental affiliation until 1986 when all Army bandsmen became affiliated with the Adjutant General Corps regiment.[39] The DUI was to be worn above the breast pocket on the Army green uniform, above any badges or other decorations worn there.

Adjutant General Corps DUI

Mess dress, the formal uniform worn during balls and similar evening functions were not worn by band members, except for the occasional bandmaster. While the band supported formal engagements (dinings-in/out, receptions, cocktail parties) on occasion, mess dress was neither provided nor required. White mess dress was even more unusual. CWO David M. Smith wore his when the opportunity presented itself.

Headgear was worn, of course, with every uniform. Throughout the years, a flat cap, generally referred to as a garrison or overseas cap, was a part of all clothing issues. This cap was worn by most enlisted. With the adoption of the Army green service uniform, however, an Army service cap (commonly called "bus driver's cap") was available. This particular cap was added to the Army band's additional uniform authorization as a part of organizational clothing. Some bandmasters preferred the bus driver cap while most enlisted detested it. Wearers found the cap difficult to handle, unwieldy, uncomfortable, and easy to damage by placing it on its crown instead of right-side-up. The Army service cap also had hat brass that needed to be polished on a regular basis. Garrison caps were far easier to handle.

Field equipment, commonly called "TA-50" was also issued by the command. The TA-50 gear included field shirts, field pants, a parka, parka liner, work gloves and inserts, waterproof boots (sometimes called "Mickey

Mouse" boots, most likely because of the air valves located in the sides of the boot that protruded a bit, lending the appearance of Mickey's ears), web gear, cold weather cap, shelter half with equipment, overshoes, and various other pieces of equipment. The Army gradually moved away from the heavy canvas canteen covers and ammo pouches, going to lighter-weight nylon material that was also employed in rucksacks, web gear suspenders, and first aid pouches.

In the early 1980s, the Army did away with the classic M1 steel pot and its associated helmet liner, opting for the Kevlar helmet which offered more ballistic protection. Nevertheless, the recognizable shape of the steel pot was replaced by a helmet that looked more like the old German "coal scuttle" from World War II. The Kevlar weighed just as much, if not more, than the steel pot and weighed things down during ceremonies.

Trombonist Dan Hermann decided to do something about this. Dan was somewhat smaller than many of the men, weighing not much more than 160 lbs. and standing not much taller than 5 feet 7 inches tall. He didn't need or want the added weight of the Kevlar sitting on his head while a two-hour ceremony progressed around him. So he designed a "Kevlar shell" mold, into which he poured a liquid resin. When dried, this resin formed a reasonable Kevlar-like shape, and when this shell was outfitted with a camouflage helmet cover and the necessary hardware to keep the object on the soldier's head, one couldn't tell the difference. Instead of 7–8 lbs., the wearer had a few ounces floating on top of his head. Dan would make these fake helmets up for a fee—enough to cover the cost of materials.

Footgear

World War II saw the 298th wearing standard combat boots and low quarters, both in russet. Harry Reinert relates, "They [combat boots] provided for a ready-made insult, e.g. 'Aw, your (mother/grandmother/sister/girlfriend) wears combat boots!'" He also recalls not having been issued any other footgear besides the boot.

The Army went to a polished black combat boot and low quarters in 1957, although issue of the russet footgear continued until depletion.

An optional low quarter shoe called "Corfam" or sometimes "Corfram" became available for purchase or was also issued as organizational wear. These shoes featured poromeric construction, meaning the uppers were made of synthetic material. They required little maintenance and remained highly shined, although in bright sunny weather they became uncomfortably warm.

When authorized, the 298th wore bloused boots with the prescribed dress uniform, as depicted in these photos:

298th AGF Band, 1947

298th Army Band, Spandau Greens, Independence Day 1987

THE BERLIN WALL AND THE JFK YEARS

The "brain drain" from the east bloc throughout the bulk of the 1950s had a dramatic impact on the quality of people who remained in those countries. East Germany and Poland were losing their best and brightest people to the West. According to Ann Tusa, this was not a surprising phenomenon – they always flowed from East to West.[40]

Rainer Mynz states that some 3.5 million East Germans emigrated to the West from 1950 until 1961, with another 500,000 from other east bloc countries alongside (Mynz, 1995).[41] This created a severe gap in working-age people in East Germany. Before World War II, 70.5% of the area encompassing East Germany was working age. Due to the flood of refugees, that number had dwindled to 61%, according to Alan Dowty (Dowty, 1989).[42] Hope Millard Harrison wrote that fully a 50% increase in the intelligentsia (teachers, lawyers, physicians, skilled workers) had been seen to emigrate, prompting analysts in the Soviet Union (Yuri Andropov being one) to report this alarming trend. (Harrison, 2003)[43]

All of this, plus Nikita Khrushchev's own fears of losing his grip on power at the upcoming 22nd Congress of the Communist Party of the Soviet Union – similar opportunities he had himself used to purge adversaries – prompted him to take bold action and authorize the erection of the Berlin Wall, posits Frederick Kempe.[44]

On Sunday, August 13, 1961, soldiers of the German Democratic Republic began stringing barbed wire along the demarcation line separating the Soviet-occupied sector of Berlin from the three other Allied sectors. In time, workers began fortifying the barrier with concrete blocks, guard dogs, watch towers, mine fields, and no-man zones. Edicts were published that forbade transit or strictly limited it. Walter Ulbricht, leader of East Germany, also concerned about the 50,000 workers (*Grenzgänger*) who lived in East Berlin but worked in West Berlin, actually had the astonishing temerity to claim that West Germany owed East Germany $17 billion in compensation.[45]

All of this was done under the guise of "protecting" the people of East Berlin and East Germany from the Western Allies occupying their own Sectors in West Berlin. The East German Council of Ministers declared that this action was necessary to address the aggressive policies of the West German government and its attempt to incorporate the Federal Republic into NATO to "start another great war" that East Germany was establishing "the forms of control which are customary on the frontier of every sovereign state," which included the "borders of the Western sectors of greater Berlin." East German citizens would in the future need "special permission" to cross to the West and official passes to work in the western sectors.[46]

The East German preparations in staging of materials, vehicles, *Volkspolizei*, and other resources was done in secret and at 4 P.M. on Saturday,

August 12, Ulbricht, operating under the recommendations of the Soviets, gave the order to begin building the Wall at midnight.[47] The movements themselves were unknown to the Western Allies and to the West Berlin government, but shortly after midnight when the S-bahn system began to run oddly, with canceled trains and broken timetables, the already heightened vigilance of the West Berlin Polizei contacted senior officers at home to inform them that "something was going on."[48]

The initial reaction by the Berlin Command, indeed the U.S. Mission, State Department, and CIA, was one of "wait and watch.' Since all indications showed that the East Germans were closing the borders rather than staging an actual invasion, and as no disruption of communication with the Federal Republic was encountered, there was no need for immediate action. Surprisingly, no one even bothered to disturb the sleep of the U.S. Commandant, Major General Albert Watson.[49]

In meetings later, the three Allied Commandants agreed that no effort would be made to tear down the barbed wire, that barriers would not be destroyed. They believed that any effort to stop the Wall's erection would quickly escalate into armed conflict and they believed that might push an already ugly situation out of control. It was quickly determined there were no contingency plans for such an event; while such plans were on hand for a possible invasion, closing the borders and erecting a wall was not anticipated.[50]

The diplomats and the politicians issued statements of protest to the Soviet commandant, to Moscow, and to East Berlin. Meanwhile, the Commandants had not uttered a squeak of protest, had not sent a single patrol to the border to demonstrate their presence.[51] In fact, it took until 15 August before that protest would be uttered (Editor, 15 August 1961).[52]

The Berlin command deferred to the politicians and the diplomats.

The 298th Army Band's role throughout this series of events was to watch and wait. The band alerted with the rest of the Berlin command, but stood by with weapons and equipment at the ready. Those who were tasked to evacuate non-combatants stood by their vehicles. But as no invasion was under way, no evacuation was ordered.

In time, construction continued on the Wall. Its 97-mile circumference was improved from that of mere barbed wire strung between posts to tall, concrete sections that were mortared together. Signs were posted, alerting people to stay away. Inevitably, graffiti in all forms, fashions, and styles appeared—on the Western side—as well.

Confrontation at Checkpoint Charlie

In the aftermath of the erection of the Berlin Wall in August, President Kennedy appointed General Lucius Clay as his Personal Representative with the rank of Ambassador. The President clarified the reporting and communication protocol in his letter to Clay, but initially left open the actual mission. The clarifications and subsequent assignment to Clay were necessary in light of Clay's expressed dismay at the Wall's presence and failure of the administration to do more than accept it. Clay arrived in September 1961 and was in place to handle the confrontation at Checkpoint Charlie personally.

E. Allen Lightner, Jr., America's top diplomat in West Berlin, intended to take his wife to East Berlin on Sunday evening, October 22, 1961, to attend an experimental Czech theater company's performance. Since the East Berlin *Volkspolizei* (Vopos) had recently insisted on seeing identity papers and conducting border inspections of Allies and diplomats traveling to East Berlin (a violation of the Four Powers Act), Lightner, encouraged by Clay, had adopted and communicated the policy of refusing to display those documents and instead, insisting on seeing a Soviet official.[53]

These border interferences and harassment actions had been ordered by East German leader Walter Ulbricht, in direct contravention of Moscow's policy of no interference for Allied travel to East Berlin. Ulbricht was incensed at Khrushchev's recent speech at the Soviet Party Congress that a peace treaty with East Germany would be delayed for at least a year and believed that asserting himself in this fashion would send a message to Moscow.[54]

Upon arrival at Checkpoint Charlie, Lightner's VW sedan processed through normally. While Lightner traversed the zigzag barriers in East Berlin, the Vopos stopped his car and demanded to see his identity papers. Lightner refused, which led into a 45-minute argument during which Lightner insisted on seeing a Soviet official. As this was a Sunday, the East German officer reported that a Soviet official was not available. During the exchange, Lightner had sent an alert to Clay through his special car phone and Clay wasted no time in marshaling forces.[55]

Initially, a single platoon from the 2nd Battle Group appeared, consisting of two armored personnel carriers and four M48 tanks mounted with bulldozers. The provost marshal monitored the activity within the checkpoint and, seeking to remove Mrs. Lightner from any sort of conflict, drove his staff car to Lightner's vehicle and invited Mrs. Lightner to accompany him away from the scene. At the arrival of the American tanks, the Vopos stood down. Lightner then drove into East Berlin, but then returned twice more, engaging in a victory lap of sorts, the final time accompanied by the Berlin command's public information officer, a man the East German news agency ADN later accused of being under the influence of alcohol.[56]

By Friday, October 27, the original four U.S. tanks had long since been recalled, but over the week, Clay had ordered armed and unarmed escorts of further traffic into East Berlin with a number of supporting tanks occasionally stationed alongside the checkpoint. By 9 p.m. Friday, Soviet T-54 tanks appeared opposite Checkpoint Charlie, their national markings obscured. The soldiers manning the armored vehicles also wore unmarked black uniforms. American tanks once again took position alongside Checkpoint Charlie.[57] The confrontation was on a hair trigger.

By this time, the entire Berlin command was on an extended alert, including the 298th. Since August, the entire command had been told to do nothing and watch the Wall rise.[58]

Through back channels and with the assistance of his brother Bobby,[59] President Kennedy made a request of Premier Khrushchev to withdraw his tanks from the East Berlin side of the Allied Checkpoint. Khrushchev did so, and by October 29, the Soviets pulled their tanks out of Friedrichstrasse. The Americans followed suit and another flash point had passed.

The Wall's presence while it steadily went up and improved required a decided Western Allied response in monitoring and patrolling.

These "wall patrols" occasionally demanded the duties of senior NCOs within the 298th. Trumpeter Ken Dodson was one bandsman assigned to this occasional duty. Monitored and supervised by the Berlin Command's G-2 Intelligence staff office, wall patrols consisted of individual jeeps driven slowly alongside the Wall, looking for reportable items of concern. Mostly, however, wall patrols provided a presence to the East Germans and Soviets that the Western Allies would not be budged and, as was seen on occasion, would render help to those escaping.

Vic St. Clair reports that a friend of his served as the driver for a battle group commander. This officer, on at least one occasion, attempted to pick a fight by driving into East Germany from the southern border from Kreuzberg, standing up in the jeep while daring the Vopos to open fire.

The President Visits Berlin; November 1963

On June 26, 1963, President Kennedy flew to Berlin as part of a four-day trip to West Germany. His speech, spoken on the steps of Rathaus Schöneberg in which he concluded, "All free men, wherever they live, are citizens of Berlin, and, therefore, as a free man, I take pride in the words, "Ich bin ein Berliner" was met with thunderous applause by an audience of an estimated 250,000 citizens. The 298th provided music for this event.

Fred Mittag, 298th bandsman and German translator from 1962 to 1964, remarked that the single event that stood out for him during his tour of duty was JFK's visit. The 298th played a presidential, multi-national honor guard when he arrived at Tegel Airport. Participants included the British, the French, and Berlin Polizei. The president stopped to shake hands with 298th bandmaster Mr. Cortese who later joked on the bus that he might never wash his hands again. Fred remembers the sea of Berliners seen everywhere behind the fence at Tegel Airport and the sound of cheers from thousands of people when Kennedy stepped off Air Force One. Fred wrote, "It was a spine-tingling moment." He still has a booklet issued by the city of Berlin to record Kennedy's visit.

Lucian Heichler, U.S. diplomat tasked with supporting JFK's arrival sequence in Berlin, noted concerning the honor guard ceremony at Tegel, "…the American Commandant, naturally enough, wanted to be first in line to shake the hand of his president. But the French Commandant argued that since Tegel lay in his sector, he should have that honor. And Willy Brandt argued that it was, after all, his city; he was the host, and therefore…" (Heichler, 2002)[60]

Heichler added, "And then there was the problem of appropriate music for the arrival ceremony: We, the Americans, wanted the three Allied military bands to play the three Allied national anthems. But the British demurred: It was contrary to British protocol to play God Save the Queen on this occasion; however, they would be glad to play the Star Spangled Banner if we would play their anthem…And the Germans, naturally enough, wanted to play Deutschland, Deutschland Über Alles, but the Allies didn't like that, especially the French, and they suggested that the Berlin Police Band play *Berliner Luft*, a popular and rather silly ditty. The Germans, naturally enough, considered this suggestion an insult to their national pride and dignity. And so it went, and in the end, of course, everything worked out perfectly."

The June day was warmer than normal and that, in addition to the huge numbers of people desperate to get a glimpse of the president, caused a few to faint from heat exhaustion. Some crowds were so thick that those suffering from heat and the press of bodies had to be passed overhead to medical help because stretchers could not be brought to them.

On Friday, November 22, 1963, at 12:30 P.M. Central Standard Time, John F. Kennedy was assassinated. In Berlin, the time was 7:30 P.M. When the news was broadcast over AFN radio, officials from the U.S. Mission, the Berlin Brigade, and U.S. Foreign Service Officers working for the U.S. Commander, Berlin, Major General James H. Polk immediately gathered in the little-used Emergency Operations Center to assess this event. They quickly concluded no international crisis existed and no need for heightened alert, so they began attending to the largely unknown issues of planning for appropriate responses/memorials to the death of a sitting president. [61]

The planners opted for a military funeral to be held on Andrews Barracks with the customary German and Allied dignitaries present. The 298th and the infantry participating in the ceremony marched to muffled drums. Echo Taps, one bugler on either side of the parade ground, was played. Mayor Willy Brandt had made an appearance in front of Rathaus Schöneberg after returning from an extended trip abroad and assured the huge crowd assembled there that he would fly to Washington to attend the funeral. But Brandt attended the Andrews Barracks military funeral just prior to departing and was so impressed with its dignity and simplicity, particularly regarding the playing of Echo Taps, that he requested Heichler to ensure that the buglers be tasked to support a memorial ceremony hosted by the city. The memorial was scheduled for Monday, the day of the Washington funeral, in front of Rathaus Schöneberg. Brandt's deputy mayor Heinrich Albertz hosted the memorial in Brandt's absence.

The request was approved and the two buglers, Sgt. John Andrews and Joe E. Pittman traveled to Rathaus Schöneberg in the evening and performed Echo Taps again. Andrews stood on the roof of the *Rathaus* while Pittman

Joe E. Pittman, Bugler

took his post on the roof of an office building across the street. Vic St. Clair, a member of the Berlin Brigade Drill Team at the time of the memorial service, but later to become a trombonist with the 298th, took a post on the platform throughout the spoken eulogies.

Meanwhile the overall protocol had directed the setup and positioning of sufficient amounts of blank ammunition to support the firing of six 105mm howitzers on Clay Headquarters. Monday, November 25, 1963, the day of the funeral in Washington, one gun fired a solitary round every minute throughout the day. At 4:30 P.M., the Berlin command prepared for a traditional Retreat Ceremony at the Clay HQ flagpole. The gunners fired their final round as the ceremony concluded. Taps was sounded, and as the smoke cleared from the courtyard of Clay Headquarters, the guns were silenced.

PARADE SEASON

Throughout the 298th's history, performing military ceremonies comprised a large bulk of the band's activities. Held in virtually any location ranging from Tempelhof Central Airport, to Platz des 4. Juli, to the grounds of Truman Hall, to Yankee Stadium on Andrews Barracks, military ceremonies remained a high priority throughout the band's tenure.

In the early years, most ceremonies consisted of the frequent honor guard and less frequent military review, which were usually larger in scope. As Harry Reinert wrote of his experiences with the 298th in 1947 and the "Army Day"

Armed Forces Day, May 1952, TCA

ceremony that June, ceremonies didn't involve the other Western Allies. However, that changed with the advent of the Berlin Wall in 1961. The Berlin command intended to show solidarity with the other western Allies and thus, beginning in 1962, the parade known as Allied Forces Day became the focus of the 298th at the beginning of parade season.

Allied Forces Day, an all-out, no-holds-barred wave-the-flag-in-their-face event involving all the western Allies, was a direct challenge to the Soviets. All three western Allies prepared representative vehicles, trained a good number of their soldiers hard, and marched them westwards along 17.Juni Strasse in the British sector of Charlottenburg. The length of the parade wasn't long— approximately a mile. The start and finish points changed, depending on traffic control and other particulars, but the intent was to categorically demonstrate to the Soviets and their East German counterparts that the Allied presence in West Berlin was a permanent one, until the political situation dictated otherwise.

Preparation for Allied Forces Day began in May of each year in which the parade was scheduled. Since this event was essentially the advent of the parade season, it was important for the 298th to train to meet this rigorous physical and musical challenge. As Allied Forces Day was typically scheduled in the third week of June, coinciding with the East German revolt against their Soviet rulers on June 17, 1953, the 298th began hitting the pavement no later than a month beforehand. Both embouchures and bodies needed to build endurance and strength.

On the day of the event, soldiers and vehicles began lining up east of the Siegessäule (Victory Column) and when kicked off, the elements began marching the short parade westwards, around the Victory Column and ending just after the reviewing stand at the U-Bahnhof Bismarckestrasse. The entire affair was spit-and-polish, the likes of which had never been seen before by most participants, save those perhaps who served in Washington.

The clanking tanks, period vehicles such as half-tracks, armored cars, artillery pieces and other examples of Allied weaponry were cleaned to perfection. Soldiers applied baby oil to the armored vehicles both for the shine and to provide protection against paint bombs. The British tended to use OD green glossy paint on their vehicles, along with glossy black on the wheel assemblies. The French also prepared their equipment accordingly. Flags flew everywhere and it was plain that a great portion of Berlin lined up to see the festivities.

The Berlin Polizei had to erect steel barricades to keep the crowd back, and they also stationed officers every few yards for the length and breadth of the parade. As with any political statement, the protesters were also out in force, and the Polizei was primed and sensitive to keeping the crowd under control. Dave Ratliff, trumpet player and later commander of the band recalls, "The only Allied Forces Day incidents I remember were in 1975—the Polizei moved in with nightsticks and stopped the demonstrators in a hurry. As you can imagine, this was the post-Vietnam era and the left wing in the city expressed their opinion on this most unpopular of America's conflicts. At that time, the Parade then was held in front of the Charlottenburger Schloss (castle) to better control the crowd. Then in 1981 or 1982 we were leading 2nd Battalion, 6th Infantry and a group of demonstrators jumped in behind the band and in front of the Battalion Commander, his staff, and the troops. He immediately gave a 'left flank' command and sidestepped the protesters.

Polizei quickly cleaned up the area and the parade went on."

Mr. Ratliff continued, "The biggest problem with Allied Forces Day was moving the vehicles through town at 0500 - they were bombarded with paint in Neukölln and Kreuzberg. But the vehicles were coated in baby oil before they left McNair and Turner Barracks and all they had to do was wipe them off and no one could tell."

Allied Forces Day was the most important marching performance of the year. It was vital that the 298th portray itself as a first-rate military band, one that not only looked impeccable, but sounded larger than it was. While the event was held almost every year from 1962, Reunification efforts from 1990 to 1993 canceled the parade. The Berlin city government requested the parade a final time in 1994.

The organizers rotated the duties as host nation between the three western Allied powers. Every three years, the Americans led the parade. In these instances, the Berlin command wished to have the host nation's band remain in a static formation near the reviewing stand. That band, the 298th,

Allied Forces Day. 1983

could not take part in the parade itself. Therefore, invitations were extended to three other Army bands in the Zone to come to Berlin on temporary duty for a week to rehearse and play the parade. Each of these bands was assigned to one of the three infantry battalions within the brigade. Their duties during the week were to rehearse drill and ceremonies and to provide martial music for their assigned infantry battalion during its own rehearsals.

The 298th in its role as host nation planned for and executed a barbeque held right on the grounds adjacent to the band hall, time permitting. Band members of the 298th set up grills, picnic tables, requested burgers, brats, and all the trimmings from the dining facility, and laid on more than a keg or two of Schultheiss beer. All participating bands caught up with old friends, made new friends, and spent time in a festive setting when the marching and playing was over for the day. The 298th also planned bus tours for the visiting bands and made sure their stay was comfortable. Billeted in various places, including McNair Barracks, Roosevelt Barracks, and wherever room could be found, the visiting bands worked hard but enjoyed their stay in the city.

The Berlin command scheduled the Berlin Brigade Review within a week of Allied Forces Day as a method for keeping marching skills fresh. This review was a warm-up for the grandest ceremony of the season—the Independence Day "Salute to the Nation" ceremony held on the national holiday. The 4-Ring served as the venue for both ceremonies and involved usually the same marching units, except that the Air Force contingent did not participate in the Brigade Review. Following the standard ceremony format, the Brigade Review acknowledged the Brigade's performance in the previous year, recognized outstanding soldiers, and otherwise made sure those marching skills did not deteriorate.

Bruce Gleason, euphoniumist with the 298th from 1988 to 1991, wrote the following article which was published in a number of professional journals for music educators. His article, entitled *Inside a Military Ceremony*, appears below and captures the mental processes of any Army bandsman performing in a standard military ceremony.

After a recent Change of Command ceremony, I wrote down everything that had entered my mind during the job. Perhaps other marching band members (military or civilian) have had similar thoughts.

> "Trumpets sound Attention."
>
> That sounded pretty good; wow, that's twice today. Man, how long can we possibly stand at attention? Don't they realize that some of us have euphoniums underneath our arms? Good Grief, this is uncomfortable. I don't remember it ever hurting this much. I suppose it wouldn't be so bad if we hadn't practiced the entire ceremony twice this morning. I guess they just want the General's Change of Command [ceremony] to go smoothly.

"Change your music."

What's next? *March Grandioso.* At least we'll be playing. This is so weird with ear plugs. I wonder if we really need them. I can only hear me, and the trombones once in a while, and the clarinets behind me, I guess. I sure am glad I don't sound like this for real. Why do they have to put the band next to the cannons? This is terrible. It sounds like I'm playing a mouthpiece. How many times did we go over this march at the School of Music? It still is a pretty good march though. Oh, that's kind of neat. I've never heard the clarinet part there. For Pete's sake, how many times are we going to do this march? We do have other music, pal. There has to be a better way to have this lyre on here; I get so tired of moving the music when we get to the bottom. Finally, the cut off.

"Change your music."

Them Basses. This one is kind of fun. Tom said it sounded pretty good from the stands when we played it this summer; I think that was for the Fourth of July. Great; we're going to play this one forty-eleven times, too. Okay sir, next march thank you. And the cut off. Horns down. Man, my mouth gets tired. This is absurd, hoping for the cut off so we can quit playing and then hoping for the "horns up" signal so we can start so we won't have to stand at attention anymore. You just can't satisfy some people.

It looks like we're going to stand at attention with horns down for awhile. I wonder if anyone would be able to tell if I reached over with my other hand to help hold my horn up? I'm sure some idiot NCO will see. Maybe I can reach behind my back. I wish I wasn't standing in the front rank. I really don't like it up here anyway. Come on, sir; this isn't a trumpet, you know. Even the sousaphones would be easier to stand with. They just sit on your shoulder. The drummers must get tired, too. I'd get tired of playing the entire time we're standing here. How many battalions are marching out here anyway?

There's the roll off. *Liberty Bell.* This is a fun one. It's strange that Monty Python would use it for their theme music. I guess that's why they picked it.

Okay, *"Ruffles and Flourishes"* and *"General's March."* This is where they fire the cannons. I think it might be better if we're playing when they shoot. Except that when I jump, I'm afraid I'll hit my teeth against the mouthpiece.

"Horns up." Wow, this mouthpiece gets cold. Good, he's letting us blow warm air through them. How many times are they going to fire? I guess ear plugs are a good idea. I hope the guys firing are wearing them.

Inspection is next. *Garry Owen*. I guess this was Custer's favorite march. It sure seems Scottish or Irish. You'd think people wouldn't use it, considering Custer's final performance. It's sure hard to play all those running passages with heavy gloves on. What note is that? The lyre is in the way again. Oh great, where does it repeat to? There. Okay. It's amazing that we can even still play. This is a good march. There's the General.

"Horns down."

Ballad of the Green Beret is next. Mary Ellen Anderson had a record of this when it first came out. We played it until it was worn out. We really thought this was a cool song. Why do we skip the first eight measures? Maybe it's a drum solo. Some time I'd like to see what's going on when we're playing.

Now the trio from *National Emblem*. This is about the only one I have memorized. Except for that note. What is it? A Bb maybe? Try that next time. We'll play it enough times to try every note if you want. Yeah, Bb. The colors forward on this, I think. *National Anthem*. I hope I remember this. It's amazing how many times I can play something, and it still scares me to play it by memory.

Oh no! "Instruments down."

"Parade Rest." Thank you, sir. What's next? Speeches. This should be interesting. I can barely hear the commander; how am I going to understand the General's speech? Well at least I can hold my horn with two hands in front of me. Who's that talking now? I wish we could just turn our heads a little. This isn't so bad. I could stand like this all day. It's just when I have to stand with the horn at my side. It sounds like a southern accent. It must be General Marsh. I think *You're a Grand Old Flag* is next. I wish we could play the second half of it some time. I think it just changes keys and then someone has an obbligato. Maybe I couldn't stand like this all day. Well, I'm starting to hurt in places not directly connected to my feet, legs or hands. That means it's time for the General to stop talking. I wonder what he said.

Yep, *You're a Grand Old Flag*. Twelve times please. Horns back down.

"Pass in Review." Finally we get to move. I wonder if my

legs still work. "Instruments up." "Forward" – here we go – "march." *American Soldier*. How many times have we played this? And I still can't play it from memory. Wow, we do sound good though, and we look pretty hot, too. Here's a corner. Stop playing. I'd rather look like I know what I'm doing than sound like it. Why is it that some people have no problem marching, playing and turning at the same time? And a counter march. Who do I go between again? Okay, here. And on line with Dan, and come to a half step. Mark time signal. And stop. Keep playing though. Why is it that at these things the General rides past the troops, to look at them and then the troops all march in front of him? Isn't once enough? Just a few more marches.

Joyce's 71st N.Y. Regiment. I hope we don't play this at circus tempo. Those boys will be running. I think this is a euphonium solo at the trio; I never noticed that before. Maybe the tenor sax has it too.

The Fairest of the Fair. This has to be one of Sousa's best.

Arirang. What a weird name for a march. It sounds like Korean Folk Song Suite. When did I play that? Tenth grade, I think. It was when we were still in the old school. Maybe both pieces were taken from the same Korean folk song. Maybe the General is going to Korea. The end.

Wait; there's the Air Force. Dave was right; that one guy does march weird. The cut off. Horns down.

It must be the *"Army Song"* next. This wasn't so bad. Why don't we ever play the whole thing? I thought I had this memorized.

Where is it that we start marching automatically? When we repeat that first theme, I think. Here it is. Great, a turn. That's it.

Are we going to march all the way to the end of the parade ground even though everything is over? I guess so. Oh well, it doesn't seem so far when we're marching.

Man, there has got to be a better way of holding a euphonium at attention.

Independence Day was unquestionably the busiest day of the year for the 298th. Beginning with formation and uniform inspections in the early morning, most 298th members had already prepared several uniforms the night before. The day's activities required multiple performances and equipment setup and teardown until midnight or later.

Taking care not to muss the uniforms, the band boarded the bus for the short trip to the 4-Ring. Offloading the bus and uncasing instruments, the band formed and marched with a drum tap to its position on the tarmac, the left-most unit in the formation with the artillery battery located about 100 yards to the band's front and to the right. Unobtrusive spray-painted markings from previous rehearsals indicated the band's position. The drum major then dressed and aligned the band while final preparations of the entire 4-Ring took place.

The ceremony officially began at 11 a.m. on this national holiday, but the troops—marshaling on McNair Barracks—had to march to their final positions beforehand. At about 10:30 a.m., the bandmaster called the band to attention and gave the downbeat for the first pre-music march. A drum cadence with a heavy bass drum continued playing after the band concluded the march. After a suitable period during which chops rested slightly, the bandmaster gave the rolloff signal and the next march was played, always with the heavy bass drum denoting the left heel striking the ground. The first units began appearing and lining up to the band's left. Drum cadences continued after completion of the second march and this process continued for about 25 minutes until all units were on the final line, dressed and aligned by their leadership.

At 11 a.m. the ceremony started with welcoming remarks by a narrator and when the Commander of Troops appeared ready to take his position on the field, this was the signal for the Adjutant to give the command "Sound Attention!" Following this bugle call by the trumpet section, the Adjutant then gave the command "Sound Adjutant's Call!" and then proceeded to march as quickly and efficiently as possible to his assigned position in front of the entire formation, a distance of about 200 yards, while the trumpet and percussion section sounded this traditional bugle call. The Adjutant tried hard not to look unmilitary, but the fast march and the sidearm bouncing up and down did lend a comical view.

The standard ceremony format then ensued, complete with a Sound Off sequence (the band's salute to the troops, which included a countermarch while performing, one of the more trickier marching maneuvers) and Honors to a Major General. The Salute to the Nation comprised the focal point with a cannon shot announcing the name of each state and territory. The U.S. Commander of Berlin (USCOB) also gave a short speech.

Immediately following the ceremony, the 298th boarded the pre-positioned bus and, with MP and Polizei escort, drove off to the Harnack House where the USCOB hosted a garden party. Elements of the 298th provided musical entertainment during this event. Depending on the musical lineup determined beforehand, approximately half the band changed uniforms, hydrated quickly, and proceeded to begin performing for the guests who were already arriving while the other half of the band ate in an anteroom off the kitchen. After a short interlude, the band halves switched, allowing the other half of the band to eat and drink water. This back-and-forth was usually very hectic, though the band did its best to remain unobtrusive.

Following the garden party, the band packed up gear and returned to Andrews. In some years, the stage band then changed uniforms, boarded the bus again, and proceeded through Checkpoint Charlie to the residence of the U.S. Ambassador to East Germany where another garden party was in full swing. The stage band performed for a rapt audience, then headed back to the band hall.

By this time, the remainder of the band had prepared and pre-loaded the necessary equipment for the evening concert. The stage band then changed uniforms, ate an evening meal, and the entire band then formed again in the late afternoon to set up for the classic Independence Day concert with fireworks. Throughout most of the 1980s, the concert was held adjacent to the Dreipfuhl duck pond near the family housing area of the same name. Americans and Berliners gathered on the lawn, spreading their blankets or setting up their lawn chairs and awaited the concert and fireworks.

In 1983, however, the Berlin command opted to hold the annual Independence Day concert and fireworks at the Wannsee. Organized by the Brian McConnell and the Community Relations section of the Berlin command's G-5 section, the 298th performed directly on the beach, aided by batteries of sound reinforcement. As the concert featured Tchaikovsky's 1812 Overture, the accompanying artillery battery that would fire its pack howitzers during the performance of that piece was situated on a barge out on the Wannsee itself. This event attracted an enormous gathering of 100,000 people, far more than the 10,000 that were initially forecast. The sun shone, the temperatures remained pleasant, and the crowds packed the Wannsee area enough to give the military police and Polizei plenty to do.

The Wannsee concert was a bit unusual. The band performed another concert on Independence Day 1990 in Potsdam, East Germany. Bruce Gleason reported:

> One of our Fourth of July performances took place at a picnic in Potsdam which is a city in East Germany across the Havel River a few miles from West Berlin. Since World War II, the U.S. has maintained a liaison mission to the Soviet military here. It was a pretty normal Fourth of July picnic with barbecued hamburgers and chicken, potato salad and baked beans, kids playing Frisbee and tag, U.S. and Russian generals sitting, visiting and eating corn on the cob together at red and white checkerboard cloth covered tables set up under ancient oak and linden trees, on the grounds of a huge Prussian mansion maintained for the Americans by the Soviets who confiscated it from the Nazis who confiscated it

from one of the Prussian royal families, with a U.S. Army jazz ensemble playing on the second story balcony while Russian uniformed soldiers played volleyball. (Gleason, 1990)[62]

By the end of the concert, irrespective of venue, equipment had to be disassembled and loaded onto equipment trucks in the dark. By the time the 298th made it back to Andrews, it was midnight or later. A day full of performances required chops of steel and as this day was the culmination of a parade season that demanded hard work, attention to detail, and more than a little bit of pain, the band was ready for two weeks of blanket leave.

BAND STRUCTURE AND SUPPORTING FUNCTIONS

The 298th's authorized strength ranged from 28 men at various points in its history to more than 100 in the early 1950s. Actual strength varied widely from a reported strength of 21 in 1947 to over 100 in the early 1950s when the band was bolstered by the 7753rd Augmentation Detachment and the 7868th Fife and Drum Unit. After the augmentation of the 298th ended in the mid-1950s, the band's strength dropped and stayed between 35-40 musicians until deactivation in 1994.

From the band's earliest days when the band received administrative support in the form of German clerks and typists to non-musician supply sergeants, the type and level of that support varied. In the mid-1970s, the Army artificially overstaffed bands in anticipation of the 1976 Bicentennial. After completion of those events, the Army reduced the strength of bands through attrition and through the actual loss of two non-musician headcount losses—a clerk-typist and a supply specialist. The loss of these support personnel created additional administrative workload for musicians, but decision-makers preferred this rather than lose actual musician slots.

The advent of technology in the form of various computer systems at various levels in the Army's systems, while useful, also created additional bureaucracies and administration procedures that all Army bands were expected to comply with. Therefore, the level of detail necessary to function within these systems became important. Bandsmen became proficient in learning how the Army did business in administration, supply/logistics, transportation, and similar systems. The necessity of completing this work tended to detract from making music, but the cost was seen as acceptable.

Chief Warrant Officer

The 298th was one of many separate or "Adjutant General" (AG) bands authorized to have a warrant officer who commanded the band. Warrant officers for Army bands were "warranted" by Congress to fulfill a designated specialty, had undergone specialized training to become warrant officers from their previous enlisted status, and usually had higher education degrees in music. Many had graduate-level degrees and were quite accomplished in their designated areas of specialization, whether in theory and composition or in conducting or in music education. In recognition of the political nature of Berlin, most Army assignment officers preferred to assign a Chief Warrant Officer (CWO) to Berlin for command of the 298th. Chief Warrant Officers assigned to Berlin usually had at least one assignment as bandmaster in their background with a corresponding promotion.

By contrast, bands assigned to divisions at the outset of World War II generally numbered about 28 musicians. This authorized number changed in later years, but the principal difference between division and AG bands concerned command: actual command of division bands was relegated to a company-grade officer, most generally the AG company commander of the division. Bandmasters of division bands did not have command authority. Conversely, due to the separate nature of AG bands, including the 298th, the bandmaster was assigned as the unit commander with the rights and responsibilities associated with that level.

The Army shifted this policy completely in the mid-1980s when command of separate and division bands was assigned to the bandmaster. This process took several years, according to CWO David Ratliff, via email. By 1988, most if not all Army bands, were commanded by their warrant officer bandmaster.

The separation of a division band from its parent AG company effectively severed the support mechanism that the AG company inherently offered to the division band. As a result, many of the administrative, supply, and ancillary duties all were transferred to the band, to be performed by musicians, technically outside of their musical skills.

Enlisted Bandleader

The senior noncommissioned officer within the band served as enlisted bandleader and throughout the 298th's history, each such soldier was male. While women served in the band beginning in 1976, none was assigned as enlisted bandleader. The initial enlisted bandleader of the 156th Infantry Band was Henry Glaviano; he served as the *de facto* enlisted bandleader with the rank of Technical Sergeant. Glaviano functioned in that position from the band's earliest days in Louisiana in 1940, through training after mobilization and the start of World War II, while in London and continuing in Berlin. Following his departure from the band, however, and continuing until 1984, the enlisted bandleader most often was a Master Sergeant. In very few cases, the enlisted bandleader was a Sergeant First Class in a promotable status.

In 1984, the Army changed the Table of Organization of all separate and division bands such that the senior enlisted sergeant serving in the grade of E-8 was assigned the "Mike" Military Occupational Specialty (MOS) identifier. The "Mike" identifier indicated that the soldier served as the unit first sergeant with the corresponding rank insignia. Beginning with Joe Bates in 1984 and continuing with the next three enlisted bandleaders (Joseph B. Martin, James (Dutch) Perry, and Michael van Winkle), these senior NCOs all served as First Sergeant of the 298th Army Band.

The enlisted bandleader's function varied, depending on the command climate and the soldier's own preference. For example, some enlisted bandleaders preferred to perform on their instruments; MSG Matlock (flutist) is a good example. Others preferred not to play their instrument and functioned as drum major or shared conducting and rehearsal duties with the bandmaster. Many others ran smaller ensembles such as the stage band or combo.

The enlisted bandleader/first sergeant attended to the day-to-day running of the band. He prepared and monitored the duty rosters, oversaw the maintenance of the facility, and kept a finger on the pulse of the morale of the musicians. The enlisted bandleader/first sergeant often served as a mentor for other NCOs in the band and provided guidance to them accordingly. The essence of the success of an enlisted bandleader was his leadership ability, technical knowledge and competency, and interpersonal skills with the soldiers of the band.

Most good enlisted bandleaders were strong NCOs, yet could relate to musicians on a musical level. MSG Nathaniel Riddick, who served in the 298th in the early 1960s, is perhaps a good example of such an enlisted bandleader. Featured in an issue of the *Berlin Observer*, Riddick was heavily involved in the musical training and execution of many facets of the 298th, as well as leading the band on a day-to-day basis. 1SG James (Dutch) Perry is another excellent example. As Dutch served for a lengthy period as a faculty member of the School of Music and from his background as a composer and arranger, he used his considerable skills in developing his subordinates.

Some 298th enlisted bandleaders/first sergeants opted to have an assistant. This soldier was often referred to as a "field first sergeant" and typically stood for the first sergeant when necessary. Several fine examples stand out: SFC Leonard "Mac" Mutter assisted 1SG Joe Martin and 1SG James "Dutch" Perry. SFC James Lindly served in the role for MSG Lou Hurvitz.

Enlisted Organization

The rest of the enlisted structure, as authorized by Modified Table of Organization and Equipment (MTOE), is generally a pyramid shape.

Three Sergeants First Class assisted the Enlisted Bandleader/First Sergeant. Relating to their respective group, whether brass, woodwind, or percussion, these soldiers provided musical leadership and senior NCO guidance to staff sergeants and below. Often called upon to lead smaller ensembles, sergeants first class also conducted the concert band on occasion. In non-musical settings, sergeants first class often functioned as platoon sergeants.

Soldiers in the rank of Staff Sergeant often served as section leaders of their respective section, whether clarinet, saxophone, or trumpet. Within a non-musical setting, staff sergeants also performed duties as squad leaders.

The number of staff sergeants assigned to the band varied, but ran anywhere from as few as five to as many as fifteen.

Junior enlisted soldiers comprised the strength of the 298th and ranged in rank from Specialist 5/Sergeant down to Private in accordance with the Army's rank structure at that time.

Stripes for Skills Program

As part of the all-volunteer Army and perhaps in an attempt to attract more musicians for the expected swell of musical requests associated with America's 1976 Bicentennial celebrations, the Army instituted the "Stripes for Skills" program for its bands. Modified throughout its history and still a hallmark of recruiting musicians for the Army band program, Stripes for Skills allowed non-prior service recruits to enlist as Privates First Class in pay grade E-3 and then renders them eligible for accelerated promotion upon successful completion of advanced individual training at the School of Music (SOM). Within eight months, a new recruit became a Specialist, a grade that other recruits generally didn't attain until they had- about two years of service.

The accelerated Stripes for Skills program started out ambitiously. Beginning in late 1973 and continuing until about 1977, soldiers who enlisted and successfully completed basic training and the SOM, plus whose band had an available E-5 slot, was almost instantaneously promoted to Specialist 5 (SP5/E-5). This program did not adequately consider the after-effects of the Bicentennial years of 1975-77. A glut of SP5 musicians created a ceiling that a few musicians could not overcome despite their skill levels. Trumpeter Dan Guth, (1981-84) encountered significant frustration with this arrangement. He confided that he could not work through that system as he had enlisted for the first time in 1973 as a Private. He rose in rank to SP4 before he left military service. Not long after he left the Army, he reenlisted as a prior service soldier, but despite his experience and the Stripes for Skills program, he could not get promoted to SP5. The promotion system made it practically impossible to get promoted, so in frustration, he left the Army a second time.

Band Support Activities

An Army band requires support in the form of administration, logistics, operations, transportation and similar functions. These jobs are common to all Army bands:

OPERATIONS: Band Operations involved the organization, transportation, and logistics associated with an Army band's performance at a venue. For musicians serving as the Operations NCO, a critical position within the band, an ability to take problems and issues and contend with them successfully was a desired quality. Trombonist Dan Steger (1974-77; 1980-84) reminisced about percussionist Chuck Ramsey (1973-79) saying that Chuck used to take all of those problems that inevitably happened while on the road and just seemed to make them go away. He did it calmly, graciously, and without a lot of drama. Chuck always kept things low-key and it primarily was because of Chuck that he became interested in working in Operations. Dan said he tried very hard to follow Chuck's example.

Band Operations personnel ranged from a single person, usually a staff sergeant but sometimes a sergeant first class, to several people coordinating transportation, training, and direct contact with the requestor. Requests for band support within the Berlin command comprised the bulk of jobs. Ranging from requesting the marching band for a ceremony to booking the combo for a formal ball, every commitment had different requirements. Very often, however, standardized questionnaires were used to assist Operations determine the details and the aspects of the job. This information formed the plan for training to prepare the band, scheduling the transportation, obtaining fuel coupons, arranging for documentation such as flag orders, and many other details.

Ceremonies posed special types of issues. Often, a unit planning a ceremony assigned a junior officer as the ceremony's action officer. Depending on the officer, band Operations NCOs could provide valuable information—but only if that information was solicited. On some occasions, the band's viewpoint was neither sought nor accepted. This often had undesired implications. For example, Charles W.T. Consaul, a guitarist by job title but occasionally pressed into service as a band representative/bass drum player during a unit's rehearsal for an upcoming ceremony, frequently brought a metronome to the rehearsal. The metronome provided steady rhythm at a tempo that troops could march to. Occasionally, the action officer had it in his head that a tempo of 120 beats per minute was the only acceptable tempo the bass drum player could provide. The reality showed time and again that 120 beats per minute was slightly too fast. The tempo of 116 provided a more natural rhythm and less need for valuable rehearsal time to practice the rudiments of marching.

The Operations staff usually included a Transportation NCO. This individual ordinarily had a military driver's license for every kind of vehicle used by the band, to include 40-passenger buses and non-tactical vehicles from a sedan to a 5-ton truck. When the band's secondary mission required the bulk of the band to be trained as bus drivers, the licensing progression took the driver up through the various classes of non-tactical vehicles. Prior to the 1960s, however, tactical 2.5 ton trucks were often used to transport the band to the job site. Musicians sat along the sides of the truck and used the center area for instrument cases.

The Transportation NCO not only had to coordinate transportation for band jobs, he also had to arrange for training and testing for those who were undergoing military driver licensing. One of the finest in this task was euphoniumist SGT Jamie Hillen (1987-89). He was always on top of the various assignments and requirements. He never failed to have transportation arranged seamlessly. He was one of those who always got the job done and handled the inevitable problems tactfully and dependably.

Chuck Ramsey smiled and said, "In my day when I was doing Operations I did all of that, plus prepare for and undergo command inspections on privately-owned vehicles (POVs) and military licenses. It really was a 20-hour per day job sometimes. I loved it, but it was a hassle at times."

Band Operations staff was heavily involved in preparing for and coordinating jobs outside of Berlin. Many times that involved traveling via duty train. Preparation of temporary duty documents, requests for the train itself (usually the band had an entire car to itself and occupied a great deal of the baggage car with instruments and gear), flag orders, rosters, itineraries, lists, and similar documents had to be typed and proofread. Bassoonist and auxiliary percussionist David Olszyk, as Operations NCO, organized these tasks, created the necessary contacts in the command's G-3 and Finance sections, and handled countless details. The band during this time (1984-1987) was frequently on the road. Dave made the job look easy.

Community Relations, an office within the Berlin Command's G-5, received and considered civilian requests for band support. The person in this post regularly consulted with the Operations NCO and the band commander regarding civilian requests. Political considerations formed an aspect of each request. Army Regulations contained guidance as to what types of events warranted band support. Certain types of events were clearly inappropriate for Army bands, including events supporting political candidates, events for which admission was charged and the band's support was not incidental to that event. This meant that if the band's performance was the main draw of the event and admission was charged, Army band participation was proscribed. Some bandmasters interpreted the regulation a bit more stringently than others.

The Deputy Brigade Commander (DBC) retained operational control of the band through a significant part of the 1980s. This officer, a colonel, decided on each request for band support, although he solicited and considered opinions by all concerned. Earlier years saw different arrangements when control of the band was held by a combination of authorities, including the Berlin Brigade G-3 Operations group, the Special Troops Battalion, and Community Relations in the G-5 section. This had led to the occasional awkward situation when, for example, a request for the band to support a battalion dining-in was denied to provide band support for a sister battalion's organizational day. At the DBC's level, those conflicts did not exist.

The DBC held regular operational meetings to evaluate and decide on current requests for band support. The DBC decided quickly after asking pointed, specific questions. While the 298th commander attended most of these meetings, the Operations NCO occasionally attended in his absence. The tempo of the meeting ran quickly; preparation for the meeting was important.

Most Operations NCOs had extended experience in Germany and many of these spoke German quite well, even fluently. From this experience, Operations NCOs knew to develop, foster, and maintain good relationships with a West German Army unit, preferably a German military band. These relationships led to joint band concerts, social gatherings, and quite often, the opportunity to qualify on German military firearms. Qualification on German military weapons resulted in award of the German Army *Schützenschnur*, a foreign badge that was permitted for wear on the American Army uniform, by enlisted only. This badge was quite distinctive and the opportunity to qualify for the badge was sought by many of the 298th. Three levels were possible: Bronze, Silver, and Gold.

An additional foreign badge could be earned. This badge, known as the *Sportleistungsabzeichen*, combined several standard track and field events along with military tasks such as an extended road march and award of the *Schützenschnur* itself. Since qualification for the badge entailed significant physical conditioning along with mastery of military skills, this badge was approved for wear by officers as well as enlisted. This badge also had three levels of skill: Bronze, Silver, and Gold.

The 298th had viable relationships with several German Army units. The *Marinemusikkorps Nordsee* (German Navy Band of the North Sea) out of Wilhelmshaven was one such unit as was the *Heeresmusikkorps 3* (German Army Band No. 3) out of Lüneburg. Operations NCO Dave Olszyk particularly remembered *Hauptfeldwebel* van den Boom, the affable, good-natured senior NCO who worked with his unit in the Hannover area. Van den Boom delighted in all things American and he quickly made friends with all who spoke with him.

Contact between the 298th and various German Army units did not occur on a sustained, regular basis. But for several years in the mid-to-late 1980s, the 298th sought out and strengthened these relationships. As a result, many 298th members qualified for the *Schützenschnur*, and others—a bit more physically conditioned and adventurous—sought qualification on the *Sportleistungsabzeichen*. Qualification for the *Schützenschnur* required excellent marksmanship skills on the German Army G3 assault rifle, the MG3 machine gun, and the 9mm pistol. Each weapon had its challenges for every firer and none of them was easy.

Success on the firing range usually meant a huge party later on in the German Army's NCO club. Trombonist Dan Hermann arrived for his second tour in Berlin in mid-1985, having arranged a military "swap" with another trombone player who preferred to leave Berlin. Dan was and is an avid gun hobbyist and extremely capable marksman. Dan did his own reloading, had his own armory at home, and spent considerable time on the range during his free time. Despite Dan's years in Germany, he never had the opportunity to qualify for the *Schützenschnur*. Once on the German Army qualification range in Kiel, in October 1989, he determined he would not settle for anything less than Gold. Dan struggled. He fired round after

Schützenschnur presentations in Kiel, L-R Perry Ralston, German NCO, Dan Hermann, Bob Barnard

round. The brass piled up. At one point the range officer designated two men to make another ammo run. The sun sank lower in the sky. But finally, he qualified. Later, in the NCO Club, Dan allowed himself to celebrate. Dan did not drink much alcohol, if at all, but he decided to celebrate this moment for which he'd been waiting so long, and a celebration it turned out to be!

TRAINING: The Training NCO, usually a staff sergeant, prepared the Training Schedule on a weekly basis and coordinated as needed with Operations. The Training Schedule was approved by the 298th Bandmaster and/or the Enlisted Bandleader. The band's operational and gig schedule played a role, as did the necessary rehearsals in preparing for those commitments. Military-related training, such as weapons qualification, physical training (PT), PT tests, weigh-ins, and the curious USAREUR invention called "Sergeant's Time" were planned and executed.

Bruce Gleason, euphoniumist with the 298th (1989-91) wrote home in a letter, "Due to the political climate in Berlin, non-combat units here do regular military training in addition to our normal jobs. So each Thursday morning is devoted to sergeant's time. This is a [US Army, Europe (USAREUR)] policy (which is not very popular); everything shuts down, and everyone brushes up on soldiering skills. This morning, each squad of about nine soldier/musicians selected their own route and went on a two hour road march throughout the city of Berlin. Our squad, which is made up of all the low brass players, dressed in our full combat gear, carrying our rifles, marched down by one of the canals past parks and shops giving friendly waves to those we met. Here is a mother pushing a baby buggy; then there are a couple of joggers; then a retired couple strolling and visiting. And then we have the low brass section of the 298th U.S. Army Band road marching in full combat uniform."

SUPPLY: A staff sergeant ordinarily served as the 298th Supply Sergeant, particularly in the band's latter years. In the 1950s, a corporal filled this position. CWO Carroll Grummish, a trained bandmaster, served as the Officer In Charge of the supply function in addition to commanding the 7753rd Augmentation Detachment to the 298th. Supply procured all manner of things needed to support an Army band—instruments, sheet music, uniforms, military equipment including weapons and basic load of ammunition, furniture, expendable supplies, and even linen for the band. Laundry service for organizational uniforms was also provided.

Guiding the 298th supply authorizations was a Modified Table of Organization and Equipment (MTOE) which provided the authority for requisitions. Throughout the 1980s, the 298th had two property books—one for organizational equipment and one for property. Each book required appropriate documentation and supporting information and was regularly audited by the Berlin command's G-4 section.

ADMINISTRATION: The Administration NCO and staff prepared the necessary documentation in the running of the 298th. In the earlier years after World War II, the 298th hired a German clerk, according to 298th trumpeter Sebby Papa (1947-48). Typing of rosters, orders, memoranda, flag orders, award recommendations comprised the first part of the job. Following up with the bureaucracy to see that actions were moving through channels was the second, and perhaps most important part of the job.

Clarinetist John Gerding (1982-86) likes to tell the story about Master Sergeant Louis B. Hurvitz's (1981-84), typing skills. "Lou Hurvitz was an amazing writer and completely commanded the typewriter. He could, and often did, roll in a fresh DA Form 638 [a multi-part form that documented award recommendations, justifications, and decision] into that thing and bang out error-free, and perfectly-worded award citations. In those days, the text had to occupy the prescribed field on the form and not a word or character more or less. And he was fast. Lou probably typed 80-90 words per minute on that typewriter."

After the Berlin Wall went up in 1961, gaining access to East Berlin required the preparation and approval of an "East Pass." The band administration function often prepared these simple one-page documents which contained the personal information of the traveler. The traveler then presented the document to the MPs at Checkpoint Charlie for processing.

LIBRARIAN: The 298th musician serving as the band librarian required flexibility, organizational skills, and ability to deal with all manner of missing sheet music. The 298th Librarian, often a junior NCO but sometimes an outstanding younger soldier, issued music pouches that contained carefully catalogued and correct parts; charts for big band (many of which were the stock charts brought to Berlin by the band from London); concert band pieces of all types and sizes, and pieces for various smaller ensembles. In the later years of the band's existence, some 35 file cabinets were stuffed full of these pieces as the band continually added to the library through procurement and purchase over the years.

ARMORER: The 298th had a secure arms room containing a number of weapons. These changed over the years from the M1 carbine and the M1911 .45 caliber pistol to the M14, the M16A1, and then the M16A2 rifles. In 1985, the Army discontinued use of the M1911 .45 caliber pistol in favor of the M9 Beretta pistol in caliber 9mm. The MTOE authorized the quantities and types of weaponry, which also included a number of M60 machine guns and M203 grenade launchers. The armorer also coordinated with supply to obtain appropriate cleaning equipment and to procure and store the 298th's basic load of ammunition.

DRUG AND ALCOHOL AND RACE RELATIONS COORDINATORS: These functions, brought on by leadership concerned with the use of illegal drugs and interested in improving race relations in a fully-integrated Army, assisted the 298th commander in addressing these issues. These functions were staffed by one responsible soldier for each. They provided information, conducted training, and processed documentation for the 298th and assisted the commander. The Drug and Alcohol Coordinator scheduled Health and Welfare inspections, coordinated with the military police and their drug-sniffing dogs, and procured the necessary equipment for urinalysis testing, which was done on an unannounced basis.

The Race Relations Coordinator ensured that the 298th received the required training, assisted in the conduct of investigations, and reported results to the Commander. This function was brought about in the aftermath of Vietnam, when racial tension throughout the Army was considered high. The function eventually morphed into the Equal Opportunity facet of military life and not only addressed racial concerns, but also those of gender in an Army band that had a number of women in it.

INSTRUMENT REPAIR: The 298th usually had at least one musician who had an interest in repairing instruments. From Sy Karpen in the early days of the 298th to Bob Frushour in the 1980s and beyond, this person took the instruments that Army bandsman routinely bang up and put them back in service, or conduct routine maintenance other than cleaning.

CWO Marion Durbin, 298th bandmaster from 1947 to 1950, complained in his annual reports about the general quality of instruments obtained through the Army supply system and took steps to get them repaired on the local economy. This would indicate that he didn't have a musician in the band with skills sufficient to handle repairs and maintenance.

Hornist/trumpeter Bob Frushour (1982-85) had run a business as a repair technician prior to his Army career. His skills were so pronounced that he was called upon to organize and lead an instrument repair course for all eight Army bands in Europe. Bob handled all routine maintenance on the Army's instruments and tackled many jobs for which he didn't have the necessary equipment.

CHARGE OF QUARTERS (CQ): The Army has always had some kind of extra duty that one had to perform. For most junior enlisted in the 298th, that meant pulling CQ. There was usually a procedure on what to do in the event of emergencies and who to call in the event of a problem, but pulling CQ mostly meant answering the phone for somebody else. For those who liked to make friends outside the gate, that often meant phone calls from those friends. One of the unwritten rules, however, concerned physically going to a person's room and informing him of an incoming phone call. Building 909 had no public address system to announce phone calls until 1986, when the building was renovated and even then, use of that system to announce phone calls was not permitted. Therefore, the CQ invariably trooped up the stairs and knocked on the door of the callee. The callee then went to answer the phone at the CQ desk. The band looked after each other in that way.

In actual fact, the CQ served as a valuable readiness mechanism. Readiness alerts certainly happened, and the CQ initiated the prescribed actions when those occurred. But the telephone provided for occasional personal phone calls both receiving and outgoing. Junior enlisted personnel customarily pulled CQ, given sufficient training in how to answer the phone and how to take messages. But in the early 1980s when the Stripes for Skills program resulted in a bumper crop of staff sergeants, MSG Hurvitz had to make a very unpopular decision. He put staff sergeants on the duty roster to pull CQ in addition to those soldiers in the rank of SP5 and SP4, the junior enlisted normally detailed for this duty. While unpopular with the staff sergeants, the decision provided an larger pool, meaning the frequency of duty was less. This meant everybody getting weekday duty about once a month and weekend duty about once every three months. This arrangement lasted until enough junior enlisted personnel arrived in the band to flesh out the duty roster, at which point the enlisted bandleader pulled staff sergeants off the duty roster.

The telephone system itself went by the nickname of "Hitler's Revenge". In the days prior to digital telephone service, using the telephone to call any sort of distance often meant screaming into the receiver to be heard. The oft-repeated joke told by many bandsmen asserted that the East German Stasi had placed so many phone taps on the entire U.S. analog phone system that those taps literally sucked the life out of it. When the band building was renovated in 1986, the archaic phone system was completely replaced with a digital system offering more clarity and more phone lines. Previously, the band had but three phone lines in which to conduct all business, a problem at times. It was nice to finally shake Hitler's ghost loose from the phone system.

Even the bandmasters sometimes had additional duties. Bill Ervin told the story of CWO Wilbur J. Moyers, who, upon returning from his duty as Officer of the Day, entered his office with his .45 pistol on his belt. A few moments later, a shot rang out. Rushing into Mr. Moyers' office, the CQ observed a very pale, very wan Mr. Moyers with the smoking .45 in his hand and a bullet hole in the wall next to his head. Clearly, Mr. Moyers hadn't been careful enough when clearing his weapon and discharged it, the bullet narrowly missing his head.

THE SEVENTIES

The years during which Vietnam waned and led toward the all-volunteer Army were not significant from a musical perspective. It was business as usual for the 298th. There were, however, several sociological issues that confronted the band.

Drugs and Alcohol

While drug use in Germany during the 1970s was seen as a problem of some concern, it wasn't as acute in Berlin. The reasons were many: first, Berlin was seen as a premier assignment and soldiers with a history of problems or issues were often denied assignment to the city. Secondly, Berlin was a city of boundless activity. If boredom were a reason to experiment with drugs, anyone could be bored anywhere. But Berlin was a city and an assignment without equal.

Certainly, some 298th members took illicit drugs. Alcohol, while legal, was a problem for a few. Some hard-core drinkers, many of them older soldiers accustomed to a different culture, did not understand that some people just didn't drink. Surprised and somewhat put off by this revelation, they sometimes viewed the non-drinkers or light drinkers somewhat suspiciously. The military began offering education in drug and alcohol use, and where the issue became a problem in select cases, appropriate administrative action was taken up to and including discharges and punitive measures under the Uniform Code of Military Justice. Drug-related inspections, generally called "Health and Welfare Inspections," were scheduled by most commanders, and in detecting the presence of drugs, trained dogs were used to sniff those substances out in circulating through barracks rooms and in common areas. More sophisticated measures, including urinalysis, became available to commanders in later years.

CWO Howard Vivian served as the 298th's bandmaster through a turbulent time in the 298th's history. In the midst of the counter-culture of the Sixties, the Vietnam War, and the era of the draftee, Mr. Vivian, a veteran of both the Korean and Vietnam conflicts, took his role seriously. He commanded the 298th and would see to it that his men behaved and performed as professionals. Unfortunately, Mr. Vivian did not relate well to the younger soldiers musicians in his command, which is best illustrated in his interactions with Lawrence "Fish" Brown, a trumpeter with the 298th from 1968-71. Fish provides a story that exemplifies the struggles seen in any Army band from time to time, but especially visible and obvious during the Vietnam era when the so-called "generation gap" separated the leadership from the musicians.

The band returned to the band hall shortly before 0900 hours after a Monday drill band session. Mr. Vivian announced an Open Locker inspection to begin directly at 0900 hours, just a few minutes away. He called the band to attention and dismissed them. Those with barracks rooms went immediately to their rooms and prepared for the imminent inspection. Fish's roommate was in a panic. He'd gone out the previous weekend and bought about seven slabs of hashish, which were about the size of Hershey Bars. He'd then bought the same number of Hershey bars and replaced the chocolate bars with the hashish slabs into the wrappers and placed them on his locker shelf. Just as Fish and his roommate opened their lockers, Fish saw that one of the slabs was only partially wrapped and openly visible on a shelf just below eye level. That's when they heard, "Atten-HUT!"

Mr. Vivian walked into the room and Fish was the first to be inspected. Fish mused internally what the consequences of a hash bust were going to be for him being in the presence of it. He knew he was clean, but could not say the same thing for his roommate. Suddenly, Mr. Vivian found a paper he'd written about an incident that happened at an official band party the previous week in which some British and French band members were present. A fair amount of beer had been consumed by several of the musicians, and Fish's colleague Warner had allowed his necktie to become loosened and his uniform otherwise rumpled. Mr. Vivian ordered Warner to put his uniform back together properly, and the beer in Warner prompted an insubordinate response. Mr. Vivian then ordered written eyewitness reports of the incident from those who had seen and heard it. Fish had written a Combined Band Party Report as a joke at Mr. Vivian's expense. It was not meant for Mr. Vivian's eyes and it was only meant to be shared with the other men. But now Mr. Vivian is pulling it out of Fish's locker! The document contained the following text, typed on a typewriter:

```
REPORT:combined band party                    last page

     20 Feb. 1970

… and as the blood oozed through the gapeing bullet
hole in his rotten guts, Mr. Vivian said: "Warner,
you stink!"
     Warner then threw his gun down on the cold,
blood-spattered ground and as the paranoic victim
collapsed into a pool of his own filthy, coagulating
body juices, Warner drove over him with his own car.
     Mr. Vivian appeared later with a sling on his arm
claiming that Warner had killed him.


                              Sp4 Lawrence R. Brown Jr.

                              /signature
```

Fish paled as Mr. Vivian's face turned red and contorted. Mr. Vivian roared, "Brown—report to my office at 1300!" as his hands shook in rage.

Then Mr. Vivian turned to the roommate's locker. The inspection thus far had unnerved Fish and he grew more apprehensive as he noted Mr. Vivian's attention directed toward the slab on that locker shelf, which was wrapped only in the Hershey's white inner paper. Mr. Vivian picked up the slab, removed the inner paper, rubbed it, turned it over in his hand, smelled it, and rubbed it again. As he did this, Fish began to shake. Then Mr. Vivian turned to the roommate, glared at him, and said, "Pxxxxxs! What's THIS!?" The roommate coolly answered, "It's a piece of sandstone, sir. I've been getting into ceramics, over at the Craft Shop." After a moment, Mr. Vivian said, "Oh," and put the slab back on the locker shelf before leaving the room to resume the inspection elsewhere. As soon as the hall was clear, the roommate then ran all his hashish down to the latrine where he crumbled and flushed it all down the toilet.

Later, at the prescribed time, Fish rapped on Mr. Vivian's office door in military fashion. Upon being told to enter, Fish opened the door, entered the office, closed the door, and marched to within two steps of Mr. Vivian's desk and saluted while barking, "Specialist Brown reports to the bandmaster as ordered, SIR!" Mr. Vivian returned Fish's salute and told Fish to approach his desk. As Mr. Vivian stood looking out the window, he turned with the typewritten page in hand and said, "Mr. Brown. You were not one of the men I asked to write a report on the incident—so what is the meaning of this and where is the rest of it!?" Fish replied, "There isn't any more, sir. That's the only page I wrote. I did it as a joke, to lighten things up among the guys. Morale is down because they see this as a misunderstanding and they're worried. Mister Warner meant no harm to anyone and has always been a good example and a source of good humor for others in the band. They are hoping you'll talk to him, sir, and bring this to a positive result, for the good of the band."

Fish noted that Mr. Vivian seemed relieved, as he himself was relieved. Mr. Vivian dismissed Fish, and as he stepped out of the office, Mr. Vivian said, "Mr. Brown, you may have some talent as a writer, but please—no more dime novels!"

Fish Brown's coming to the 298th actually started with his having fallen short on the teletype speed requirement for the Communication Center Specialist job at Ft. Gordon. That earned him a ticket to Ft. Dix, where he was slated for training as a mortarman. Fish went to the Ft. Dix band, auditioned, and passed the audition on trumpet. Unfortunately, there were no openings, so Fish went through the mortarman training course at Ft. Dix and did well enough to be sent to Berlin, where he took one of two slots. Intent on staying involved in music despite his assignment with the infantry, Fish started a pickup band called "The Group" and further developed his instrumental skills. The Group was good enough to be sent on special duty tours, but one such tour had to wait, because Expert Infantry Badge testing was on the company agenda. One of the challenges was a 12-mile march with full equipment through varied terrain in the Grunewald. Fish ended up with a half-dollar sized blister on each heel and couldn't march in a planned Review on the 4-Ring the next day. The annual Allied Firing Demonstration was also scheduled and the minimum rank to participate in this inter-Allied event was Sergeant E-5. Fish was only a Private, so the company commander ordered a Sergeant who was about his size to lend Fish his spare uniform dress greens coat. The captain said, "Okay, Brown. Just walk around, look good and tell 'em where the latrines are."

Fish did so and while looking the part of a Sergeant E-5, his ears followed the music of the 298th. The band was playing under a tent whose sides were rolled up and secured from the sun and wind. Fish listened a bit, arranged for and passed another audition, and was assigned to the 298th. The first sergeant and commander of the infantry company were not amused at this turn of events, but Fish packed his bags and headed over to Andrews Barracks and his new home. Fish continued his off-duty music-making by jamming at establishments like the Badewanne and the Jazz Galerie. His efforts in forming a jazz-rock group called "The Gasoline Band" were instrumental in cutting an album and providing a venue for him and several others to remain in Germany following their enlistments.

Within the 298th itself, the business of making quality music required some good, fundamental leadership from the senior NCOs. The 298th found it in the musical skills and direction of SFC Al Nelson, tenor and baritone saxophonist. Leader of the 298th stage band, Nelson knew his business, for prior to his arrival in Berlin in 1971, he'd had a lot of experience fronting big bands. He continued in that role, though Al does recall having some personal differences of musical opinion with Mr. Vivian. Despite these differences, he led a group that had a sizeable following and featured such budding stars as Tim McWright, who later became the NCOIC of the Army Blues, the Army Band's premier jazz ensemble. Tim played alto like a man possessed, and Al gave him plenty of room to express himself.

Changes and More Turbulence

In January 1975 CWO Richard "Dick" Saddler and Master Sergeant Tom Easley closed down the 76th Army Band in Worms, Germany. They were ordered to the 298th in Berlin and brought along a contingent of musicians from the Worms band, as well as the bulk of the equipment. This had the rather discomfiting effect of swelling the numbers of musicians and leadership in the 298th. CWO Al Tapia, the sitting bandmaster in Berlin at the time of the Saddler/Easley reassignment, had to make room for this influx of people.

Trumpeter Dave Ratliff, who arrived in Berlin with his wife Kay in February 1974, said the 76th Army Band guidon (unit flag) was moved out of Worms to Kaiserslautern due to more Army-wide changes made in band structure due to the upcoming Bicentennial. The rest of the musicians in the Worms band were moved to other bands around US Army Europe. Mr. Tapia was due to return to the States in late 1975, so Mr. Saddler was moved to Berlin. Mr. Saddler was senior to Mr. Tapia and therefore became commander of the 298th. Dave recalled that when he arrived, SFC Ed Greene was the enlisted bandleader he left for the School of Music in December 1974. MSG Juan Martinez del Carmen was the enlisted bandleader during the latter part of 1974.

Vic St. Clair said that Easley had it a bit easier, as he simply moved into the enlisted bandleader position as his predecessor, MSG Juan Martinez del Carmen, had already departed Berlin. "Mr. Tapia did not like Mr. Saddler taking over," Vic said, "but he was just outranked. They kept it professional, though, and I appreciated it from both of them."

Mr. Ratliff said, "There were some distinct adjustment issues, despite the professionalism of both officers. This eventually resulted in reassignment of several 298th members to other bands in Germany. As Mr. Tapia was in the latter part of his Berlin tour anyway, he got a curtailment and left in the summer. Once these events took their course, the 298th gelled and became a wonderful band. We started traveling due to Saddler and Easley's connections with U.S. Army Europe's Public Affairs Office. Until then the 298th took only one trip a year to West Germany."

The Women Arrive

Saxophonist Cheryl Wason enlisted in the Army in July 1974 with the idea of serving as an Information Specialist. While processing in at basic training, the Women's Army Corps (WAC) Band at Ft. McClellan, AL, posed routine questions to all female basic trainees such as, "How long have you played a musical instrument?" Cheryl's drill sergeant later called her in and told her she would audition at the WAC Band. After passing the audition in January 1975, Cheryl graduated basic training and went to the WAC Band the next month, assigned as a Private E-2. Female soldier-musicians were assigned exclusively to the WAC Band at Ft. McClellan. Cheryl's first impressions of the WAC Band were strong. Ably led and known for extremely high standards of military appearance, the WAC Band leadership insisted on professionalism in all aspects of behavior and duty. She recalls standing up on the bus on the way to performing a ceremony to keep from wrinkling her "cords," the female version of khakis. She learned and retained those high standards throughout her tenure with the WAC Band, earning recognition as the Soldier of the Quarter at Ft. McClellan. In the mid-1970s, the Army integrated the sexes in non-combat jobs, including bands. In 1976, the WAC Band played its final concert and would thereafter be known as the 14th Army Band when male soldier-musicians started appearing at Ft. McClellan.

Cheryl previously had indicated an interest in an assignment in Germany and arrived in Berlin in September 1976 as the first female musician in the 298th. Dan Steger recalls another female assigned to the 298th before Cheryl's arrival, but she was not a trained Army musician. Up to this point, Building 909 had been strictly a male facility and plans weren't yet complete to designate a female barracks area. Cheryl was assigned a barracks room in Building 904, a short 100-yard walk from the band hall. Other women within this designated area were assigned to other units. That arrangement held until June 1977, when a section of the 3rd floor of Building 909 was cordoned off and secured for the women, who were beginning to join Cheryl. Complete with padlocks and other controls, Cheryl found the approach a little excessive, but the effort revealed a genuine desire to protect her.

Cheryl recalls with appreciation how MSG Tom Easley and Mr. Saddler openly welcomed her and made her feel at ease. MSG Easley invited her to Thanksgiving dinner with his family. Clearly supportive, they went to many lengths to incorporate her skills and talents into the 298th. Cheryl said, "It seemed that Mr. Saddler understood that my being there was an historic time. He took many opportunities to showcase me and make me feel welcome." Cheryl heard from her friend SP5 Barry Farley, French Horn player, that when MSG Easley had formation shortly before she came to the 298th· he told the band, "We got a member of the WAC band coming in. That's a pretty strac [disciplined] unit. The Old Man wants you to keep your stuff straight! This is important to him!" She said that Barry remembered the guys anticipating the change and thinking it was going to be a cool thing.

Every band takes official photos from time to time. The 298th treated these events like gigs. Cheryl remembers getting dressed in the Class A green uniform and taking the bus down to the Brandenburg Gate and the Reichstag with these iconic places and the Wall as backdrops. She felt strange about being so close to the Wall and knowing that they were surrounded by this wall and on an island of freedom in the middle of communism.

Once the band was in formation, MSG George Pledger assumed his position as Drum Major as he customarily performed in that role. But Cheryl previously had expressed an interest in the job and had undergone some training at the WAC Band while she was there. Mr. Saddler then told Cheryl to take the mace and be photographed in front of the band as Drum Major. She found the experience exhilarating and an honor and believed this was yet

Cheryl Wason, Drum Major

another example of how she was accepted as a member of the 298th. Soon other women began arriving. Deborah Boyd (sax), Diana Vargas (flute), Laurie Everett (clarinet) and Denise Brochares (clarinet) all arrived to accompany Cheryl as the newest females in the band. Cheryl had been the sole female for about eight months before the second female arrived. She had had time to adjust and offered encouragement to the new members. By this time, the necessary renovations were complete up on the 3rd floor of the band hall, and all the single females moved in.

Cheryl remembers some ribbing on the bus that went a little too far. Choosing to address the inappropriate comments herself, she successfully shut down the exchange and demonstrated the limit of her acceptance of less-than-professional talk. She had the impression that her assertion skills were being tested and did well to stand up for herself. Nevertheless, she later learned that the same individuals kept an eye on her and her safety as "big brothers" do for their sisters.

Einhausen

An Army band performs for the community in which it is located as a measure of community relations. Performances for the Berliners were common or less so, depending on the bandmaster and the overall command climate. Various relationships between the 298th and areas outside of Berlin developed over the years, despite the distance involved and of the perceived value of maintaining that relationship. Mr. Saddler and MSG Easley brought the Einhausen gig to 298th in 1975 when they closed down the Worms band, and as a result, performing for the townspeople over the weekend that the band spent there was one of the highlights of the year.

In the mid-1970s, a very young David Ratliff showed up at the 298th with his trumpet and a degree from a well-respected university. Dave watched his leadership and learned and realized that he had what it took to become a bandmaster in his own right. Less than five years later, he showed up again in Berlin for his second tour, this time as the 298th commander. During Dave's first tour in Berlin, he had encountered the town of Einhausen for the first time, and became enamored of the town's hospitality, generosity, and unhesitating support for the members of the band. When he returned as the bandmaster, he learned that the relationship had withered since his departure, but he quickly set about to reconnect the 298th to the small town with the big heart. He did so by taking the band on side trips to Einhausen while the band was in the general vicinity performing other commitments. For example, the American military community in Worms booked the 298th to support the German-American Festival. Following this festival, Mr. Ratliff brought the band to Einhausen, only 15 kilometers from Worms, to play an unscheduled pouch concert directly in the middle of the village. This had the effect of bringing out the mayor and other officials from within city hall for this unexpected treat. The relationship quickly grew enthusiastic again and the band enjoyed several encounters with the Einhauseners while Mr. Ratliff was bandmaster/commander.

In November 1976, the 298th traveled through East Germany to get to West Germany and Einhausen. Cheryl Wason was on board the duty train for one of her first out of town performances. She could not know on her trip down that the coming weekend would change her life. Once arriving in Einhausen, Cheryl learned she'd be staying with the Schumacher family. Her presence as the sole female in an American Army band that had previously had only men, fascinated the townspeople of Einhausen, who welcomed her with flowers and open arms. The concert went on, and while Cheryl took a break and was greeted by many in passing. One young woman approached her and introduced herself, "Hello, my name is Elgin Tessereaux and I would like to practice my English with you!" She and Cheryl went on to study together at the University of Heidelberg two years later, and they are dear friends to this day.

The logistics of getting to Einhausen/Worms were a bit more complicated than supporting a simple *Platz* concert in Berlin. The Berlin/Frankfurt duty train provided the bulk of the transportation. Leaving on a Thursday evening in November, the band traveled overnight, arriving in Frankfurt early Friday morning. The Einhausen organizers arranged for a commercial bus to pick up the band at the Frankfurt *Hauptbahnhof.* Meanwhile, the band sent an equipment truck with at least two band members as drivers through the East German corridor. Once the band arrived in Einhausen, breakfast was served at the restaurant "Zum Engel," owned and operated by Adi Schumacher and his family. Then the band members sat down to wait for their host family to arrive and pick them up.

Band operations had previously coordinated assignments of the band to townspeople willing to share their homes with one or more 298th members. Many things were considered. For example, those 298th members who spoke at least some German were assigned to those families who spoke little or no English. Host families stopped by Adi's restaurant to pick up the individual members as their schedules permitted, so this process took several hours to complete.

The rest of Friday and Saturday morning were set aside for friendship, conversation, plenty of food, wine and beer. Some band members would take advantage of the location and engage in sporting activities in the area, most notably Volksmarching. Volksmarching, a sport originating in Germany, simply entailed hiking marked courses. Distances hiked (or run) and the events themselves were tracked in an official notebook.

Saturday evening's concert would be a long affair. The band arrived in the late afternoon and staged equipment in the cramped and crowded civic hall, located in the center of Einhausen. As the band of the Einhausen Volunteer Fire Department, an organization that began under Adi Schumacher's tutelage in 1967, would also perform, the small hall's stage and backstage area became full of concert gear. Meanwhile, the townspeople gathered, speeches were made, refreshments were made available, and the concert started with the fire department band. Complete with traditional and more contemporary costumes, festive decorations, intricate dance numbers, and entertaining music

from a wind band of about 25 musicians, the Einhausen band played their favorites for over an hour. A break was necessary to set up the 298th's gear and then the concert continued. The 298th stage band, full concert band, or other ensemble provided most of the entertainment and the evening became a showcase extending a genuine thanks to the people who never ceased to make the 298th welcome in their small community.

After this lengthy and happy concert, the party often continued in various venues throughout town. Host families provided those venues or simply wished their charges a good evening, providing a key to the home, and at least some of the 298th found a different setting until the wee hours. As the duty train would not leave Frankfurt until early the next (Sunday) evening, there was no rush to leave Einhausen the next morning. Another round of delicious meals, socializing, and farewells took place until the bus departed for the main train station. The equipment truck departed, the band boarded the duty train, and then disembarked the train in Berlin early Monday morning.

Einhausen was an experience that most 298th members had never encountered. Instead of sleeping in a German Army barracks room or in less comfortable venues throughout Europe, the band members were brought into the homes of attentive, considerate, and gracious host families. Despite the language barriers, communication occurred; long-lasting friendships developed and life-changing events were influenced by this small town in southern Hesse.

The relationship between the 298th and the town of Einhausen ran with only periodic interruptions from 1975 to 1990. Reunification and other priorities assigned to the 298th ended the opportunity for performances in Einhausen, but that did not keep Cheryl and others away. She and other veterans of the 298th have visited Einhausen many times over the years and have continued to share their news with old friends. After having become a German teacher herself, Cheryl took many of her students to Einhausen for the experience of immersing into the language and culture. Some years later, Cheryl saw an opportunity for Shoreview, Minnesota, a suburb within the Twin Cities area, to extend a hand in friendship to Einhausen as Sister Cities. This effort also succeeded and in 2014, Cheryl returned from yet another trip to Einhausen to deliver and celebrate a huge 9-foot rooster (the rooster is the town's mascot) as a symbol of their friendship.

Cheryl was also instrumental in arranging a concert tour for the Einhausen Volunteer Fire Department Band in the northern Midwest in 2012. The band started their tour in Chicago, where Cheryl's husband Jeff Gottwig, also a veteran of the 298th, and others met them at their hotel. The Einhausen band traveled north into Wisconsin and then into Minnesota for two weeks of festivals, touring, fun, and lots of playing.

Cheryl and other veterans of the 298th have grown to love the town of Einhausen and the people in it. She stops to marvel at the strange twist of life that led her to Einhausen on that November day in 1976. "Thank you Richard Saddler. You were a big part of starting this," Cheryl says with passion.

SECONDARY MISSION

All military units are assigned missions according to their specialty. Army bands are no exception. During wartime, the tactical situation may preclude Army bands from performing its customary mission—music—and thus may be required to perform a different mission, such as security, providing medical assistance for casualties, or any number of routine jobs.

Commensurate with the accomplishment of any mission, commanders ensure training is done to prepare their unit for completion of that mission.

The 298th Army Band and its precursor the 156th Infantry Band had several secondary, or tactical missions, over the years. Local commanders directed what bands would do when and if war came to Berlin. No specific wartime doctrine for a band's mission was adopted for Army bands until the mid-1980s. As a result, the band's normal secondary mission became blurred and changed at the whim of the local commander. Despite this lack of consistency, several secondary missions assigned to the band were identical with other Army bands and two were unique to Berlin.

Tactical Mission

An Army band begins to prepare for war by learning to live in a field setting. Band soldiers learn the need for tactical security, light and noise discipline, basic infantry skills such as map and compass reading, and small unit tactics. The band may move to its objective by road marching and once there, prepares its bivouac and operational areas using those skill sets. Glaviano wrote in his book on the 156th Infantry Band that the unit frequently participated in road marches of 20 miles with full packs and 30 miles with field packs during the year the band spent after mobilization in 1940 to active duty. That included six months in Camp Blanding, Florida; several months in southern Louisiana, and an extensive period in North and South Carolina. This continual period of living in a field setting, while difficult, brought cohesion and unit esprit.

Field exercises often pit an aggressor against a defender. These events reveal significant competitive spirit with the requisite differences of opinion, so umpires are typically used to decide matters based on the tactical result of the exercise and the performance of the combatants. On occasion during the extensive maneuvers in preparing for World War II, 156th bandsmen were used to assist umpires in communicating or performing other routine tasks. In other instances, bandsmen were used in assisting battalion commanders as runners.

While in Berlin, the 298th continued to participate in field exercises throughout its history, more often than not held in the *Grunewald*. These exercises were generally short in duration and often were held in conjunction with a called "alert" in which the band's notification system was used. Typically, the band's Charge of Quarters was notified that an alert was in progress. The CQ then employed a telephone notification tree to bring in those members who lived off the kaserne and also manually notified members living in the barracks. As members arrived, they reported in, collected equipment or weapons, and awaited further instructions. On occasion, the band deployed as a portion of the exercise to gauge how quickly the unit responded to the alert.

Bill Ervin, drummer with the 298th in the early 1950s, remembered in an interview, "Oh, yeah, we'd go out to the field two or three times per year. Usually it was headquarters security, that sort of thing. We weren't necessarily fond of that type of thing, but we did what we were supposed to. That's when we became very familiar with the Grunewald and the 'Gruney Pigs' that ran through the area (Ervin, 2005)." The "Gruney Pigs" were wild boars that made the Grunewald their home. The swine encountered American GIs while military training went on. Those encounters weren't always pleasant.

Tactical equipment at the unit level changed considerably through the years. While canvas for tentage remained largely unchanged, the use of the "Multiple Integrated Laser Engagement System" (MILES) gear came to the Army in the early 1980s. This system incorporates the use of a laser-emitting device that fits on the barrel of a rifle and "fires" when the firer squeezes the weapon's trigger. Battery-powered with a 9-volt battery, the system could "kill" an opponent by the use of receiving sensors that each soldier wore in the form of web gear and a helmet cover. If the soldier was "hit" by a beam, a high-pitched, distinctive squeal was heard that could only be extinguished by an umpire with a key. Soldiers learned to game the system by using strategically-mounted paper clips, which provided an "automatic fire" capability without using blank ammo. Many more "kills" than should have been recorded were the occasional result.

One alert that culminated in an exercise occurred in 1984. The band responded to a called alert, got to the band building and uploaded weapons, gas or "protective" masks, and the rest of the usual tactical gear including web gear, steel helmets, and Nuclear, Biological, and Chemical (NBC) equipment. NBC gear included the gas mask, a chemical suit with rubber booties and rubber gauntlets.

The band then loaded up onto trucks and convoyed over to Parks Range (also known as "Doughboy City") for an overnight exercise.

Doughboy City was constructed as a small city and expressly intended to provide a venue for urban warfare. Located in South Lichterfelde and butted up against the Wall separating West Berlin from communist East Germany, this area comprising perhaps 10 acres featured concrete shells of buildings with open frames for windows. An odd array of junked cars, building materials, and similar objects provided attackers and defenders the detritus that any urban war would offer.

Given the order to get dressed in the chemical, biological, and radiological configuration known as Mission Oriented Protective Posture (MOPP) 4, the most stringent, obstructive, and uncomfortable level of chemical and biological protection available to all soldiers, the band suited up and started to sweat. The gas mask, charcoal-permeated suit, rubber booties and rubber gauntlets formed a steam bath for everyone and those uniform items, along with the rest of the combat gear made things decidedly uncomfortable.

Those involved in that particular exercise assumed a defensive position inside a concrete structure representing a church. Remaining in a static position partially solved the sweating problem, but the exercise didn't include communicating the battle plan to those awaiting the pending assault. After six hours of MOPP 4 and no assault, the "All Clear" was passed and the protective masks removed. Breathing could once again become a priority.

Setting up and dismantling camouflage was a frequent part of field exercises and alerts. Camouflage netting consisted of various pieces of nylon netting material in which individual pieces of camouflage-colored plastic (off-browns, shades of green, taupe) were woven. These pieces of netting could be laced together to form pieces large enough to erect over tentage, large vehicles, or weapons systems. Poles and "spreaders" were used to get the netting high and were then tied down with the used of guy ropes and stakes. Like any task, the 298th needed practice in rolling out, selecting the correct color camouflage, and then erecting it. The netting frequently got caught on protruding objects which made for occasional frustration in getting the netting up quickly.

Bruce Gleason, euphoniumist with the 298th from May 1989 to August 1991, recalls, "Due to the political climate in Berlin, non-combat units adhere to regular military training in addition to our normal jobs. So each Thursday morning was devoted to "Sergeant's Time." This is a brigade policy (which is not very popular); everything shuts down, and everyone brushes up on soldiering skills. This morning, each squad of about nine soldier/musicians selected their own route and went on a two hour road march throughout the city of Berlin. Our squad, which is made up of all the low brass players, dressed in our full combat gear, carrying our rifles, marched down by one of the canals past parks and shops giving friendly waves to those we we met. Here is a mother pushing a baby buggy; then there are a couple of joggers; then a retired couple strolling and visiting. And then we have the low brass section of the 298th U.S. Army Band road marching in full combat uniform."

Not all military training was work. Some of it was actually fun. Bruce continues, "Last week we went to a West German army post in northern Germany (Kiel) to qualify on German weapons – pistol and automatic rifle. Most of us qualified bronze, and there were two silvers and one gold. The badge called the *"Schützenschnur"* is huge and is attached to a silver cord which hangs down from the right shoulder to the second button of our dress uniform and looks quite nice."

Medical Mission

The 156th Infantry Band knew when it was mobilized in 1940 that its mission shifted from that of music to that of bearing litters during combat. Colonel Kuttner, the 156th Infantry's regimental commander, directed that the band allocate all its training time toward the accomplishment of the medical mission, in addition to other duties as message bearers, kitchen police, guard duty, and similar field duties. During its one year of mobilization prior to the declaration of war, the 156th spent six months in Camp Blanding, Florida, and the remaining time in southern Louisiana during which the band trained in those tactical missions. After declaration of war in 1941, the band prepared for deployment in Texas, North Carolina, and South Carollina and continued its medical training there. The band was directed to participate in regularly scheduled ceremonies such as Retreat; however, no training time was allocated for that daily task.

Bearing litters sounds easier than it is. Two men must bear the load of another through terrain and weather of all types, all while synchronizing their carry so as not to deposit the wounded man on the ground. Bearing litters required physical strength, communication, and good judgment.

Medical training was a crucial element of the overall medical mission and instruction was given not only in tactical/field settings, but also within the Berlin Army Hospital. From the late 1970s through 1984, the 298th's secondary mission was that of hospital corpsman. Unannounced alerts were called to measure readiness and during these, the band often traveled directly to the hospital to assist in patient care or undergo first responder training.

First responder training consisted of addressing the immediate medical need. Maintaining breathing, stopping arterial bleeding, performing cardio-pulmonary resuscitation (CPR) and even the Heimlich Maneuver to dislodge food or other objects from the throat were elements of such training. Medical authority conducted such training per accepted Red Cross standards and issued certificates afterwards. Practicing CPR on life-sized mannequins was an element of such training and certificates of completion were issued to graduates.

Tactical Operations Center (TOC) Security

TOC Security was by far the most prescribed secondary mission assigned to the 298th. As all TOCs are centers of command and control, they are also targets for the enemy. Commanders want to safeguard their capabilities and communication networks, so they call a small contingent of soldiers to provide the physical security necessary.

While on shift, the TOC access point was guarded with at least a couple soldiers. These soldiers maintained a written access roster and those who wanted access to the TOC needed to be on that roster. If they weren't on that roster (ID cards were requested for examination), the band soldier requested an explanation. In the event of questions, an NCO was consulted to assess and make a decision. The NCO needed to be on task, but sometimes wasn't. Another exercise, largely a simulated exercise involving no actual troops, occurred out of Clay HQ. A senior NCO not known for his tactical skills nearly as much as his ability in arranging music quickly and accurately decided to take advantage of a slow spot in the middle of the night and began arranging an entire concert band piece—in his head. And then put it on paper. The band commander came in to check on things and discovered the NCO immersed in his music and not so immersed in the tactical situation at hand.

Another exercise involved the band working 12-hour shifts while in the field, but then returning to the band hall to turn in weapons, grab a shower and get some sleep in a real bed. The shifts repeated in that fashion for about a week. This exercise took place near Doughboy City and was characterized by an attack that was beaten back thanks to SFC Dan Hermann's tactical sketches of their machine gun positions and other military-oriented data. The aggressors expected to route the band's squad, but instead got "killed" themselves.

Not all of it was serious business. Larry Hill, low brass player, recalls, "I remember our perimeter being constantly tested by 'MRE Kids.'" Perhaps harkening back to a time when children continually begged chewing gum, chocolate, or field rations from American GIs, these kids had become technologically savvy. Larry continues, "Besides wanting to trade cans of Coke for anything MRE, their other favorite request was 'Have you chemlight for me?'"

Chemlights were disposable "sticks" manufactured of plastic in which both a liquid chemical and a breakable bubble containing another chemical were housed. When the stick was bent and the internal bubble broken, the two chemicals mixed, creating an effervescent glow that was quite effective in providing muted, long-lasting light. The kids loved them as toys. When the chemical reaction ran its course after several hours, the chemlight was discarded.

Larry continued, "This was also the time our squad of mostly woodwind players, led by flutist Karla Hillen, was sent out to be ambushed by the Drill Team. The Drill Team was very disappointed when they were soundly trounced by a bunch of clarinet and flute players."

Other activities involved improving camouflage and staving off boredom.

There was a bit of time for levity—Berlin being a larger city and with some of the aforementioned detritus in the area, looking for that blue light

Buy One, Get One Free...

special in the mud became the project of the moment.

SFC Randy Hamilton related an account of the band's two weeks in Grafenwöhr (a major Army training area in Bavaria) in Fall 1991 that featured time spent in "The Box," a euphemism for being in a strictly tactical environment. Multiple tactical scenarios were presented to the band and opportunity given to address the scenario in the prescribed way. Failure meant repeating the exercise until standards were reached or exceeded. This was a grueling, exhausting field exercise that had surpassed all previous encounters with living in a tactical environment and represented the length to which the Berlin command went with respect to the 298th.

Still another long 17-day encounter in a field exercise occurred for the band in 1992 in Hohenfels (another major Army training center located not far from Grafenwöhr). Several photographs from Sally Gerry (clarinet and drum major) depict the scenes. Sally recalled that the 298th took their own tactical equipment, anticipating correctly that Headquarters and Headquarters Company, Berlin Brigade, would not. Radio call signs were "X-Men" and "Halls of Justice", obvious depictions of popular movies of the day.

Sally also noted that the band working the perimeter of the TOC continually captured infiltrators from Brigade S-2.

The band also brought instruments and played concerts on occasion, a practice that indicated a band's primary mission—music—was never far removed.

Mixing exercises with real deployments, Sally also recalled the band's flight to Macedonia to support the Berlin Brigade Task Force in Operation Able Sentry, a United Nations effort to maintain peace and security in that region of the Balkans. The band, accompanied by the Berlin Brigade Commanding General Brigadier General Walter Yates, flew in to play a single ceremony. The ceremony was characterized by the presentation of medals to the Commander of Troops of the formation and his staff, which promptly fell off during the Pass in Review sequence.

Transportation and Drivers

Still other secondary missions became known to the 298th, including that of providing transportation. In the event of war, noncombatants were to be evacuated. The secondary mission assigned to the 298th centered on transporting noncombatants (family members, civilians, and other support personnel) out of the war zone, typically via bus. The 298th provided bus drivers, all of whom needed training. Consequently, one of the band's expected activities when a new arrival showed up was to introduce the soldier to Transportation Motor Pool (TMP) and get the individual licensed on all types of wheeled vehicles.

The process of licensing an American driver to German traffic laws took place in stages. The first item was to introduce the new man to the study manual and the various signs. European signs were often very different than American signs. Furthermore, the right-of-way laws were different. The process required serious study, but average American driver who had been behind the wheel for a few years didn't take the process seriously. Therefore, the new man usually failed the sign test, which was much more difficult than it seemed. The written test was also not easy, especially the right-of-way laws.

Once the testing phase was complete, the new driver was then evaluated by German testers behind the wheel of a basic sedan. The process gradually moved toward larger and larger vehicles until the driver passed the driving exam on the largest buses.

All this time spent for a newly arrived 298th member to train for and obtain the various driver licenses did not sit well with the band as it was very disruptive to the band's primary mission. The individual was needed to participate in rehearsals and performances. The new man needed to understand how the 298th did things and the more time spent behind a wheel meant less time spent on the instrument.

Trumpeter Richard Lant, due to his infantry background, was designated as the commanding general's tactical command van driver. He was therefore in high demand during alerts and field exercises. Lant also did some of the more routine things like erect tents and perform guard duty/security.

Lant told the story of how he, in the commanding general's command van, drove and parked the van in the vicinity of Truman Plaza. As this was clearly not a tactical area, explaining this to somebody might be a little problematic, so Lane paled a little bit when the general himself spotted his command van and came over to investigate. He and Lant spoke for several minutes with just pleasantries and small talk and never questioned why Lant had the command van up at Truman Plaza. Lant felt as though he had dodged a bullet.

Ken Dodson, trumpeter who served in the early Sixties, related that NCOs in the 298th would patrol the Wall for the Berlin command's G-2 or Intelligence section. This was akin to a Staff Duty NCO additional duty.

Deploying to the hospital for alerts or camouflaging the TOC weren't the only methods of field training for the band. The photo nearby shows Cheryl Wason and her colleagues as they gear up for a four-mile road march. Combat gear included steel helmet, web gear, weapon, and spit-shined boots.

Whatever the tactical mission, one thing consistently rang true: the Berlin command looked for the 298th to provide common-sense solutions to field exercise problems. The band routinely exhibited professional capability and was sought for the type of security that kept the commanding general and his staff in the fight.

OFF DUTY

Berlin—a major European city, international in texture—awaited the 298th member. So many things to see and do, it was difficult to absorb it all, even over time. The best thing to do involved going out in incrementally larger circles from the band's area.

American Facilities

The Berlin command itself offered various opportunities to delve into entertainment, work on a hobby, craft, or even repair your car. Movie houses and theaters were found in all larger facilities—the "BB" (the general area including family housing, Truman Plaza, Berlin American High School, and surrounding facilities across from Clay Headquarters) area, Andrews Barracks, McNair Barracks, Tempelhof Airport all had theaters that offered English language films. The British also offered a movie theater for their patrons as well at RAF Gatow, across the Wannsee.

Harry Reinert recalls seeing a stage play in the spring of 1947 from within the small compound known as Onkel Tom's Hütte, where the 298th was located from 1945 to 1949. A movie "Kino" was also available there at the OTH compound, next to the U-Bahn.

The September 25, 1945 edition of The Berlin *Sentinel* makes reference to the first American all-soldier musical that presented itself in the city. "You're On Your Way," hit the stage of the Titania Palast, which happened to be the alternate movie theater in the early years of the occupation. Andrews Barracks also had a small theater in which dinner theater events were sometimes offered. One in particular, a musical, solicited several musicians from the 298th for a performance in the spring of 1983. Trumpeter Dan Guth, trombonists Shawn Holtzapple and the author, along with reedmen Mike Carroll and Bob Armstrong were crammed onto a small shelf 8 feet above back stage surrounded by mutes and music stands. Singers, dancers and actors came from the Berlin community. Dropping a mute or a mouthpiece cap weren't options during performances.

The Berlin command became well outfitted with sports and craft shops of various types. The Rod and Gun Club at McNair Barracks offered guns, ammunition, fishing tackle and associated gear for authorized patrons. Registration of recently-purchased weapons in US Army Europe was mandatory before the weapon could be picked up. Intramural sports such as softball, football, and even bowling leagues were offered. Cole Sports Center had a bowling center in the basement and even Andrews Barracks had a 4-lane facility in the basement of the swimming pool for a time.

The golf club was located west of the Wannsee and close to Glienicker Brücke, the westernmost point of West Berlin. The 18-hole golf club had the customary club house, golf pro shop, and even a caddy service. Oboist Carl McGuire (1973-74) related that he was on the course one day, doing badly. Observing his play, an older gentleman dressed in civilian clothes asked Carl if he was a regular player. Carl answered no, he was a beginner. The gentleman then somewhat impatiently asked Carl if Carl knew who he was. Carl answered no, he didn't. Carl then asked the gentleman the same question whereupon the gentleman answered no, he didn't. Carl's response was "Good," as he walked away. The gentleman turned out to be the Berlin Brigade commander. Carl encountered him later in a formation and hoped the gentleman didn't recognize him.

Individuals signed up and played baseball and softball such as clarinetist Roger Woodrum (1949-53), who achieved the rank of Sergeant Major before he retired in 1978. Roger recalled that he played on the Berlin Bears baseball team as a pitcher and on the basketball team of the 7782^h Special Troops battalion, in which the team never lost a game in three years. Roger got the support he needed from Mr. Durbin and Mr. Trumbull, who himself was an outstanding first baseman on the softball fast pitch team in which Roger caught for John "Buzz" Rhoads. Roger was proud of the Berlin championship his team won in 1952.

The 298th also put together an intramural team consisting of tubist Eric Percoski, trombonist Richard Heard, drummer Douglas "Dallas" Millar, bassist Bruce Malone, and others, all of whom played in the 1980s. Andrews Barracks featured a well-tended softball field, as did McNair Barracks and "BB".

Dedicated swimmers such as bassoonist David Olszyk (1985-89) regularly used the Andrews Olympic-sized swimming pool that also featured a 10-meter diving platform, as did euphoniumist Bruce Gleason (1989-91). Jerry Larson, oboist from 1987-92 remembered that percussionist Bobby McGuffin (1987-89) organized a water aerobics course held at the pool. Olszyk, trumpeter Bob Wagner, and tubist Eric Percoski would occasionally participate in swim training over at the pool adjacent to the Cole Sports Center at "BB". Oboist William Berliant (1977-79) related in a Facebook posting that he did a physical training session in the Andrews pool and missed an emergency "Happy Birthday" gig for the battalion commander next door. He said that missing this emergency gig "went over big" with the band commander. Charles "Frogg" Consaul, guitarist and keyboardist (1987-94) remarked that the 298th occasionally trained in the Andrews pool. Swimmers inflated BDU camouflage uniform trousers to make life preservers.

Craft shops featuring pottery-making, photo developing, lithography, and similar skill sets were available. Euphoniumist Allen Thompson (1954-56) made regular usage of the photo lab, which happened to be in the basement of the Andrews pool and when he wasn't doing that, he swam laps in the pool located just above the photo lab. He also notes a window through which one could see the swimmers, a perspective he found interesting.

At one least 298th member mixed business with pleasure. PFC H. Ward Beyer won the U.S. Army Europe song-writing contest in December 1953.

Beyond the Berlin command's offerings, the city of Berlin had plenty to do and see including performances of every type imaginable, restaurants, clubs, museums, all of that and more.

The Neighborhood Kneipe

Berliners call their neighborhood bar or pub a "Kneipe." "Kneipen" are everywhere and have the same purpose as an East London pub—provide a beverage, usually beer, and possibly a snack to the average person. People gathered to talk, solve problems, watch a sporting event on TV, or even play various card games (Skat) or dice games (Liar's Dice or Chicago).

The area just outside the main gate of Andrews Barracks featured many Kneipen, snack stands, and restaurants, though most of these were set up to appeal to the average American GI.

- Märkischer Hof – a combination butcher shop, restaurant, and Kneipe, this business was owned by Wolfgang and Kristal and was a band favorite during the 1960s and 1970s. Trombonists Vic St. Clair and Paul Creighton occasionally popped over there for a bit of a refresher during concert band breaks. The couple eventually sold the business, which then became an Italian eatery named "il Mulino's."

- "il Mulino's" or "al Mulino's" – known for its classic Italian fare such as pasta, pizza, salads, and snails, most patrons were offered an after-dinner shot of Sambuca, a anise-flavored sweet aperitif that was served aflame. Adorned on the top rested 2-3 coffee beans, which leached out a bit of oil as the liquor heated up. Many 298th new arrivals were invited to Mulino's and other nearby establishments to sample the food and drink, including a fiery schnapps named Ratzeputz. This liquor became an initiation rite as the new arrival was instructed to down the shot rather than sip on it. As this liquor was distilled from ginger root, the resulting sinus-clearing, eye-watering reaction invariably resulted in a cough and a good-natured slap on the back to help him recover.

- Home Bar – more of a classic bar that did not serve food, this watering hole stayed open till the early morning hours. Located just to the west of Mulino's, the business was eventually purchased by a Turk named Ali, who also purchased the snack stand directly next door and on the northeast corner of Finkensteinallee and Kadettenweg.

- Ali's Imbiss – this Turkish snack stand featured the classic Turkish "Döner kebap", a sandwich comprised of seasoned meat (mostly lamb) that had been formed and pressed onto a spit, then later roasted on a vertical grill, carved into slices and set upon seasoned leavened bread. Topped with chopped romaine, a little red cabbage, onions and a pungent garlic sauce, onions, and wrapped in a foil napkin, this sandwich for DM 5 was a nighttime favorite with many who were returning to Andrews after a night on the town.

- Frank's Pig Pen – located at the corner of Marthastrasse and Kadettenweg, this combination restaurant and Kneipe was operated by Frank, an American. His establishment was very popular for a number of years in the 1960s and 1970s. The building is now a residence.

- Speakeasy – owned and operated by Carolyn, a Briton, this Kneipe offered Weizen (wheat) beer in either gold or silver varieties (meaning with or without visible yeast in the bottle), other beer in the bottle, shots, darts, and lots of smoke. Frequented by a number of 298th members some of whom worked part time for Carolyn, the Speakeasy was also popular with soldiers from other units, including Field Station Berlin. Carolyn owned a medium sulfur-crested cockatoo and a caricature of the bird was the pub's logo.

- Linda's Lounge. Another nearby pub that also stayed open late, this watering hole was open in the 1960s and 1970s.

- Tony's Imbiss – located just outside Andrews Barracks main gate, this tiny snack stand offered traditional Berliner street food – currywurst, Buletten (tiny meat loaves cut in small pieces and doused with curryketchup, a sweeter and less tomatoey concoction infused with curry powder), bratwurst, and the ubiquitous French fries served with ketchup and mayonnaise for many. Tony's was a stand-up eatery and thus wasn't necessarily popular in inclement weather, unlike Ali's Imbiss across the street which had indoor tables.

The "Kastanieneck", a classic Berliner Kneipe that did not cater to the American GI, was located about a half-mile west of Andrews Barracks. Most 298th members who went there, preferring the Berliner Kneipe rather than the American-tinged bars located closer to Andrews, referred to the place as "Mom's". Owned and operated by a woman whose name was Waltraud, she ran the place efficiently, getting a bit frazzled when things got busy. She offered Löwenbräu beer from Munich, a real treat for those 298th members who had spent some time in Bavaria, along with a standard Berliner beer, Schultheiss. She also served the German schnapps such as Dornkaat and Bärenjäger, keeping several of these bottles in a small freezer, along with the tiny bottles of a "Magenbitter" such as Kuemmerling. Food was limited to snacks that were heated in a toaster oven. During the soccer season, the small television with rabbit ears presented the game of most interest and it was on this television on January 28, 1986 when the world, including the clientele within Mom's at the time, watched the space shuttle Challenger explode a few seconds after liftoff. Many members of the 298th happened to be in Mom's that afternoon and witnessed this sobering event half a world away. Bassoonist Dave Olszyk remarked that Americans couldn't buy anything in the joint that night and gave thanks to trombonist Kevin Entwistle for the ride home.

Mom's was also a popular hangout for a group of NCOs that became known as "The Ten." This group, approximating ten in number, would frequently stop in, have a beer or two, and solve the world's problems. The venue occasionally changed, for example, a session of "The Ten" occurred periodically at the Roosevelt Barracks canteen (headquarters of the 6941st Labor Service Battalion) where beer was significantly cheaper.

There were many such Kneipen all over Berlin and some in the immediate area of Andrews that were also visited, but these were the principal establishments. The further away from the American facilities that one traveled, the more typically Berliner the establishment.

Venturing Out

Recognizing the potential good to Americans and Berliners, the Army instituted a program called the School of Standards (SOS). This two week course, attendance at which was mandatory for all enlisted and most officers upon arrival in Berlin, introduced the soldier to life in Berlin and Germany. The School was instituted in the 1970s and featured German language training as a component.

German language training was taught by Ingeborg Schwanke, a short, blonde, feisty lady who delighted in all things American. She began her tenure with the School of Standards in the mid-1970s and quickly became an icon of the SOS staff, especially the commandant. Inge was especially fond of the band and had arranged to conduct German language lessons at the band hall during Mr. Jaynes' time as bandmaster. She was also known to be effective in organizing brewery tours.

Inge Schwanke and friends, Engelhardt Brewery Tour, 1987

The training intended to introduce the student to a few basic sentences, numbers, and other basic elements of the German language. Most students did not progress beyond those few rudimental expressions, but some 298th members became quite fluent. These chose to immerse themselves into the language and study it formally and informally. Some of these—Bela Bobasçy, Dan Steger, Vic St. Clair, Bobby Hawkins, Fred Mittag, and others including the author, became translators for the band.

Born in Hungary and emigrating to the United States in 1956, Bela Bobasçy was one of those musicians who had a great time no matter what was played. He played his alto sax with an abandon that was infectious. Using a wide vibrato and a tone quality reminiscent of the Guy Lombardo band, Bela (a.k.a. "Booby") was a real crowd pleaser. Extroverted and gregarious, he talked to Berliners in fluent German, occasionally mixing it up with some of his native Hungarian, and laughing it all off in English. Bela married a Berliner and the two of them eventually bought a house in Rudow, at the southeastern corner of the American sector.

Bela served in Berlin on two different assignments, the first in the mid-1970s and the second in the early 1980s. He retired in 1987, but not before several interesting situations developed.

Booby Hits the Lottery
by David M. Smith, CW4, US Army, Retired

Not unlike "hitting the wall" sometime before Mile 26 in a marathon, the 19th year of a US military career can seem to alter time and space as they bend, stretch and sometimes contract toward retirement eligibility at 20 years' service...it affects everyone differently.

Bela "Booby" Bobasçy might well have had what seemed to be the longest 19th year of active federal service on record...

As a boy, he sang in Budapest's prestigious Kodaly Institute Choir, under the direction of Zoltan Kodaly himself. When Booby was 16, Soviet tank divisions rolled through the capital to put down what they deemed an uprising by the Hungarians.

During the turmoil, many Hungarians...Booby included...seized the opportunity to flee to the West. Booby escaped through Austria and eventually came to America, where he joined the 82nd Airborne Division, served a hitch at Fort Bragg, then went to college at Arizona State and eventually decided to come back on active duty and make a career of Army Bands.

When I got to Berlin, Booby had around 17 years in the service and he had been stationed in the city for what seemed like forever. His wife was *eine Berlinerin*, and he and Dorit lived out on the Economy in Berlin's Neukölln district with their daughter. Booby kept extending his "overseas" tour to stay in Berlin...close to her family in Berlin and also close to his family, still in Budapest.

Shortly after Booby began that 19th year of service, he received word that his mother had passed away in Budapest and we processed an extraordinary emergency leave for him to go to Budapest. He had gone back before on ordinary leave and had never experienced any problems, either going or coming...his choice was to either pack up his Chrysler New Yorker (for years I couldn't see a silver New Yorker and not think of Booby) and then he set out to drive to Budapest or to fly from Flughafen Berlin-Schönefeld in East Berlin.

Today, the drive is about 650km in a direct line between the two cities; in 1986, the drive was more than double that at 1450km because of entry and exit point travel restrictions.

Booby was pretty flustered when the time came for him to travel, and making the long, circuitous journey by auto on short notice was not going to cut it. He had driven home before, but had usually had a great deal of time to plan the trip...getting the clearance to go under normal conditions usually took an extended amount of time which allowed him to plan the trip. Since this time he pretty much had made a mad dash to the East German airport, Booby made the mistake of transporting too much Western currency into Hungary...normally he would have thought this through and planned accordingly...when he arrived in Budapest and went through customs, he had what was arbitrarily considered too many greenbacks in his wallet...it wasn't like he had a suitcase full of banded $100 bills. The upshot was that he was cited for currency violations and his passport was taken pending "resolution of his case."

Everyone has heard the stock response in an Army formation "All present or accounted for"...it literally means that everyone is either actually, physically present at that location or that they fit into a pre-described status from the morning report...sick call, on pass, on leave, absent without leave, etc.,. It turns out that we had to carry Booby on the books as "held by a foreign power, not incarcerated" which was the first and only time that I ever heard of that status or its use.

Even before his mother's funeral, Booby went to the US Embassy in Budapest to try and sort things out. While he was at the embassy, his father keeled over and died.

Another funeral and no movement from the Hungarian government on Booby's status.

The Brigade Commander was in daily communication with the military attaché in Budapest, but the Hungarian government was not budging an inch on the return of our sergeant...days turned into weeks and weeks into months...Booby remained "held by a foreign power, not incarcerated".

We finally got a call from Brigade HQ—Booby was being allowed to return to Berlin...for compassionate reasons.

Dorit was hospitalized in Klinikum Steglitz. While Booby was being held in Hungary, she had been diagnosed with breast cancer and his release had been allowed on the grounds that he should be there for her scheduled surgery and relieve some of the emotional burden from their daughter. Booby made it back just in time to be by her side—until he was doubled over in pain while sitting in her hospital room.

He went to the Berlin US Army hospital and was told the pain was just a reaction to the immense stress that he had been under...they medicated him, but the pain persisted, really intense and localized in the lower right quadrant of his trunk—about where the appendix is located—which was confirmed when he was rushed to the operating room to remove his burst appendix. Booby made a fully recovery in time to play the televised New Year's Eve gig to usher in 1987 and the 750th anniversary of the founding of Berlin.

He said to me (in his unique accented English), "Chiff, I hope that my luck changes in the New Year."

I replied, "Booby, it's gotta get better, 'cause it just can't get any worse for you than it was in 1986."

About two and a half months later, Booby rushed into my office very agitated and red-faced, closed the door and asked if we could talk.

Having gone through the previous year with him, I was waiting for the other shoe to drop so just a little tentatively I said, "Sure, what's up?"

"Chiff, I haven't slept in two weeks and I'm going bat-shit crazy...but you gotta promise not to tell anyone at all about this..."
[he gets the nod from me...oh crap, what now?]
"...I'm afraid I'm gonna lose everything..."
[drugs? gambling? what?]
"...but you CAN'T tell ANYONE, okay?..."
[I nod again]
"...What if I really screw this up?...You're NOT GOING TO TELL ANYONE, RIGHT????..."
[vigorous nodding...get on with it]
"...I hit 20 in about four months and then I'm going to retire."
"I won the West German Lotto for [he mentioned an eight-figure amount of Deutsche mark...which was still well into a seven-figure amount of US dollars] and I don't know what to do...Chiff, I never had nothing in my life and now with all this money, I could really mess it up, you know?"

Okay, this was one counseling topic that was never covered in any of my Army training so I simply tried to talk him down off the ceiling and let him use me as a sounding board for what he thought were his preliminary plans, reassuring him that what was said was in the strictest of confidence. He left the office a bit calmer and a little more self-assured.

For some reason, the roll call formation the next morning was held outside in the parking lot. It might have just been the first really nice Spring day and the First Sergeant wanted to enjoy the day—except that Booby wasn't in formation, and he wasn't accounted for, and my mind began to spin with the horrible possibilities of where Booby might be and why he wasn't present for duty—until a horn honked and everyone turned to see Booby drive up in a fire-engine red Mercedes 300SL cabriolet with the top down and the biggest shit-eating grin that any of us had ever seen, before or since.

So much for keeping his "secret." To his credit, Booby finished his 20 years honorably and retired to the city of Berlin.

Nightlife

When Berlin recovered from the war and sustained the *Wirtschaftswunder* (economic miracle) that the rest of West Germany also enjoyed, there were more and more places to go and things to see. The Kurfürstendamm ("Ku-Damm"), West Berlin's principal shopping and downtown area featured a number of venues for eating and drinking. The Europa Center, essentially a skyscraper-sized strip mall directly adjacent to the remnants of the Kaiser Wilhelm Memorial Church, contained Restaurant "Alt-Nürnberg", the Irish Pub, a Mövenpick ice cream stand, and a large disco on the top floor, among other attractions. Sandwiched in between were offices and businesses.

The Ku-Damm ran for 2.2 miles and had every conceivable type of luxury boutique in Europe. The flavor of the Ku-Damm continued east of the Kaiser Wilhelm Memorial Church on Tauentzienstrasse. One of the more popular shopping venues located close to Wittenberg U-Bahnhof, the Kaufhaus des Westens (KaDeWe) is the largest department store on the European continent. Now consisting of 60,000 square meters, the store attracts thousands of shoppers daily. The 6th and 7th floors are devoted entirely to food, both fresh and prepared, and the quality, freshness, and sheer variety are all hallmarks of this store.

The side streets off the Ku-Damm offered piano bars, jazz clubs, movie houses, and cafés. Café Kranzler on the corner of Joachimstalerstrasse and the Ku-Damm is renowned for its coffee, bakery, and opportunities for people-watching. The west end of the Ku-Damm is less commercial, but nonetheless features more apartments and homes which are known for their exclusivity and prices.

One of the most popular jazz clubs, and a favorite with many 298th members, remains the Quasimodo. A small club holding not more than a few hundred people not far from the Ku-Damm, this club nevertheless attracted a number of well-known and respected musicians. All the big players played the Quasi—Dizzy Gillespie, Chet Baker, both Wynton and Branford Marsalis on the stage together, Johnny Griffin, Lew Soloff, and Lou Donaldson, among others. Going to hear Dizzy play one evening, 298th saxophonist Paul Dickson approached Dizzy after the first set as they both made their way to the restroom. Paul asked, "How are you doing, Diz?" Dizzy replied, "Great! Where are you from?" Paul replied, "North Dakota." Dizzy shot back, "North Dakota? Wow, I've been to that cold-ass place!" On another occasion in the Quasimodo, Lew Soloff (former lead trumpeter with the jazz-rock group Blood Sweat and Tears) played an old, beat-up trumpet with leaky valves. Lew was asked during a break if that trumpet was a Mt. Vernon Bach, as all Bach trumpets have a distinctive shape. Lew looked surprised at the question, but answered, "Yep, sure is!"

Saxophonist Willie (P.K.) Pollock, another musician assigned twice to the 298th and resident of the city after conclusion of his service, performs in the Quasimodo on a regular basis. Herbie Hart, also a saxophonist, and trumpeter David "Skip" Rinehart remained in Berlin after their tour of duty as well, and make their living as musicians in the city.

Trumpeter Fish Brown, mentioned in an earlier chapter, participated in several regular jam sessions, occurring at the *Badewanne* and the *Jazzgalerie* and in 1969 started making plans to co-found yet another group with a slightly

Fish Brown & friends in the Badewanne, 1970

more creative name this time – "The Gasoline Band." Originating after recording a studio demo tape containing original music, Fish and co-founder Fred Schwartz, composer from New York, brought in other 298th members. Brian Bevin, guitar and vocal; Major Wilburn, tenor and soprano saxophone; Jerome "J.J." Johnson, trombone; Bert Thompson, bass; and Bob Howell, drums comprised the original members, along with Fish. The band changed its name to "Children of Fools" but then changed it again in 1971 to "FishBrown" after having grown to 10 members. Fish reports the group was offered a recording contract in London under the "Gasoline Band" moniker. But he wound up leaving Germany in December 1971 for the States, but not before leaving an indelible mark on those around him.Seeing an opportunity for more gigging opportunities, Fish was able to secure an early release from the Army and thus he began his European career.

Trumpeter Dan Guth and saxophonist Mike Carroll gigged often in the city in the early 1980s. Mitchel "Mike" Kaufman on guitar often joined them and when the opportunity presented itself, the group named Brandenburg Express pumped out some rock, rhythm and blues, and soul enough for much of the area. Lee McPherson's vocals and bass playing added flavor. Mike Haskell on drums, Robert "Chico" Cordero on keys, Sully "Fred" Frettoloso on bass (replacing McPherson), along with Paul Dickson (saxes), David "Skip" Reinhard on trumpet, and Lindsay Lioen (tenor) were some of the regulars, along with two-tour Willie "P.K." Pollock on alto.

For those who liked dancing, but didn't like traveling all the way to the Ku-Damm, the Eierschale (eggshell) near U-Bahn Podbielskiallee in Dahlem was an option. The Eierschale appealed to a number of younger Berliners. It was loud, boisterous, and made for great fun for those who enjoyed the style. Another club located near the Eierschale directly on Breitenbachplatz in Dahlem was the Nashville. This, of course, was country music oriented. Many, many Berliners enjoyed American country and western music and sought it out regularly at the Nashville, and similar venues.

Gambling didn't have a big following in Berlin, except if you consider machines that offer games of chance as "gambling". If that's the case, Berlin was rife with gambling. Every Kneipe and most every Imbiss that wasn't physically on the street had at least a couple of these colorful, noisy, and for some, enticing machines. They would periodically chirp, rumble, burp, and flash their lights to get your attention. Playing the machine took only 30 pfennig to start and for many just having a drink, it was a way to occupy the time. For those who liked to play the machine, "timing" the blinking lights was the key to winning and losing. Each successful "hit" got the player further up the ladder until cashing out or running out.

Performances and Concerts

The Metropol, a concert venue that was once a theater, lay on Nollendorf Platz, not far from the eastern end of the Ku-Damm. This seedy building's interior was painted in flat black, stripped of seats, and hosted many contemporary artists. Bluesman John Lee Hooker performed at the Metropol in 1984.

Musicians who enjoy classical music took special delight in the many offerings in East Berlin. The Staatsoper and its related orchestra, the Staatskapelle Berlin, routinely presented fine performances. Master Sergeant Lou Hurvitz, Enlisted Bandleader for the 298th from 1980-84 and formerly of the West Point band, wrote of his experience in attending an opera in East Berlin:

Little did I realize when I applied for my Wall Pass that my excursion to the Soviet-controlled sector would be so interesting. A friend and I had planned to attend a performance of Madama Butterfly in East Berlin's Komische Oper. My usual routine for an East Berlin trip was to depart Andrews Barracks early-to-mid afternoon with a friend (or a group of friends), cross over to East Berlin via Checkpoint Charlie, purchase music at Der Musik Freunde, eat dinner at one of the wonderful East Berlin restaurants, and return to West Berlin. This occasion, however, included the added feature of the opera.

At approximately 12 noon, Wednesday, 17 February 1982, I picked up my wall pass at HHC on Andrews Barracks. Because I would be attending the opera, the Army dress blue uniform was appropriate. A friend and I drove into East Berlin and we ate a sumptuous lunch at the Budapest. My entrée was roast duck with all the trimmings. Wine accompanied the meal. The cost of my meal, including a handsome gratuity, was approximiatley $7.50 (American). Heading down Karl Marx Allee, we ambled into Der Musik Freunde and I purchased a great many musical scores, to include the vocal-piano score, full-sized, hard-cover edition, for Puccini's Madama Butterfly. The stark difference between the Communist East German economy and the American economy was amazing. While stationed at West Point during the period 1972-1978, I often purchased scores at the Joseph Patelson Music House, directly across 56th Street from the Carnegie Hall stage door. Because of the high cost of printed music in the United States, I could only afford to buy one score per visit. Scores in America averaged between $30 and $75. Contrast that with the price I paid for the Madama Butterfly score in East Berlin: the equivalent of $1.92 (American). It was fortunate that I purchased this score as this Edition Peters edition of the opera was the resource used for the production that we were to hear that evening. Of course, no East Berlin trip would be complete without obtaining Meissen and crystal. After completely filling the automobile's trunk, my friend and I adjourned to Ganymed for a wonderful meal of chateaubriand, featuring an almost endless supply of cooked vegetables, potatoes, and other side dishes. Of course, another bottle of wine was consumed. The Ganymed house "band," consisting of an elderly violinist and a pianist, held forth and did its best in entertaining us. The moment we were seated they began performing American standards that spanned the period from the Roaring Twenties through the 1940's. Again, we paid only a pittance for our superb meal. After leaving a fine gratuity for the waiter, we left approximately 50 East Marks on the piano for the combo, an amount that put broad smiles on their faces.

Adjourning to the Komische Oper, we purchased excellent tickets from the opera house's ticket kiosk. The seats were located in the first loge of the first ring and cost approximately $2.00 apiece. Prior to this evening, I had attended performances of Madama Butterfly at New York's Metropolitan Opera and at the Deutsche Oper Berlin (in West Berlin). This production was, in comparison to those others, quite unusual. Most noticeable to me was the departure from using period costumes. The American characters were clothed in post-World War II Army uniforms. This, of course, flew in the face of accuracy. Not only did the costumes not depict the proper era, they represented the United States Army. The opera's American characters are, of course, United States Naval personnel. The reason for this departure from artistic accuracy is that there was only a tiny American naval presence in Berlin; however, there was a significant United States Army population in Berlin. Because Lieutenant Pinkerton is not a very decent person and because the Americans and the Soviets were, at the time of this production, facing off, toe-to-toe, in the Cold War, the uniform issue was another way to advance negative propaganda about the Americans. As the opera progressed, I caught many an East German audience member casting a disapproving eye in my direction. I was highly identifiable in my dress blue uniform. The arts have always been a strong propaganda tool and this was a very real example. During the only intermission (between the first and second acts), we went to the front of the house for coffee. Again, disapproving eyes were cast in my direction.

This was not paranoia as the Cold War and the very negative American part in the opera were present. The audience reacted favorably to the performance. I felt that it was adequate, however it paled in comparison to the Metropolitan Opera offering. The condition of the "front" of the opera house disturbed me. The facility had fallen into disrepair. It was in serious need of a fresh paint job and the plumbing had been seriously neglected. In contrast, the auditorium, itself, was in considerably better condition. So once you completed negotiating the lobby, the hallways, and the toilet facilities, the experience improved. And, after all, the performance was the primary reason for my presence.

The cast was quite good. It consisted of Jana Smitkova as Tscho-Tscho-San, Friederike Wulff-Apelt as Suzuki, Hanns Nocker as Goro, Elisabeth Ebert as Tscho-Tscho-San's mother, Perry Price (Adjunct Instructor of Music and Applied Voice at Western Connecticut State University) as Pinkerton, Rolf Haunstein as Counsel Sharpless, Christa Noack as Kate Pinkerton. The music director was Joachim Willert.

Immediately following the performance, we returned to West Berlin via Checkpoint Charlie and enjoyed some of Kranzler's magnificent ice cream creations. This was indeed an interesting evening.

Cultural Attractions

Museums abounded. A visitor to Berlin could spend a month and see a different museum every day and still not visit them all. Most of the more eclectic museums were in East Berlin in a special section near the Berlin Dom (Cathedral) called Museumsinsel (Museum Isle). Here the National Gallery, the Pergamon, and the Altes Museum round out some of the choices. For a bit less formality, one could visit the museum at Dahlem-Dorf and get a glimpse at life in Berlin 400 years ago. Featuring street fairs and festivals, Dahlem-Dorf offered participants in period costume, selling examples of locally-prepared food and wares.

Arranged by Inge Schwanke, the School of Standards German teacher and good friend of the 298th, the band visited the Music Instrument Museum in the early 1980s and again in the mid-1980s. This repository of ancient and priceless artifacts, located not far from the Philharmonie, has up to 3,500 specimens in its collection. From the smallest piccolo to the Mighty Wurlitzer Organ, built to accompany silent films in cinema halls, many of these instruments can be heard at various listening stations through recordings. The museum also has a workshop where certain specimens are repaired and restored.

Classical music enthusiasts appreciated the artistry of the Berlin Philharmonic as the orchestra performed at the acoustically-rich Philharmonie

Ray Claes, Instrument Museum

concert hall. Conductor Wilhelm Furtwängler reassumed the directorship of the Berlin Philharmonic in 1947 and from that time until his death in 1954, conducted some of his most memorable performances. Herbert von Karajan assumed the directorship of the Berlin Philharmonie in 1955 and remained in that capacity until his own death in 1989. Claudio Abbado served from 1989 until 2002. All three were giants in the conducting world and left behind recordings and performances that are models of artistry. Dozens of 298th members attended performances of this world-class orchestra during their assignments.

The Canadian Brass, a brass quintet of international fame, performed in the Philharmonie in the late Eighties. This performance included their standard "A Closer Walk with Thee" as they strolled through the audience in reaching the stage, arriving in time to complete the opening hymn and get into the up-tempo Dixieland section to close the tune out. This particular performance wasn't quite up to their usual highest standards of excellence. Trumpeter Ronald Romm struggled with the theme and variations to "Carnival of Venice." Traveling takes a toll on musicians and jet lag must have played a part as Romm's recordings of the same piece were flawless.

The Berlin Philharmonic also performed open-air concerts directly in front of the Reichstag. This venue attracted tens of thousands of people to hear the orchestra. Setting up a picnic with blankets, lawn chairs, and then sitting back to hear the orchestra play well-known pieces was a hallmark of summertime Berlin.

Die Waldbühne, an outdoor amphitheater located close to Olympic Stadium in the British sector, offered open-air concerts of all types, from the Berlin Philharmonic to Billy Joel. All manner of current popular musicians performed there. The setting was idyllic, the sound perfect, and the crowds appreciative. 298th bandsmen of any but the earlier eras enjoyed summertime concerts at the Waldbühne.

Food

If there is one dish that is classically Berliner, that dish would be Eisbein. A pork knuckle, simmered until tender and served with pureed potatoes and sauerkraut, is a meal that is available—but you have to look for it. By far, most restaurants in Berlin stem from other countries. These run the gamut from Italian, Greek, Yugoslavian, Argentinian, and even the ubiquitous McDonald's, where your French fries are served with a small plastic fork.

The good thing about Italian and Yugoslavian food is that it was relatively cheap. A pizza, served whole and not sliced like you find it in the U.S., was single-serving, plentiful and easy on the wallet. Yugoslavian restaurants offered enormous portions of food for reasonable prices. Yugoslavian food was generally very flavorful with liberal use of herbs, especially paprika. A table condiment consisting of raw, chopped onions mixed with liberal doses of spicy paprika was on every table.

Italian restaurants served up not only pizza and pasta, but also very flavorful salads. Pasta was served in true Italian style, meaning the pasta was cooked al dente, then finished in the pan of sauce (marinara, meat sauce, or cream sauces of various types). Also in typical Italian style, sauce was portioned very sparingly. In the early winter, mussels were available and many patrons enjoyed this seasonal seafood.

Greek restaurants were also very common in Berlin and many offered classic and delicious fare that went far beyond that of the usual gyros. Stuffed grape leaves, classic salads with feta cheese and huge Kalamata olives, dressed lightly with oregano and oil and vinegar accompanied main dishes such as Souvlaki, Bifteki, and seasoned meat patties filled with feta cheese and charcoal grilled. Greek wines rounded out the dining experience.

Street food includes the items already discussed earlier in the chapter. The *Döner kebap*, while Turkish in design, actually originated in Berlin. Street festivals in the summer exhibited many snack stands offering these standard food items, along with sweet items such as American-style cotton candy. In winter, the Christmas market in *Alt Rixdorf*, adjacent to the borough Neukölln, offered *Glühwein*, a warm, mulled red wine, and samplings from the neighborhood schnapps distillery. Hot bratwurst off the grill, slathered with mustard and jammed into a small Brötchen went down well.

Sporting Activities and People-Watching

A club popular with the Nazi gentry was confiscated at the end of the war and converted into a facility for American troops and re-named the Wannsee Recreation Center. Offering many activities, the Rec Center was a favorite spot for many 298th members for sailing, rowing, swimming, or other pastimes.

Indeed, the Wannsee was only a part of the many types of water-based activities available in the western portion of West Berlin. The Havel River provided additional sites for summertime activities of all types up in the French sector, including rowing, fishing, and nude sunbathing. A nude beach was even in the Grunewald and was a little closer to home for most Americans – even though swimming was discouraged (except for dogs), there were plenty of other "sights" in this mecca of the unadorned.

Hornist Dave Lytner, (1986-89) thrived on all manner of physical exertion, as long as it took at least 8 hours to complete. He ran miles effortlessly. He and Dave Olszyk, bassoonist from 1986 till 1990, competed with each other in this manner – they, and trumpeter Robert Wagner, ran the 100 km marathon at Davos, Switzerland. Through thunderstorms, past dumb-struck cows, out in a rock-strewn path all night long. Sixty-two miles of running, up and down 3,000 meter mountains. This event was the extreme marathon in which he had participated several times. What got him there was an association with the *International Volkssport Verein* (IVV) or International Volkssport Federation.

The IVV formed in Germany in the mid-1960s and quickly spread throughout Europe with the expressed goal of encouraging people to get out in the fresh air and experience exercise and the benefits associated with it. The structure of the organization rested in clubs that organized events of their choosing under the IVV's tutelage. The events followed three sporting functions: hiking, swimming, and cycling. In some cases and weather permitting, cross country skiing was included.

Most 298th participants took part in the "volksmarches" but instead of hiking, participants ran these courses. Lytner, Olszyk, Wagner and others all participated regularly in the sport, amassing "event" credits and a total kilometer count. Books, purchased for a modest fee, were stamped upon completion of each event and became part of aspiring toward the next level.

The activities were normally held on weekends and were publicized in various volkssporting publications (including the Stars and Stripes newspaper), and featured specific distances at various levels of ability.

The purpose of the sport is simply to move the body. There is no race. There is no competition, except from within the participant himself. There is no time limit for completion of the course, within reason.

Members of the 298th who participated in these activities traveled extensively to get to the venues. Scattered throughout Germany and Europe, a typical weekend volksmarch took place in central West Germany. Traveling on the autobahn from Berlin through East Germany, the trip took a minimum of two and one-half hours to arrive in West Germany. Once into West Germany, the drive might take another hour to arrive in Hannover or similar place. Once at the volksmarch site, marchers register by paying a small fee at which time they are issued a Start card. Courses in different lengths are offered, usually 10 and 20 kilometers. The marcher decides on the length of the course he wants to complete (10 km, 20 km, sometimes 30 km and even full marathons at 42 kilometers, 195 meters), and sets off. The course(s) were marked, usually tape of a specific color hanging from a tree or sign.

Checkpoints along the way monitor progress. The volunteer at the checkpoint stamps the Start card and offers a sweet tea as refreshment. After this short break, the trail continues. The courses were usually laid out in the woods and fields ringing the town where the event was held. Twenty kilometers, a common distance, might take two hours to complete. Marathons took anywhere from three to four hours, depending on the runner and the actual distance, which were sometimes imprecise. Volksmarches took advantage of trails, hiking paths, bicycle paths, even roadways at times and they took place regardless of weather conditions. The main point was to complete the course and have fun doing it. Exercise was a key motivator for many 298th members in keeping weight manageable.

The IVV had a minimal presence in Berlin, but events were offered at times, perhaps two or three per year. These courses were organized and held in various places, but most often they were held in the French sector and in the Wannsee area.

The IVV concluded that the people wanted the type of course that wasn't monitored, as a weekend course might be, but still sanctioned. To meet this need, a special type of course was set up for marchers. These courses were called "Year-Round" events because the courses were set up in a permanent state, marked, and then described in written instructions for marchers to purchase. One such course was called the Berlin "Rundwanderweg." Marchers wanting to participate in this year-round event paid DM 10 for a booklet. Inside this book were stickers. Start and finish points were designated at various U-Bahn and S-Bahn stops in the text. To prove that a person took part in a given course at a given time, the marcher inserted a sticker into the ticket canceler at the entrance to the U-Bahn. The time and date were printed on the sticker. The marcher retained the sticker, ran or walked the course along which he had to be alert for the Checkpoint—ordinarily a sign hung in a tree. The marcher was expected to record this number in his book. Upon completion, the sticker was inserted into the canceler again and the sticker then affixed to the book showing the time and date of course completion. Ten courses were offered, ranging from 10 kilometers up to 29 kilometers, totaling 200 kilometers for the entire event.

The courses took the marcher up into the farthest reaches of West Berlin and always, with one exception, took him into the woods. One aspect of participating in these runs was seeing just how much forest there actually is in a large city like Berlin.

One December afternoon in the late 1980s, the band had a light duty day.

Plans were made to take off early and run the 24 kilometer course through the Grunewald. This course, a very hilly course, would be challenging enough without the snow. When the marchers started, there were four inches on the ground with the snow still falling. A typical cadre of participants included Lytner, Olszyk, and a few others.

Bobby McGuffin, a very capable drummer, small, but packed full of energy, was a veritable hummingbird. He talked fast, he moved fast, he was always in motion. He decided he was going to go out with the group that day and airily described how he was going to excel in negotiating this course. Nobody doubted that Bobby was incredibly fit—he routinely maxed his Physical Fitness tests—but everybody was pretty certain he didn't run these kinds of distances, and certainly not in those snowy conditions.

The group took off, leaving from the U-Bahn Krumme Lanke in Zehlendorf at about 1300 that snowy afternoon. At the start, it was fun—lots of talking, ribbing, carrying on. Bobby decided to hotdog it a little bit, racing ahead through the snow, ribbing everybody else about how slow they were. The response was, "Yeah, okay, Bobby. Let's get about 22 kilometers of this done and let's see who's left."

Time went on. One hour, two hours. The falling snow grew deeper then finally stopped. When the course was just about ready to come out of the Grunewald and along the Schlachtensee for the final three kilometers, dusk approached and seeing the trail became difficult. The course wasn't marked very well to begin with and with the gathering darkness, the few markers were not easy to pick out.

Bobby was finished. He couldn't even walk very well, much less run.

This would have been funny had it not been potentially very dangerous. All the runners were sweaty and that combination, in cold weather, all too often yields hypothermic conditions. Dave Olszyk and another runner pressed on, leaving Dave Lytner to help Bobby make it back. Eventually, everybody did make it back – tired, sweaty, a little dehydrated, but safe aside from some wrinkly feet brought about by the constantly wet conditions. The next day at work, Bobby didn't say much. He was still recovering.

The Tiergarten provided dozens of walking paths through the central part of the city, all of which left the concrete and asphalt behind. Popular with many Berliners, this part of Berlin was a focal point. Bicycle paths parallel with all major streets provided a safe way to get through the city. Bicycle riders were expected to comply with traffic laws. American drivers in Berlin quickly learned to look for bicyclists on the right at traffic lights.

Off Duty Outside Berlin

While Berlin offered a great deal of entertainment of all kinds—music, dance, theater, opera, city tours, brewery tours, cabaret shows, festivals of all kinds, and even a suitable number of more "blue" offerings, there would come a time for everybody just to escape the city.

Some people felt hemmed in. Being 110 miles behind the Iron Curtain had a profound impact on many people, especially family members who weren't otherwise employed elsewhere. It became necessary to occasionally depart the city and there were several ways to do that.

The most convenient was probably via privately owned vehicle (POV). Documentation in the form of "Flag Orders" was necessary, but this document on which was typed the traveler's name, identification number, and dates of travel was easily available. Upon receiving this document and equipped with the necessary ID card or passport, the individual processed through either Checkpoint Alpha (at the border between East and West Germany near Helmstedt) or Checkpoint Bravo (at the entrance to the American sector in Berlin near Dreilinden). These "checkpoints" were manned constantly by trained and capable military policemen who would review the travel documents and issue a travel pack if everything was in order.

Flag Orders

For the person who had never traversed the 110 miles between Berlin and West Germany, a detailed briefing was given showing the mile markers and suitable landmarks where exits were necessary. Appropriate warnings were given not to delay, but to adhere to a steady 100 kph speed limit. Arriving at the other checkpoint earlier than two hours would earn one a speeding ticket and failing to arrive within 3 ½ hours would also result in questions.

Strict instructions were given to ignore the East German transit points and to follow the markings to the Soviet checkpoints, located approximately a mile from either Allied checkpoint.

Once beyond all this and upon arrival in West Germany at Helmstedt, driving the German autobahn to points south toward Munich, or south and west toward Frankfurt, or even north toward Hamburg and Bremen were all possible. Authorized drivers with the command-sponsored vehicle registration could buy gasoline coupons through the PX. Gas coupons were rationed; an authorized driver could buy up to 400 liters per month. The coupons could be used at any Esso station in Germany. Once outside Germany, however, a person had to resort to paying the high prices that the normal civilian would have to pay.

Another popular option—and inexpensive—was to take the American duty train, as discussed elsewhere in the book.

Since the duty trains traveled through and were processed by the Soviets, flag orders were required for duty train travel. Flag orders and travel documents had to be surrendered to the military policemen upon checking in at the Rail Transportation Office prior to departure.

The British duty train traveled during the day, opposite of the American duty trains. This train left the British rail station and traveled on as far as Helmstedt, then returned the same day. Their train featured an on-board restaurant and it was quite a treat to ride the rails through East Germany and see things during the day that couldn't readily be seen at night on the American duty trains.

Finally, flying was a quick option. A quick 45 minutes in a jet out of Tegel Airport in the French sector would see the traveler landing at Frankfurt International. Flag orders were not required for air travel.

EVENTS OF THE 1980s

The Vietnam era and the policies inherent to that conflict gave focus to a new voice of protest and resistance. Seen in the U.S. in the most extreme form by the shootings on Kent State University students by National Guard troops in May 1970 to the more usual "sit-in" protests elsewhere, the universities and centers of higher education formed the backdrop for many expressions of disapproval. These voices were usually associated with young people, many of whom expected to serve in the military if called up in the draft.

The voices of protest about Vietnam extended from the U.S. to Europe, becoming more politically oriented and much more violent. The Baader-Meinhof gang, a group of German terrorists comprised primarily of a group of former students, journalists and intellectuals, were also known as the Red Army Faction. They, along with the Red Brigades in Italy, espoused an anti-imperialist, antiwar, anti-capitalist ethos, and sought to kill German politicians and industrialists, as well as striking U.S. interests (Montgomery, 2005).[63]

Terrorism

Terror strikes on U.S. bases and interests in Europe, principally Germany, began in the 1970s and ran until the latter part of the 1980s. These included:

- May 12, 1972. Officers Club near the U.S. Army V Corps Headquarters in Frankfurt bombed by Baader-Meinhof gang, killing one U.S. officer and injuring others (Huffman, Frankfurt V Corps HQ Bombing Damage #1, 2011).[64]
- May 24, 1972. Campbell Barracks, Heidelberg, Headquarters of U.S. Army Europe and 7th Army bombed by Baader-Meinhof gang, specifically in response to bombings in Vietnam, kills three U.S. soldiers (Huffman, May 24, 1972 Heidelberg, October).[65]
- August 31, 1981. Ramstein Air Base, Rheinland-Pfalz, bombed by Red Army Faction. Twelve U.S. military and two German civilians injured (Editor, 30th anniversary of USAFE headquarters bombing, 2011).[66]
- August 8, 1985. Rhein-Main Air Base, Frankfurt, bombed by Red Army Faction. One U.S. airman and one U.S. family member killed (Tagliabue, 1985).[67]
- November 24, 1985. Military Exchange (PX) shopping center in Frankfurt, bombed by persons unknown, however an Iranian and unnamed accomplice were the subject of an international police investigation and charged with the crime. At least 34 persons were injured in the car bomb (Markham, 1985).[68]

Terror attacks occurred elsewhere throughout this time period by differing groups and for different reasons.

On April 5, 1986, at 1:50 A.M., the La Belle Discotheque in the Friedenau subdistrict of West Berlin's Schöneberg District exploded from a 2kg bomb made of Semtex explosive encasing shrapnel. The blast killed Sergeant Kenneth T. Ford outright, along with a Turkish woman. A second U.S. infantryman, Staff Sergeant James E. Goins, died of his wounds two months later. The disco was known to be frequented by many U.S. servicemen. More than 200 were injured, included 37 (Fleshman, 1986)[69] other U.S. military, all of whom were awarded the Purple Heart for sustaining wounds at the hands of terrorists.

The attack on the LaBelle was seen as revenge for the sinking of Libyan patrol boats and destruction of a Libyan missile control site by U.S. warplanes in March 1986 when those planes were attacked by up to six Libyan surface to air missiles (Gerstenzang, 1986).[70] U.S. intelligence indicated Libya's involvement in the LaBelle bombing, so President Ronald Reagan ordered retaliatory strikes on the leadership and government of Muammar Khadafi 10 days after the disco bombing (Connolly, 2001).[71] F-111 bombers and other aircraft flew out of their bases in England and hammered targets in Tripoli and Benghazi.

CW3 David M. Smith, commander of the 298th at the time of the LaBelle disco attack, recalls receiving a phone call at his quarters at about 0230 – a scant 45 minutes after the bomb's detonation. He was instructed by the Berlin command's Emergency Operations Center (EOC) to initiate a unit recall/alert. Mr. Smith was informed that there had been an "incident" downtown with mass casualties and that a solid headcount was needed to determine personnel accountability.

Mr. Smith immediately phoned the 298th's Charge of Quarters and instructed him to execute the band's alert roster/phone tree. Mr. Smith added the instruction that this was no drill.

At about 0315 hours, the band was fully assembled or accounted for. Mr. Smith submitted the appropriate report to the EOC. The band was then instructed to stand fast and await further instructions. Later that morning, the band stood down and went about the normal duty day.

Mr. Smith further recalls planning and conducting two Battalion Funeral Parades per Army regulations and field manuals, commensurate with the death of each soldier. Noteworthy about these parades was the parade to the McNair Barracks chapel was conducted with the respective battalion commander and his staff leading the formation, with no guidon (unit flag). The band's drums were draped in black and the snares on those drums were turned off. Mr. Smith had directed to play a Beethoven dirge on the way to the chapel.

From the chapel following the service, Army procedure stated to undrape the drums and turn the snares on. Mr. Smith ordered uplifting patriotic music to be played, characterized by the band's performance of Sousa's *Washington Post* march.

After the fall of the Berlin Wall in 1989 and the opening of secret files of the East German *Staatsicherheitamt* (Stasi), evidence indicated direct Libyan government involvement with an intercepted radio transmission to the Libyan embassy in East Berlin with orders to attack "with as many victims as possible." Telegrams supported the charge of Libyan involvement.[72]

Major Arthur D. Nicholson – the Last Cold War Casualty

On Sunday afternoon on March 24, 1985, Major Arthur D. "Nick" Nicholson, dressed in battle dress uniform and riding in a vehicle with United States Military Liaison Mission (USMLM) license plates, approached a Soviet tank storage building near Ludwigslust, East Germany. Armed only with a camera, Nicholson began to take photographs of training posters affixed to the building's walls (Stacey, 1988).[73] Nicholson's driver, Staff Sergeant Jesse Schatz, maintained a watch for any Soviet personnel. Unseen by either American until just before the first shot rang out narrowly missing Schatz, a Soviet sentry fired again hitting Nicholson, who cried out he'd been hit. The sentry fired a third round, hitting Nicholson a second time. Schatz exited the vehicle with first aid kit in hand and gestured with it to Nicholson, who lay on the ground and twitched. By this time, the sentry had approached both Americans. The sentry pointed his weapon at Schatz and with his finger on the trigger, forced Schatz back into his vehicle. More than two hours transpired before Nicholson was medically examined and by this time, he had bled to death.

Major Nicholson and Staff Sergeant Schatz were both members of the USMLM, a coalition of Soviet and Western Allied intelligence personnel formed in the aftermath of World War II under the terms of the Huebner-Malinin Agreement. The missions organized under that agreement created opportunities for the exchange of information relative to the occupied zones of East and West Germany. USMLM was based on Potsdam, East Germany, approximately 20km from Berlin command headquarters. From Potsdam, agents from USMLM and their Western Allied and Soviet counterparts undertook missions to observe and report on each other. Ostensibly, the purpose was to ensure and otherwise monitor the others' activities to reduce the possibility of misunderstanding and confusion.

The reaction to the shooting was swift and various military and diplomatic officials were consulted and notified.

Major Nicholson's body was returned to U.S. control at 5:15 P.M. on March 25 by passing over Glienicke Bridge, the scene of various spy transfers throughout the Cold War. An honor guard without band support met Major

Nicholson's body and transferred his remains to an ambulance for transport to the U.S. Army Hospital.

The 298th supported an honor guard ceremony at Tempelhof Central Airport which began at 10 P.M. the same night. Mr. Smith again recalls that Major Nicholson's widow specifically requested "I Know That My Redeemer Liveth" as it was her husband's favorite hymn. As Mrs. Nicholson and her young daughter looked on and the international press pool photographed the sequence of events, the pallbearers bearing Major Nicholson's remains made their slow, solemn march toward the aircraft. As the final chord of the last hymn drifted into the night, Mr. Smith turned and faced the aircraft rendering a hand salute. As he faced about toward the band again, he noted how the gravity of the event and the music had had a profound effect on the band. Even in the semi-darkness, he noted many in the band had tears in their eyes.

Major Nicholson was buried in Arlington National Cemetery with full military honors. He was posthumously awarded the Legion of Merit, the Purple Heart, and was promoted to Lieutenant Colonel.

Some months later, the 298th performed at the dedication of the Berlin command's library, located on Clayallee just north of Truman Plaza. The library would hereafter be known as the Arthur Nicholson Memorial Library. The library was built in 1979, but had not been named until this event. The Nicholson Library continued to serve the community until deactivation of the Berlin Brigade in 1994. Today, the Nicholson Library is void of books, but the building remains as part of the Allied Museum which is a private enterprise located in the former Outpost Theater next door.

Other Events

The 298th's move from building 909 on Andrews Barracks to building 904 during 909's complete renovation occupied a significant amount of time, in addition to the normal workload of rehearsal, performances, and travel. Already discussed in an earlier chapter, the result was a facility that met all the 298th's needs and provided a stellar place to live and work.

In October 1985, a significant uniform change came in the form of the Specialist 5 rank insignia, which was abolished. Those dozen or so 298th soldiers in that grade were transferred in grade to Sergeant E-5. Organizational uniforms, such as dress blues, for those soldiers were changed per the new authorized rank insignia.

The illness that became known as AIDS, made highly visible in July 1985 by the actor Rock Hudson's publicist that the actor had contracted the disease, prompted a mandatory program within the Berlin command. All soldiers were required to submit a blood sample for analysis. Any soldier's sample found containing evidence of exposure to the AIDS virus led to immediate action by the Berlin command to reassign the soldier from Berlin to the United States.

Two soldiers within the 298th were so identified and reassigned as a result of this program.

The year 1986 was a calamitous one for most Americans, at least insofar as world events were concerned. The earlier Chapter "Off Duty" discussed the January 28, 1986 tragedy of the space shuttle *Challenger*'s explosion 73 seconds after liftoff. Several members of the 298th were in Mom's Kneipe when a news broadcast on the small television showed the dramatic and fiery disaster. A catastrophe of this magnitude had not been seen in the American space program since 1967 when a fire during a training event claimed the lives of the three Apollo 1 astronauts. The vaunted space shuttle program, highly successful until this point, underwent a thorough review.

The LaBelle disco bombing comprised a big element in the Berlin command's day to day operations, as the security levels on all American compounds were increased. Inspections of vehicles were required for a time, even when the resulting traffic backlog at the Clay HQ, Andrews and McNair gates created problems. Pedestrian traffic into the Truman Plaza area also required presentation of an ID card. Fences were erected around the Truman Plaza area, along with the emplacement of large concrete flowerpots. These flowerpots were more than decorative—they served as barriers to keep unauthorized vehicles from attacking the area in the same fashion as the 1983 car bomb attack on the U.S. Marine Barracks in Beirut, Lebanon that had killed 241 servicemen.

On April 26, Reactor #4 at Chernobyl, Ukraine, USSR, exploded during an experiment, creating the world's worst nuclear accident in terms of severity and resulting deaths. The Chernobyl explosion released more than 400 times the amount of radioactive material into the earth's atmosphere than had occurred with the Hiroshima atomic bomb (Editor, Ten Years After Chernobyl: What Do We Really Know?, 1996).[74] During the 10 day period of maximum releases from Chernobyl, volatile radionuclides were continuously discharged and dispersed across many parts of Europe and later the entire northern hemisphere. For example, relatively high fallout concentrations were measured at Hiroshima in Japan, over 8,000 km from Chernobyl. In terms of surface area, Belarus and Austria were most affected by higher levels of contamination However, other countries were seriously affected; for example, more than 5% of Ukraine, Finland and Sweden were contaminated to high levels (>40,000 Bq/m2 caesium-137). Forty-four percent of Germany and 34% of the UK were similarly affected. In terms of total deposition of caesium-137, Russia, Belarus and Ukraine received the highest amounts of fallout while former Yugoslavia, Finland, Sweden, Bulgaria, Norway, Rumania, Germany, Austria and Poland each received more than one petabecquerel (1015 Bq or one million billion becquerels) of caesium-137, a very large amount of radioactivity (Fairlie & Sumner, DPhil, 2006).[75]

The effects of Chernobyl are still being measured today, 28 years after the catastrophe.

On June 4, 1985 Jonathon Pollard, an intelligence specialist for the U.S. Naval Intelligence Command, pleaded guilty to espionage. Pollard's sale of classified information to Israel resulted in his conviction and a life sentence. West Berlin, a center of intelligence activity, noted this case and others similar to it.

The election in June of former United Nations Secretary General Kurt Waldheim as President of Austria in June caused a furor in Europe. Waldheim's service as an officer in Germany's Wehrmacht and his registration as a Nazi prior to the war were examined and reported in detail. Waldheim continued serving as president until 1992 at which point he retired.

Berlin's 750th Anniversary—1987

CW3 David M. Smith, commander of the 298th, relates that in preparation for the upcoming 750th anniversary of the city of Berlin in 1987, the 298th pre-recorded music for a show taped on December 31, 1986 in one of Tempelhof Central Airport's (TCA) large halls. This large hall had previously served as the airport's arrival and departure center for travelers. The purpose of the show, produced and taped by German radio and television broadcaster ZDF, was intended to usher in 1987 and the celebrations that occurred from April through October. For many in the band, pre-recording music and then "faking playing" while executing marching maneuvers through the hall was new. It took several takes and two hours or more to get it right.

President Ronald Reagan's visit to Berlin on June 12, 1987 incurred the expected participation by the 298th. But due to security concerns, the 298th needed some help. Three performances by military bands were planned: the incoming honor guard, the 750th anniversary celebration "birthday party" inside the Tempelhof facility, and the outgoing honor guard. The 298th could not negotiate the security cordon following the indoor anniversary celebration back to the outdoor honor guard due to the time the protocol took to execute, so the 33rd Army Band, also known as the U.S. Army Europe (USAREUR) Band out of Heidelberg, commanded by Major Stan Cornett, made the trip to Berlin to play the outgoing honor guard.

Air Force One was preceded in flight by a 747-121 aircraft containing over 300 journalists. This large aircraft was only the second 747 to ever have landed at the relatively small Tempelhof airfield outside of test flights to confirm that capability (RonaldV, 2013) (Editor, Flughafen Berlin-Tempelhof).[76,77] The 298th performed the incoming honor guard on the tarmac and then, while President Reagan departed to speak at the Brandenburg Gate with the Wall as a backdrop, moved into Tempelhof hall for the Berlin 750th anniversary celebration to be attended by President Reagan after his

Brandenburg Gate speech.

The USAREUR Band was designated to play the outgoing honor guard following the indoor anniversary celebration and waited on bleachers for the entire event to unfold.

Mr. Smith, conducting the 298th on the tarmac throughout the long rehearsals prior to touchdown of Air Force One and the honor guard itself, recalls that the 298th played the U.S. National Anthem, and the Trooping the Line by President Reagan to inspect U.S. Army, British Forces, and French Army troops, in that order. He described the formation as a rough "L" shape with the 298th forming the base of the "L" and then American, British and French troops (in that order) forming the upright of the "L." Air Force One then provided the other side of the upright "L" thus becoming a "U" formation. The entourage would then disembark the aircraft and, beginning with the band, troop the line.

As very few ceremonies of this magnitude escape at least a little drama, Mr. Smith related the incident of the British infantry soldier whose toes bordered the red carpet on which the president and his entourage marched. Evidently, the soldier had grown ill just as Air Force One was landing due likely to the long rehearsals and poor ceremony "technique."

"Even as he began to waver like a long-stemmed flower in a stiff wind and just before the very long arm of his regimental sergeant major plucked him from the front rank, [the soldier] had the presence of mind to remove his headgear and puke into same, sparing soiling the red carpet."

Mr. Smith went on, "The other oddity that I had not ever experienced was the Brits 'grounding the Colour' (their regimental colours literally thrown across the path of the red carpet) in salute to a foreign head of state. The president was a bit shocked and did a shuffle step as though he didn't wish to walk on the regimental flag.

"My most vivid memory was doing an about face, executing 'Eyes Right' as the President hit the band's right flank and marveling at how tall Reagan was. I don't know why this was so shocking, but I remember having to adjust my position ever-so-slightly so as to make eye contact with him.

"We played the 'birthday party' in [TCA's hall] with various silly stuff including a simply terrible arrangement of 'Footloose' for an elementary school dance troop. I had fought this one at the planning meetings...pushing for use of recorded music...and lost. So we ended up playing a throw together arrangement of this otherwise forgettable tune."

Trombonist Dan Hermann recalled how full the band sounded, even four times larger than its actual size. The overhang under which the honor guard place provided an acoustic echo chamber which amplified the sound to give that impression.. Dan also remembered how, during President Reagan's short address, a balloon popped. President Reagan quipped, "They missed me" eliciting a chuckle from the audience.

Due to the aforementioned security protocol, the 298th remained on the tarmac while the president traveled to the Brandenburg Gate with the Berlin Wall as backdrops. There, in a 25-minute speech, the president spoke his challenge, "General Secretary Gorbachev, if you seek peace, if you seek prosperity for the Soviet Union and Eastern Europe, if you seek liberalization: come here to this gate. Mr. Gorbachev, open this gate. Mr. Gorbachev, tear down this Wall!"

Less than two and one-half years later, the Berlin Wall came down.

The U.S. Army Field Band out of Ft. Meade, Maryland arrived in Berlin to assist the Berliners in celebrating their 750th year. Over approximately a 3-day period, the Field Band performed a formal concert in West Berlin's most prestigious concert hall, the Philharmonie, a venue in which the Berlin Philharmonic also regularly performed, and provided a larger American musical footprint for the Berliners. The formal concert was well attended and the Field Band put on a professional, exciting program.

Planning and orchestrating the arrival, billeting, messing of the Field Band required the work of two senior NCOs, Master Sergeant Mike Demeo and Sergeant First Class Dominic Fiaschetti, within the Field Band who, while non-performers themselves, nonetheless worked over the details while the operations staff of the 298th assisted by providing local knowledge, transportation, and administrative support. Most of the Field Band, including the commander, Colonel William E. Clark, was billeted and messed at McNair Barracks.

Rudolf Hess in Spandau Prison

The sole occupant of Spandau Prison, Rudolf Hess, committed suicide at the age of 93 within the prison walls by hanging himself with an electrical cable. This was not Hess' first attempt at suicide—he had tried three times; the first time in June 1941 in England,[78] the second time in early 1945, also while imprisoned in England and the third time in 1977 while in Spandau Prison (Nesbit & van Acker, 2007).[79]

The Four Allied Powers, France, United Kingdom, the Soviet Union, and the United States, all shared in the management of Spandau Prison from receipt of the first prisoners—all of whom sentenced at the Nürnberg Trials—in 1946 until Hess' suicide in 1987. The Four Allied Powers provided military guards and staff sufficient to run the prison on a rotating monthly basis.

The 298th Army Band did not support Spandau Prison. While U.S. infantrymen were detailed to serve as guards when the U.S. had its monthly rotations in April, August, and December of each year, band support was not provided.

Spandau Prison was demolished in the immediate aftermath of Hess' suicide. The bricks comprising the prison were ground up and either shipped to the North Sea for dispersal, or transported to the British airfield at Gatow for burial. Definitive plans had been made beforehand to obliterate the prison, thereby eliminating a possible Nazi shrine.

General Secretary Gorbachev's policies of *glasnost* (transparency) and *perestroika* (restructuring [of the Soviet Union's political and economic systems]) were items of interest in the news. Initiating these policies intending to improve the Soviet Union's economic and political system, Gorbachev set about creating a new "openness" by which the Soviet Union could embrace those changes. These had a profound effect on the rest of Eastern Europe.

1989

Eastern Europe paid attention to Comrade Secretary Gorbachev and began restructuring their own socio-political structures in their own countries, usually nonviolently. Beginning actually before Gorbachev's rise to power, Lech Wałęsa founded Poland's trade union Solidarity in 1980. Wałęsa's influence increased sufficiently for him to win the Nobel Peace Prize in 1983.

Solidarity's pattern, reaching far beyond that of a normal trade union in forming coalitions with the Catholic Church and anti-Soviet organizations within Poland, advocated non-violence (Editor, Solidarity (Polish trade union)).[80] Solidarity's impact, financially supported by the U.S. labor union AFL-CIO against the wishes of the Carter and Reagan administrations (Puddington),[81] grew in strength throughout the 1980s and resulted in a series of worker strikes that forced the Polish government in 1988 to acknowledge and address those grievances. In order to end the strikes, the ruling Polish government then agreed to a bicameral legislature. As Gorbachev's own policies had ended the so-called Brezhnev Doctrine (the active interference by the Soviet Union in the affairs of one of their satellites), this effectively ended Soviet domination over the country, the first Soviet satellite to break free. Solidarity then defeated the Polish Communist Party in 1989's elections, setting the stage for other countries to begin their own processes in breaking the shackles of communism.

Hungary was the next country to adopt a non-communist government. In January 1989, the Parliament adopted a "democracy package" which included trade union pluralism, freedom of association, assembly, and the press; a new electoral law; and a radical revision of the constitution, among others (Editor, NY Times Archives, January).[82] Hungary's next action was to begin dismantling the 150-mile barrier between Hungary and East Germany. This resulted in thousands of East Germans illegally crossing to the West through Hungary to Austria over the summer and into autumn, an act that destabilized both East Germany and Czechoslovakia.

Demonstrations and protests then appeared throughout Eastern Europe. East Germans, particularly in Leipzig, took to the streets on successive Mondays in September and October, petitioning the government for the right to travel freely and to elect a democratic government. The numbers of demonstrators grew over these weeks from just 1,800 to over 70,000, to 120,000 to more than 320,000 in a city of 500,000 people. The East German military stood by, but took no definitive action. This "Peaceful Revolution" is recognized as the catalyst that resulted in the fall of the Berlin Wall on November 9, 1989 (Editor, Peaceful Revolution).[83]

THE 298TH ARMY BAND—PERSPECTIVES OF ITS COMMANDER

CWO David M. Smith commanded the 298th from 1984-88. Some years after his retirement from the Army, he had occasion to write the essays appearing in this chapter. His stories are humorous, readable and typically have a message. More than anything, his stories offer a perspective that could not be replicated in any other way. Mr. Smith graciously permitted these stories to appear in this book.

Volksfest Milkshakes

Part county fair, part embassy-level cultural exchange, part musical revue, part beer fest, [the Volksfest] has always been a hot ticket for the locals.

Away from the music and the rides, the Volksfest was a showcase of foreign (American/Tex-Mex) food that never failed to amaze the Berliners. This was a time when many of the food items that we take for granted were just making their appearance in Germany. The band once played a supermarket opening (yes, a supermarket opening—just like a faded/fading obscure rock tribute band supermarket opening) in support of the Embassy Econ Section because the market chain was highlighting American foods. The biggest stir of that crowd was this rare imported cheese...such a novel delicacy...by a company whose name in German meant "strength". The crowd was simply stunned and amazed by the display of Kraft American single-wrapped cheese slices with comments about this Brave New World like, "They pre-slice their cheese," "Strength cheese?" "Look at the color...it must taste fantastic," "They pay a worker to wrap each slice?" What an amazing thing marketing is...

At my very first Volksfest, just before or after a gig, I was walking in uniform down the midway near the La Raza Unida booth (I guess looking like I might have an answer) when a very, very old German lady stopped me for a question. Could I please tell her what this "Chilisuppe" was?

My first attempt was to list the ingredients, but the whole was greater than the sum of its parts—just listing them out didn't translate to something that she could wrap her head around and make the decision whether or not to commit DM 1,50 to purchase a bowl of the stuff. How could I relate this to something in her experience? After a few more feeble, impotent attempts, FINALLY...it's like Gulaschsuppe, but with sharper spices...much sharper spices. She got it. And then she got some.

That attempt at explaining Tex-Mex came in handy later that year. We were in Einhausen [Germany] in October, 1984 and watching a news story on German television about the first Tex-Mex restaurant to open in Germany—on the outskirts of Frankfurt. Rather than try to explain how a whole cuisine could be based on the same seven ingredients, we piled into the car and drove to the restaurant to sample the food. A picture may be worth a thousand words, but handing a friend a taco to eat loses nothing in the translation.

The big hit that year at Volksfest was an American beer. No, not Budweiser—that had been around forever, but it couldn't be sold on The Economy since it didn't meet the restrictions of the German Beer Purity decree.

In 1516, Wilhelm IV and Ludwig X, co-rulers of Bavaria, proclaimed the Reinheitsgebot that in part stated "...in all cities, markets and in the country, the only ingredients used for the brewing of beer must be Barley, Hops and Water. Whosoever knowingly disregards or transgresses upon this ordinance, shall be punished by the Court authorities' confiscating such barrels of beer, without fail." It was adopted as law throughout Germany in 1919. Bavaria refused to join the Weimar Republic unless the Reinheitsgebot was made the law of the land. Until it was struck down by the European Court in 1987 as a restraint on free trade, the Reinheitsgebot made it impossible to sell foreign beer in Germany. Every bottle of beer had always had the inscription "Gebraut nach dem deutschen Reinheitsgebot" on the cap or label.

Then came along an American outfit called Sam Adams, the first American beer to meet the restrictions of the Reinheitsgebot and to be legally sold on the open market. If Berliners went a little gaga over the silly yellow cheese, imagine the major event that the introduction of this beer was at the Volksfest.

The Berlin Chapter of the US Army Warrant Officers Association (USAWOA) had a booth that sold milkshakes and American candy bars. We would don our USAWOA-logoed T-shirts—they were a dark chocolate brown, the branch color of Warrant Officer Branch (feel free to take a minute to compose your own joke on how it was decided to make brown the WO branch color...okay, everyone past that?)—which did a great job at hiding any spills of chocolate syrup.

Leo Ott and Dick Gadarian, two retired-in-Berlin warrant officers led the effort. We served vanilla and chocolate shakes out the front of the booth for DM 1,50 and, to trusted colleagues and the occasional Berliner Polizist, Leo's special shakes (vanilla with a hefty shot of booze) out the back door of the booth for a wee bit more. The Germans didn't have softserve ice cream and there was always a line to the front of the booth. At really busy times, the normally unflappable warrant officers began to resemble Lucy and Ethel in the candy factory during times of what seemed like fast-paced, never ending demand.

We developed a shorthand for each order that would have impressed the staff of The Varsity in Atlanta (or the Soup Nazi on Seinfeld) for its brash brevity and ruthless efficiency. As the next customer came up to the counter, we would bark, "Shoko oder Vanille? Wie viele von jeder?" and we would then fill the order.

During a slack time, a German grandmother with her 4-5 year old granddaughter in tow came timidly up to the booth and requested, "Eine Shoko, bitte." When I presented her with a chocolate shake, she was a little embarrassed (apparently she did not know our shorthand for orders) and explained in halting English that she had meant a chocolate candy bar.

I looked back over my shoulder and saw the display of various Schokoriegel on the shelf—M&Ms, Baby Ruth, Zagnut, Reese's Cups and Hershey Milk Chocolate Bars—any and all for DM 1 apiece. We did such a landmark business in the milk shakes that I really hadn't taken much notice of the candy and Oma was the first person to ask about them all week.

I did the ubiquitous grunt-and-point routine down the line of candy bars to try to ascertain which candy bar she wanted. M&Ms? Baby Ruth? Of course, the last one in the line—the plain old-school Hershey bar.

She explained that during the Berlin Airlift, about 35 years before when her family lived in Tempelhof, she was introduced to Hershey Bars through the good offices of the Rosinenbomber who repeatedly parachuted them to the children of Berlin as each flight made its final approach to the airfield day after day in support of Operation Vittles. She said that, many times, that candy was the only thing that she had to eat and she wanted her granddaughter "to know the taste of American kindness."

I gave her the shake and as many candy bars as she could comfortably carry for free. She summed up what we were doing in Berlin back then better than I could ever hope to express.

Kaiserstraße

The Berlin - Frankfurt and Berlin - Bremerhaven Duty Trains not only left daily from these cities but also provided a departure from a certain "sameness" that affected other US Army bands. When you start out and finish any road trip with a ten to twelve hour train ride—each way—there are endless possibilities for a variety of experiences.

The stated purpose of the daily trains was to overtly maintain the concept of free access to and from the City of Berlin. Each evening, two trains would leave Berlin headed for either Bremerhaven or Frankfurt and from each of those cities, a train would head toward Berlin. There were planned stops at railway Checkpoint Alpha and railway Checkpoint Bravo, the lesser known cousins of the famous Checkpoint Charlie, where the Soviets checked flag orders and afforded our Hungarian woodwind group leader [Bela Babocsay] the opportunity to help me to increase my foreign language vocabulary as he hurled pointed insults in gutter-Russian to the sentries along the track. Amazing what we got away with.

The train track in the DDR that was assigned to the Duty Train was the least-maintained rail bed in all of the Warsaw Pact. The transit of the 110 miles inside East Germany, less than a third of the distance to Frankfurt, ended up taking over half of the travel time. And, due to the ill-maintained rail bed, the trip felt as though the sleeper car that we were assigned had square wheels. After an uncomfortable night's sleep, we would then get on a Reisebus to complete our travel in the West.

Travel in either direction required that the unit muster at the Rail Transportation Office (RTO) at approximately 1700 or so to be included on the manifest for an approximate 1930 departure. This usually wasn't a problem in either Berlin or Bremerhaven; however, on return trips from Frankfurt we usually ended up with 3-4 hours of free time before the manifest muster. Consequently, the Bahnhofsviertel (the train station quarter of Frankfurt in the same sense as the Latin Quarter pertains to the City of Paris or the French Quarter to New Orleans) presented unique challenges for the band and these recurring segments of free time.

Most of the immediate area just outside the Bahnhof didn't spark much interest with young military musicians; however, if you had proceeded straight ahead, dodged the streetcars [at that time] and negotiated the automobiles-used-as-weapons traffic, you would have found yourself at the entry to Kaiserstraße—the main street of the Bahnhofsviertel.

The street began at the train station plaza and extended about eight long blocks ending at the Hauptwache U-Bahn station. But it was the first few blocks that were noteworthy. To be sure, there were an ample number of restaurants and even a Burger King (a very rare sighting back then) if you wanted a sort-of-a-kind-of-an-impression-of-a little taste of back home, or a Wienerwald restaurant that quickly served a terrible Schnitzel dinner. These were the cultural highpoints offered by Kaiserstraße. After all, the museums were all on the other side of the Main River.

Since the band's only commitment was to be present for movement and we had no other duties facing us for 18 hours or so, it was okay during the 3-4 hour layover to grab a beer—except this was the Bahnhofsviertel.

Kaiserstraße was bereft of a normal tourist area's shops. Parfumerie Douglas, souvenir shops, other than a few restaurants, it was a collection of sleazy clubs. The usual scam in these joints was that when an American Gomer entered the club, a hostess offered a beer to the unsuspecting GI—who would reach out and take the beer—to the sound of the German equivalent of "Ka-Ching" as the poor GI now owed the bar DM20 or more (about $10 for a $1 beer). And this was in the more upstanding places.

It became the custom in the band that on a first Duty Train trip from Frankfurt, the applicable section leader would give the newbie a tour of the Kaiserstraße—especially showing places and behaviors to avoid and places that were relatively okay.

For example, in European society, a sex shop like Doctor Müller's is considered just another business and I'm told that band members gave a good effort in trying to blend in with the locals in this regard by going in for regular check-ups with the good doctor. But once again, the section leader orientation included an explanation of the nature and layout of the store so that the newbie could avoid any undue embarrassment by being in the wrong place at the wrong time.

This also allowed everyone the freedom, based on the knowledge of what was out there, to remain in the train station and wait for the manifest muster. I never received a report of any of the band members getting into trouble on the Kaiserstraße; however, there was one incident that did occur in the train station itself.

On one trip, [saxophonist] Johnny Hanson (1985-91) felt the call of nature and chose to use the facilities in the US Army RTO in the train station which were cleaner and more private. What could possibly go wrong? It seems that Johnny was still in the crapper doing his business when it came time for the RTO personnel to close up and do their thing with the flag orders and manifest sheets. It might have even been a little ahead of schedule for them.

Johnny looked at his watch and knew he had to hurry to meet the manifest muster at train side, so he pulled up his pants and headed for the RTO door—which was locked. With a deadbolt lock…tick-tock, tick-tock…what to do?…tick-tock, tick-tock…aha, pound on the door…tick-tock, tick-tock.

You know how in a big city people will walk right by the oddest things and pretend not to notice…tick-tock, tick-tock…that's what happened to Johnny…tick-tock, tick-tock. He was sure he would be cited for missing movement (for those of you with scorecards, that would be Article 87 of the Uniform Code of Military Justice…tick-tock, tick-tock.

Johnny's answer: pick up the otherwise never-used fire extinguisher, throw that sucker through the RTO window, and climb out of there—right into the arms of two Frankfurt Polizei who immediately apprehended him for trying to break into the US Army RTO. Johnny explained, of course, that he wasn't breaking into the RTO; he was breaking out of the RTO.

Help came on the horizon as the First Sergeant and the RTO personnel arrived looking for our lost sax player and took charge of Johnny who had quite literally been caught with his pants down.

Mons and Doudou

Every year in Mons, Belgium, the city hosted an International Military Band Show that had 10-12 NATO and non-NATO military bands performing. The Berlin Brigade Band was first invited in 1986 as the US Army Europe

Band in Heidelberg had a conflict in scheduling, so the gig fell to Berlin. We ended up returning the next year.

The gig was held in conjunction with its Ducasse du Mons festival, held each year 47 days after Easter, that capped off week-long festivities...a torch light parade, daily rehearsals for the show, platz concerts in surrounding villes during the day and nightly concerts on three stages in La Grand Place right outside l'Hotel de Ville (City Hall), which sported a brass monkey statue that, for reasons never explained, brought the passersby luck if they rubbed its little brass head.

Last but not least was a remnant from the Middle Ages, the physical trial of all the young men of the town in battling St George's dragon, known locally as Le Dou Dou.

La Grand Place was not a small little village square and on the Feast Day and for our concerts, it would be packed with thousands of people.

El Dou Dou is this great wooden Dragon...from nose to tail about 40 feet long...most of it being tail with a rather compact head and body. There is a horsetail affixed to the very end of the wooden shaft that was the tail...it is considered to be the best of luck for the upcoming year for any young stud who could pluck a hair from the dragon's tail. Sounds pretty easy, but not necessarily. Dou Dou's helpers (the gentlemen all dressed in white) spin the dragon body around at a high speed, gradually lowering the tail down into the crowd. Like a centrifuge, the end of the heavy wooden tail is literally cracking the whip as it descends into the crowd. Fortified by as much Chimay Bleu beer as they can stand, the truly insane then leap up to try and throw their torsos into the path of the tail to slow it down so their buddies could pluck a hair or two. The Belgian Red Cross would treat literally hundreds of broken bones (ribs/arms/noses/etc.) over the course of Le Dou Dou's procession through town.

There is La Chanson du Dou Dou—a snappy little number in 6/8. For those who've played the song before, I will not be responsible for trying to wash the tune out of your head. If the tune becomes a chronic companion, I've included the lyrics at the end of this article.

Here's the story:

The actual week that the Berlin Brigade Band spent in Mons, Belgium was in celebration of the Ducasse du Mons (Dedication of Mons), a celebration dedicated to the local patron saint, St Waudru who, in 1349, answered the prayers of the townspeople and delivered them from the Black Plague that had decimated the region. The fest has been held 47 days after Easter every year since 1353, with the exception of 1803, when Napoleon took exception to it and during WWII, when Hitler did the same.

There is the religious part of the celebration, but El Dou Dou is centerstage in the Combat dit Lumecon du Mons (basically the combat in Mons of Good and Evil). Good is St George in his yellow tunic and evil is The

Dragon (El Dou Dou). They process (accompanied by the good/evil helpers) through the town to La Grand Place where the real fun begins in a sand-covered area in the square.

Two things:

Dou Dou's heavy wooden tail is approximately 8 meters long and really whips around.

The videos and still images on Youtube give a small look at the throngs of people at this thing.

The dragon is carried by the "White Men" who make him turn in a counterclockwise direction to deliver coup de queue (tail blows) to the young men who are encircling him...they're trying to snatch a horse hair from the tail for good luck. It's some high-speed, terminal velocity of a heavy timber, dangerous, break your nose-ribs-arm-leg stuff.

St George rides around El Dou Dou for a half hour trying to run him through with his lance, which continually breaks. In an Indiana Jones moment, St George finally throws down the spear, pulls a gun and shoots El Dou Dou.

C'est la vie...

Lyrics to El Doudou:

1. Nos irons vir l'car d'or
A l'procession de Mon
Ce s'ra l'poupée St Georg'
Qui no' suivra de long

(Refrain après chaque couplet)
C'est l'doudou c'est l'mama
C'est l'poupée, poupée, poupée
C'est l'doudou, c'est l'mama
C'est l'poupée St Georg' qui va
Les gins du rempart riront comm' des kiards
Dé vir tant de carottes
Les gins du culot riront comm' des sots
Dé vir tant de carot' à leu' pots

2. El' Vieill' Matant' Magu'ritte
Trousse ses falbalas
Pou fair' boulli l'marmite
Et cuir'ses biaux p'tits pois.

3. Les Dames du chapitre
N'auront pas du gambon,
Parce qu'ell' n'ont pas fait
El tour d'el procession

4. Voici l'dragon qui vient!
Ma mère sauvons nous!
Il a mordu grand'mère,
I' vos mordra itou

5. V'là qu'el Lum'çon commence
Au son du carillon
Saint Georg' avec sa lance
Va combat' el dragon

6. Dragon, sauvag' et diabes,
Saint Georg' éié chinchins
Ess' tourpin dédins l'sabe…
On tir', c'est l'grand moumint.

7. V'là l' dragon qui trépasse
In v'là co pou in an;
Asteur faisons ducasse
A tabe mes infants.

Café Moskau

For the Berlin Brigade bandmembers and their families, the strange thing about the Wall was that every morning that you got up in Berlin you saw the Wall. And every time was almost like you were seeing it for the first time. You were immediately reminded of why you were in the Army and that US Army Bands weren't just some whacky extension of the National Endowment supporting wind musicians.

Having said that, most of us took ample opportunities to secure an East Pass and make fairly frequent trips to East Berlin.

After crossing the border at Checkpoint Charlie, my usual route was to drive 10-12 blocks on Friedrichstraße and then make a right on Unter den Linden—passing first the mounted statue of Friedrich der Große in the middle of the boulevard, then the ornate Staatsoper on the right.

Almost immediately on the left was the Neue Wache, originally built as a guardhouse for Prussian troops, it's been used as a war memorial since 1931. Then there was a richly-ornamented bridge with Baroque statuary that crossed onto Museum Island—all of which served as counterpoint to the ultra-modern-out-of-place-as-anything-you-could-ever-imagine Congresshalle and giant TV tower where the boulevard became Karl-Liebknecht-Straße and entered the center of Berlin - Alexanderplatz.

I never felt totally comfortable in Alexanderplatz back then—for two reasons. First of all, there were multiple surveillance cameras on the corner of every tall building trained down to cover and actively monitor every inch of the shopping district. You could actually look up and see the cameras turn to follow you as you made your way from store to store to the point that it was simply disturbing.

Secondly, although the shopping complex was meant to show the success of the system to its people and the abundance of goods that could not be had anywhere else in the East Bloc, the scarcity of some of even the most basic clothing and other items was a pathetic reminder of how spartan the conditions were in the East.

I usually made another right onto Karl-Marx-Allee.

Karl-Marx-Allee had been rebuilt in many places with Stalin-era Brave-New-World-style apartment houses. These were massive blocks of poorly conceived and even more poorly executed megastructures which were absolutely hideous. However, as you got away from Alexanderplatz, more and more 18th and 19th Century buildings survived. This boulevard had traditionally been the main thoroughfare out of Berlin toward Frankfurt an der Oder and the old eastern boundary of the City was consequently called Frankfurter Tor (Frankfurt Gate).

Karl-Marx-Allee was where the East German military held its May Day

Parade. Just picture streams of troops, armored vehicles and missiles simply pouring down this wide, very Parisian-scale boulevard.

The parade stretched from the old Frankfurter Tor in the east toward the parade's end at a reviewing stand just before Alexanderplatz, all in a nonsensical contest of one-upsmanship and who has the big/bigger/biggest missile—bordering on a kind of armament exhibitionism. To be fair, our side did the same thing with our Allied Forces Day Parade.

In that same spirit of competition, all of the Warsaw Pact countries built and maintained restaurants and/or cultural centers to showcase the best of each of the member nations. Cuisine, folk art, music, recordings, artwork.

Perhaps the strangest entry in this particular endeavor was the Soviet eatery, Cafe Moskau.

Built in 1959, Cafe Moskau was rendered in a style diametrically opposed to the titanic apartment blocks. While the apartments were 20-25 stories tall, the showcase restaurant was built in that curiously transparent architectural style known as 1950's California Gas Station—one thin slab of nothing but horizontal lines and glass hunkered down close to the ground. Any visible means of supporting the structure with verticals was coyly hidden from view. This was a total renunciation of the Workers' Apartments.

Even the roof was flat, except for one teeny tiny concession to the aforementioned one-upsmanship contest. As a not-too-subtle reminder that they had been first in space, the restaurant sported a model of the Sputnik I satellite on its roofline.

The first thing that greeted you at the entryway was a very large, laboriously-executed mosaic. It was 15 meters wide and 9 meters tall...three car lengths wide by one and a half stories tall. It showed an idealized view of the Workers' Paradise...all executed in mosaic tiles, each less than 1/4" – 1/2" square.

As you can see by this interior shot, once you entered the main salon, everything was in black-and-white.

Okay, not really—but it seemed that way.

The totalitarian ambience was in keeping with the surliness of the Russian wait staff which proved a perfect match for the "interesting" cuisine. Four years in Berlin and after my one-and-only visit, I could say that I had been there.

The irony of all of the mine-is-bigger-than-yours effort lies in the street's name...Karl-Marx-Allee wasn't always called Karl-Marx-Allee. Originally, from before the Middle Ages, it had always been the very wide boulevard that ultimately led out of Berlin to the east and thence to the next largest town of Frankfurt an der Oder.

In German, the street had always been named die Große Frankfurter Straße.

How could they have possibly known back then?

Luxembourgisch

One of the Berlin Brigade Band trips to the Benelux [Belgium, Netherlands, Luxembourg] was in support of a Community Relations request from Hautcharage, Luxembourg, a tiny town of about 1200 residents in a tiny country of about 400,000. Even so, the Hautcharage local festival beer tent was standing room only with an audience of 6,000—but the Grand Duchy of Luxembourg is one contradiction after another.

It is a separate country, but our entry into it by tourbus was the first time that I had experienced crossing an international border at 50 kph. There was no passport control point or customs shack—just a small sign on a pole and a yellow line in the road to let you know you had crossed the border.

The entire country is about 40km wide by 60km long and much of the northern portion is covered by the Ardennes forest. After leaving the unlimited speed of the German Autobahn, the max speed limit in Luxembourg of 50 KPH is like driving through Jell-O. But I think their intent was so you wouldn't fly right through and miss the country entirely.

We programmed away from our German selections since, like the Belgians, there was that pesky history that Luxembourg has had with Germany.

The mayor picked me up and drove me to the gig in his auto. As small talk, I asked him "Remy, what is the cradle language here in Luxembourg?"

"Why, David, but of course it is Lëtzebuergesch...in English Luxembourgish."

"Remy—there are only 400,000 people in the country. You have your own language?"

"Well, it is a patois of French and German and English and Flemish, what was called Franconian in ancient times. For instance, we would say, "D'Fra ass grouss." What do you think this means?"

I told him and he threw back his head and roared laughing as we hurtled down the expressway at 50 kph (32 mph). "No, no, no; that might be true. It might be rather large but this means the woman is tall."

"Oh...hmmm...Let's say I wanted to say 'Good Evening Ladies and Gentlemen' to the crowd tonight. What would that be?"

He replied,"Gudden Owend...Allegra," at which point, we fell silent except for the murmur as I chanted the mantra under my breath of, "Gudden Owend, Allegra...Gudden Owend, Allegra...Gudden Owend, Allegra."

At the end of the first number, I flipped on the mike and in an accent that was more reminiscent of the piazza in front of Saint Peter's than a beer tent, I waved my hands to the crowd in what must have looked like a benediction and said, "Gudden Owend, Allegra."

All 6,000 went absolutely bat-shit crazy in a frenzy of cheers and applause and stamping of feet on the temporary wooden floor. The joint was absolutely rocking. An American officer that spoke Lëtzebuergesch? Unheard of...

It felt so good, I hit them with it again, but louder and with more assurance. We got the same response, but louder and even more frenzied. If you listened closely, you could hear the echoes of Jeeps rumbling through the flower strewn streets 40 years before.

As was our custom, before we left Berlin the First Sergeant and I had reminded the band to get over to American Express and get some walking around money in the local currency. Because we travelled so much and there were so many local currencies, we always used the phrase "Make sure you get your zlotnys before the trip."

The band ended up taking their Luxembourg Francs back to Berlin with them. The crowd wouldn't allow them to spend one zlotny that night.

Namur, Belgium

The Berlin Brigade Band did quite a few jobs in the Benelux and each was memorable in its own way.

The band was scheduled to do a live broadcast TV show from the shopping district of Namur and a couple of gigs in outlying villes. We scrapped our normal German-oriented program, replacing Prussian marches with French and keeping our lighter fare.

We began the show with what in America is called The French National Defile March [in France the full title is Pas Redouble: Le Regiment de Sambre et Meuse] (if you've ever seen Ohio State University's band do Script Ohio, you've heard this march).

We then played through the program and, in an effort to quell the heavily-accented shouts of "Glenn Miller" "Glenn Miller" that followed us wherever we went on the Continent, we ended, as we almost always did, with the ubiquitous In The Mood, as a sax feature with the sax section fronting the stage.

At the end of the broadcast, the mayor of Namur came up for what was usually the obligatory "It was so nice having the band" thing. But no, he said words to this effect:

"Oh, Mr Smeeees, the program was brilliant. Here on a bandstand in Namur you began the show with the march that celebrates an epic battle...no, no, no THE epic battle of the Franco-Prussian War. It took place where two rivers meet—the river directly behind you is Le Sambre and it meets the River Meuse a mere half kilometre to your right. That would have been superior in itself, but then to finish the show honoring our most famous son, the inventor of the saxophone, Adolf Sax.

"In the ensuing 25 or so years, the good natives of Namur-Dinant have erected a statue to give visiting conductors a clue...

"...whose birthplace in Dinant is a mere half kilometre to your left. Brilliant! What exquisite planning you have done to make this special for us...magnificent...what an honor for Namur to have had the Berlin musicians here today." [this went on for another 5-10 minutes or so]...

I didn't have the heart to tell him that it was simply blind dumb luck. There simply isn't a more French march than the Defile, unless it's Marche Lorraine and, as I mentioned before, it was impossible to leave a stage in Europe without playing some Glenn Miller.

Belgium was always a challenge when it came to accommodations for the band, but the trip to Namur stands out as the worst place the band ever spent the night—beating out the time the band was stranded and ended up sleeping on the floor in the Judge Advocate General's courtroom in Bad Hersfeld during a once-in-a-100-year ice storm.

We were put up at the Belgian Commando Barracks outside of Namur. This was the mid-1980's and the senior folks in the band told stories of the "old days" of how rough the barracks were, with gang showers and that peculiarly Gallic invention, the squat-and-aim hole in the floor and Le Pissoir.

Two footprints. User would be facing the target hole. Grab bar as a concession to the Americans.

The first-timers individually and collectively responded with "Really?" "Huh?" "Nuh-uh" "When was THAT? The 50's?" "Why'd they do THAT?" and we boarded the Berlin-Frankfurt Duty Train for the first leg of the trip and then a Tourbus into Belgium. Let the trauma begin...

After the fairly lengthy ride, the entire unit exited the bus and went directly to find the facilities, conveniently located about a block and a half from the sleeping quarters—an unheated unisex gang latrine and shower area, so when I entered, I was surprised to find small groups of 5-6 bandmembers clustered around the various squat holes. Did I mention that this was the Belgian Commando Barracks? None of that sit-down-while-you-do-your-business thing for them. My folks were too shocked and awed to actually use the facilities. Then they were hit with the combination punch that followed—the barracks itself.

The barracks, like the epic battle at the two rivers above, dated from the Franco-Prussian War—say about 1870 or so. Think of the stage set for the Dickensian orphanage in Annie and double the dreariness factor. Ancient cracked and rotted wainscotting to about 30 inches off the floor topped with absolutely filthy, dingy fly-specked windows that completed every interior wall topped with institutional green paint on the load-bearing exterior walls. This was also the instance when the band realized that many other armies of the world do not issue mattresses and linen to the troops—just blankets and moderately clean straw that is placed on plywood shelves. The bus had left; the bus driver actually went into town to find a place to stay, and the band did what they always did the best—they soldiered through the situation.

About 11:00 that night, as I was reading in my officer-hovel, I thought that the barracks were abnormally quiet even for that time of night. (The only other time that I experienced barracks that were this still was when the band played for a week in Norway—all of the gigs were in the evening and ran really late, so our initial formation of the day was around 4:00 PM. I asked 1SG Joe Martin where everyone was, but he stood up for his guys and didn't tell me. I later found out that everyone had discovered the nude beach two tram stops away from the Norwegian barracks. But that's another story...)

I couldn't help it, I had to find out where everyone was. I went outside and heard what sounded like a party in the Enlisted Club on the Belgian Kaserne. In an effort to be anywhere-other-than-the-barracks-rooms-from-hell, the band had talked the manager of the Club to stay open later than usual. Their answer to the adversity was to watch videos (in French, although the story lines of these particular videos were fairly explicit and easy to follow) on the club's TV system and to support the Belgian Morale Welfare and Recreation Fund by buying many, many drinks from the club. I slowly backed out of the Club and quietly closed the door.

The next morning, everyone lined up at the chow hall for breakfast. The Belgian cooks were gracious enough to attempt an American breakfast, complete with fried eggs. Deep-fried eggs—deep-fried, like french fries. Fried eggs—it's a cultural thing in the land of Pommes Frites. SSG Willie Pollock ("PK"), curiously enough one of those sax players who so honored Adolph Sax the day before, went behind the food service line and mimed some instructions to the Belgian cooks who began to furiously crack two eggs each into little bowls while PK scraped the grill clean to the welcomed cry "How you want your eggs?" that is bellowed out by US Army cooks each morning the world over.

East Berlin – Random Thoughts

Excerpt from President Reagan's speech, June 12, 1987:

"Years ago, before the East Germans began rebuilding their churches, they erected a secular structure: the television tower at Alexanderplatz. Virtually ever since, the authorities have been working to correct what they view as the tower's one major flaw: treating the glass sphere at the top with paints and chemicals of every kind. Yet even today when the sun strikes that sphere, that sphere that towers over all Berlin, the light makes the sign of the cross. There in Berlin, like the city itself, symbols of love, symbols of worship, cannot be suppressed."

For technically adept East Berliners who could rig their televisions sets, Western TV shows also could not be suppressed—which which caused me a few awkward situations.

While US Forces were free to cross Checkpoint Charlie and had access to East Berlin, one of the rules was that we remove our nametags as a passive counterintelligence effort. If they couldn't readily read your nametag, then close contact was that much more removed from the equation.

On a number of occasions, usually during a shopping trip out on the street, an East Berliner who had seen coverage of one of the Brigade Band's performances on TV would say, "Look, it's the American Kapellmeister! Oh, sir, we love your music. Can we have an autograph?"

East Germany was a police state after all and by definition that meant at least a cop or two on every street corner. The unwarranted attention from my well-wishers usually prompted me to start looking, on their behalf, for Stasi (DDR Secret Police) or at least an interested Volkspolizist (normal cop).

Question: How do you double the value of a Trabbi?

Answer: Fill it with gas

DDR *humor, circa 1985*

The police couldn't have done anything to a member of the Occupation Forces, but it would have made a bunch of trouble for my newfound fans. As I made my way to the late 70's silver Oldsmobile that I eventually sold to Al Lawless—like THAT didn't stick out among all of the Trabants (Trabbis). The Olds was a diesel. It even sounded odd in the East and disappeared in a large black cloud of smoke, a la David Copperfield.

An exception to the uniform, Orwellian grey pall that fell across East Berlin streets were the bright spots of color provided by the Ampelmännchen...the little guys on the lights at all the crosswalks.

Crosswalk signals anywhere in the world were unknown before the 1960s—and they've taken various forms across the world. In the states, initially words were used (WALK...DONT WALK). West Germany devised a pictogram of a svelt figure in stride—a figure in repose, as well as a green bike/red bike for bike trails and a special signal for Straßenbahn crossings. The newest signals in America now show a green walking figure or a red palm-extended hand, as well displaying the time left to cross all in LED lights.

The original design in East Germany was Ampelmann—walking-with-a-purpose-with-a-big-stride in green, and arms extended in the Polizei signal-that-everyone-learned-in German-driver-license-course-that-meant-HALT in red...both with that outrageous fedora from the 40s-50s.

Economics being what they were in the East, Ampelmann remained unchanged from his original 1960's incarnation...thru the 70s and 80s all the way up to Reunification...then, even with the economic means to modernize the crossing signals, the choice was made to keep the little guy just the way he was. Nostalgia won the day for the Ampelmännchen.

In Dresden, they've even recently given Ampelmann an Ampelfrau.

Mädchen Musikzug Neumünster

We had just finished a parade to kick off the Soap Box Derby competition in the Berlin district of Tempelhof when the leader of one of the other marching units stopped me to ask whether or not the Berlin Brigade Band would be available to play in a town called Neumünster in a joint concert with his band.

This exchange was overheard by a number of Berlin Brigade bandmembers who were packing up instruments and when they saw that the guy had been followed by three of his bandmembers, my guys immediately began to lobby that it would be very proper to reach out to our allies in our host country through the universal language of music, and in the spirit of friendship, accept the guy's most gracious offer—to endure the rigors of the road and travel to Neumünster to perform with his Musikkorps.

Their fervor might have been the reaction to the three Musikkorps bandmembers that tagged along with their director—dressed in their uniform tricorn hats, red jackets, very short white skirts and boots, the uniform of the Neumünster Mädchen Musikzug. An all-girl (and pretty much all-blond) band.

Stinky Cheese

The Berlin Brigade Band ranged across most of northern Europe playing in excess of 200 gigs each year. In most cases, the sponsor would host a reception for the band and the local bigwigs would all attend.

We would finish the gig, quickly put away the instruments and then proceed to the reception venue. Because of the time delay, there was usually a crowd of local folks waiting for the double doors to open into the reception hall. As we made our way through the assembled townsfolk, the doors would open and, if it was anywhere northwest of Hamburg in the German Jutland heading towards Denmark, we would be smacked in the face by the overpowering odor of what the band called stinky cheese, as in, "Ahhhh maaaan, gee sir, they're serving stinky cheese at this one, too."

This was not always the case. We played a gig somewhere in Belgium and the reception was the exception—a sitdown dinner in a restaurant. I was seated next to the mayor and the meal was simply superb: meat, potatoes and vegetables (not our usual road trip diet).

The meat had been encrusted in locally-produced mustard and then roasted. Knowing that the mustard was a local source of pride, when the mayor asked how my meal was, I replied that "the meat was wonderful but your regional mustard is simply a thing of beauty" or some such thing.

He smiled broadly—quite literally beamed at the compliment, and then turned away while motioning to one of his henchmen/bodyguards to come to the table. He whispered something to the guy who did his best imitation of being placed in the StarTrek transporter and all but got shimmery/sparkly and immediately disappeared.

He returned about 30 minutes later. It's after midnight and it seems the mayor had the guy wake up the proprietor of a local store, open the place up and secure a 5 liter crock of the mustard as 'un petite souvenir.'

Petite it wasn't—think of a Heineken keglet.

I accepted the offering on behalf of all the American people in the spirit of friendship shared by our two great nations, etc. Pictures were taken for the Local Bugle/Register/Enquirer to publish and we finished the evening. Fast forward to next morning as the bus is getting ready to depart.

What am I going to do with this office-waste-basket-sized jar of mustard? This was the first job on a fairly extended road trip and we have many more stops before we return to Berlin.

I can't leave it here...they'll know.

I can't leave it in the next town...they'll see where it came from and perhaps taunt the guy who gave it to me, to paraphrase, "You see, Jacques, zee Americains do not really honor zee mustard of your town. Shall we return to you your pathetic leetle geeeft?" (Think Belgian-French accent as opposed to

Al Pacino here.)

Or the next town.

Or the next.

The mustard became not only my travelling companion, but a dear friend. Except for jobs and receptions, we were never separated. We sat together on the bus. I lived in a very real fear that the jar would break turning my Army Blue uniforms into Army Greens. I invited it up to my room at every stop and put it in a place of safekeeping.

It wouldn't fit in the suitcase, so at every new town as the mustard and I got off the bus, I was greeted with astonished looks from our new hosts that simply screamed, "Who knew that Americans were so devoted to mustard?" It got to the point that I tried to conceal the thing under my raincoat. I'm amazed one of the sponsors didn't stage an intervention and suggest a 12-step program to deal with what must have seemed like a secretive, shameful and unnatural fetish right out of a Fellini movie.

I was seriously facing the prospect of returning to Berlin and answering my pre-teen daughters' "What did you bring us, Daddy?" question with a rather lame and whiney, "A lifetime supply of mustard?"

But I digress. The mustard was resting in my room in whatever town we were in and there was a gig followed by a reception. And the band just simply knew that a stinky cheese moment awaited them behind the closed double doors.

Experience is a hell of a teacher—after just a first few road trips, even the rookies in the band could acquire the target of the stinky cheese table from the reception hall doorway and divert their course to the cold cuts table and then the beer table.

The doors open. The band picks up the scent as it enters the reception hall, confirms the presence of stinky cheese and with the zeal of a swarm of hungry squirrels sighting a pile of acorns in late Autumn, heads toward the cold cuts en masse.

I had been diverted upon entry, so I'm watching this from near the doorway. The front-most chow hounds slam on the brakes causing a Three Stooges-like pile-up. Then the entire blue-suited swarm veers off to the left and ferociously attacks the stinky cheese table, reveling and exalting in their good fortune in finding stinky cheese and sandwich makings and that the beer table was very well-stocked.

Who knew that the local delicacy in this town was pork tartar?

THE PERFORMANCE PROCESS

Audiences see a musical ensemble such as the 298th take the stage and begin a performance, not always realizing that the moment at which that ensemble takes the stage is the culmination of a chain of events that started long before. First, the organizers have scheduled an event that requires musical support. They then make application to the 298th to check on availability and perhaps approval. The organizer provides detailed information to address the logistical needs of the band and, depending on the details and availability, the band is booked.

Event organizers did not pay the 298th Army Band or the U.S. Army for the band's services. But organizers did have to take normal logistical matters into consideration such as transportation, billeting, meals, and, where required, pay to provide those amenities. Particularly important, due to the 298th's location in West Berlin, was transportation.

These criteria all had to be addressed irrespective of the type of request received. All the same, the 298th's support of the Berlin command came first. By far, ceremonies comprised the majority of jobs requiring the full band. These jobs were the most basic, requiring nothing more from the sponsor other than the vehicles normally provided for the band. These vehicles ranged from 2.5-ton trucks to plush motor coaches.

Ceremonies, then, are an Army band's "bread and butter." The commander wants to honor and decorate his soldiers and see them together in one setting. Ceremonies bring help bring esprit to a military unit and while a band isn't required for a commander to have a formation and observe his troops, a band adds the acoustic and the visual effect to make the effort worthy. The unit sees that good performance is rewarded and that provides incentive. The unit coalesces and solidifies. The commander gets a more combat-ready force, which is his objective.

The 298th and 300th Infantry bands received movement orders in mid-1945 to support the Potsdam Conference by providing appropriate music throughout the event. The photographs depict lawn concerts and ceremonies. The two bands, acting as one, served another key function by supporting the initial flag-raising ceremony at the Allied Control Council near Kleistpark in Schöneberg. This most important of ceremonies at the site of the former supreme court of the state of Prussia known as the Kammergericht heralded the United States' official beginning of occupation duties. President Truman and Generals Eisenhower, Patton and Bradley, along with many others, attended this ceremony thereby demonstrating the importance of this event; it culminated the entire European war's effort and signified the long-desired peace. President Truman's remarks spoken without notes underlined his desire that the Peace for mankind and prosperity for all still remained the goal for the United States, thereby requiring the continuance of the war in the Pacific. Reparations, territory, and similar spoils of war taken by a conqueror were not objectives and would not be sought, Truman said.

This ceremony characterized the nature of the assignment to Berlin. Attended by various politicians and senior military leaders, this ceremony and many others like it that followed spoke of hope and determination. Truman's words were prescient.

Colonel Frank Howley documented the contentious atmosphere of the Allied Control Council in Berlin, particularly involving the Soviets and their style of obfuscation, deflection, and outright lies. It didn't take long for this kind of behavior to alienate Colonel Howley and others. In an effort to smooth over the relationship, decision makers assigned the 298th and a Soviet band, presumably stationed in East Berlin, to participate in a concert on every fourth Sunday. Those efforts didn't work. On March 20, 1948, Marshal Vasily Sokolovsky, U.S.S.R.'s representative, walked out of the council. The Soviet Union never attended another meeting. Use of the 298th in partnership with another Allied band attempted to use music to overcome political agendas and while it was unsuccessful, the effort reveals the power of music to overcome adversity, even on the international level.

As the Allied Control Authority worked on the whole of Germany, the Allied Kommandatura formed the military governing arm specific for Berlin. The officials of the Kommandatura worked out of a smaller building in the sub-district of Dahlem, located not far from Clay Headquarters.

One specific ceremony occurred in front of the Allied Kommandatura in 1983. The ceremony's purpose is long forgotten, but Tripartite ceremonies such as this required elements of the three Western Allies. The 298th was called on to provide music for the ceremony, but British forces organized this particular event. British regimental sergeants major have a distinctive quality when they are addressing their charges. Their approach consists of unintelligible screaming of drill and ceremonial commands, understandable to the British Army soldier, but generally indecipherable to any other nation's soldier. This particular RSM enjoyed his craft, which required considerable vocal cord strength and endurance.

Over the months and years to come, the 298th participated in all manner of ceremonies. Ranging from single buglers sounding Reveille to the entire band's presence while Taps was sounded, most ceremonies involved a change of command, honor guard, or Retreat. Special ceremonies included the Salute to the Union on Independence Day and the funeral ceremony for President Kennedy on Andrews Barracks. Another special ceremony occurred in 1985 when the 298th played separate battalion funeral parades for two soldiers who were victims of the LaBelle disco bombing. Irrespective of the occasion, the 298th Army Band's purpose was to support the ceremony and lend a martial air to it.

Honor guard ceremonies, particularly in the early years of the 298th's assignment in Berlin, comprised a large portion of the band's performance schedule. Held at either Tempelhof Central Airport or at Office of Military Government, United States (OMGUS)/Clay Headquarters, these short ceremonies provided an official welcome to political leaders, military officials, and even some Hollywood celebrities. Wallace Beery, for one, visited Berlin in 1947.

CWO Marion Durbin's historical reports chronicle the more significant honor guard ceremonies. They averaged about two per month.

Political leaders also visited Berlin, including President Kennedy in June 1963, President Nixon in February 1969, merely five weeks after he assumed office; and Vice President Humphrey in April 1967. President Reagan visited twice; the first time in June 1982 and the second five years later. Before and after his presidency, Mr. Reagan came to Berlin in November 1978 and September 1990, respectively. General Lucius Clay also received an honor guard welcome upon his re-arrival in Berlin in September 1961 as President Kennedy's envoy, and also at his departure in early 1962.

All of these ceremonies required preparation and at least a measure of logistical support. Training and drill band generally took care of the musical preparation, and band personnel took care of the logistics, through the support of the event organizer.

The 298th performed more than just ceremonies. Clarinetist Harry Reinert spoke of Sunday afternoon concerts on the lawn of Truman Hall, just across the street from OMGUS. The stage band often performed at Club 48 in those early days. Christmas and holiday concerts using the full concert band entertained the American community, as did scheduled and impromptu performances by smaller ensembles in the Clay HQ foyer. Bandsmen pressed into service as vocalists sang Christmas carols on Christmas Eve in 1952 on the staircases leading up to the U.S. Commander, Berlin's office suite, conducted by the bandmaster, CWO Wilbur Moyer. One characteristic about the foyer in "Building One," foyer was that it featured marble floors and stone walls. These hard surfaces provided a "live" sound with much reverberation that carried throughout the entire building.

Vocal performances occurred periodically, but not regularly, throughout the 298th's existence. Trumpeter Lawrence "Fish" Brown details his own activity within a combination Berliner/American glee club. Outfitted with stylish sport coats with a distinctive blazer pin, this group found opportunities to sing throughout the city. Clarinetist and Woodwind Group Leader John Gerding formed a temporary vocal group to sing at the Harnack House Officer's Club in the early 1980s in commemoration of West Point Founder's Day. In the late 1980s, clarinetist Todd Mastric used his music leadership skills and formed the Berlin Brigade Soldier's Chorus. Comprised of singers throughout the Brigade other than the 298th, Todd developed a program patterned on airborne paratroopers and used choreography along with the vocal work to entertain. Very popular with the soldiers performance in the Chorus, the Chorus was nonetheless broken up when higher headquarters realized that non-musicians were used to perform music-related tasks.

Despite the skills and abilities of any single musician, the ensemble assigned the job had to prepare for its performances. This meant rehearsals and individual practice to sustain those skills and increase endurance.

Musical Support for the Berlin Command

The German-American Volksfest, a collection of carnival-type rides, events, and entertainment that featured an American theme, began running in late July 1961. The 1961 Volksfest ended precisely on the day the East Germans began building the Wall, August 13, 1961. This event was hugely popular with the Berliners, many of whom traveled across the city to partake of some typical American wares.

298th Stage Band, led by Al Nelson

The 298th supported the Volksfest in many ways, using the full capability of the band. Ranging from short parades through the festival grounds to full concerts on the main stage, the 298th usually performed in one fashion or another each day of the festival, to include the official opening. Photographs provided by trumpeter Robert Jones (1966-69) depict the 298th marching band dressed in the Class A green uniform with music pouches marching through the festival grounds. Al Nelson led the stage band in the early 1970s; James (Dutch) Perry led the stage band in the late 1980s; and MSG Lou Hurvitz played piano in the early 1980s at each Volksfest.

Lou describes his participation in the 1983 Volksfest, "I was heavily involved as rehearsal and performance pianist/accompanist for the 'Cotton Blossom Revue,' centered around the Jerome Kern musical, Showboat. The performances took place on the "Riverboat Stage...." Dressed fully in costume typical of the era, that is, a red and white, vertical striped, vest and derby hat, Lou performed on a daily basis bringing a bit of America to the onlookers, day after day. In developing the show, Lou described said that the planners were not permitted to perform Showboat's most famous piece, Ol' Man River. The Brigade Commander, Brigadier General Leroy Suddath, believed the piece depicting Negro slaves in 19th Century America was inappropriate for the times.

One of Lou's very many talents was his ability to perform on the fly. Lou said via email, "I recall one performance featuring the vocal soloists and me performing an afternoon show at Truman Plaza. For one selection, a recorded orchestral accompaniment was used and my piano services were not needed. So, I stood up and stretched my legs. As luck would have it, the power went out, ending the recorded background. I quickly jumped on the piano bench and provided the background for the singers. After the performance, each of the female singers came up to me and gave me a big kiss on my (facial) cheeks. They were all wearing VERY red lipstick. Prior to taking the duty shuttle back to Andrews Barracks, I did my best to obliterate the marks."

The 298th commander often used the full concert band in Volksfest performances. Playing any number of rousing patriotic marches to more contemporary music of the day, the concert band's performances were well attended and appreciated. CWO David M. Smith conducted a particularly good arrangement of Billy Joel tunes in the 1984 Volksfest. Programming Billy Joel's music as played by the concert band brought that style not to just the audience, but to the band itself. Programming lighter fare for an audience that might be sipping on an American beer or eating American ice cream worked better than a heavier classical piece.

The 298th performed alongside the railroad tracks when Berlin Brigade troops returned from extended training exercises in West Germany. Known as "duty train gigs," these required the band to form at about 4:00 a.m. and take a short bus ride up to the Lichterfelde West S-Bahn station. The Berlin command's Rail Transportation Office (RTO) and the terminus for both duty trains from Frankfurt and Bremerhaven lay adjacent to the S-Bahn station. A battalion at a time, soldiers disembarked the train, found their platoon and company, formed, took accountability, then either marched to McNair Barracks or climbed aboard other vehicles for the ride home. Throughout all of this activity, generally occurring at 5 a.m., the band played pouch music—sometimes rather loudly.

Band members, sometimes half-asleep themselves, found the atmosphere associated with duty train gigs a little surreal. Lighting conditions led to problems in reading music, even of familiar pouch tunes selected to welcome home tired, dirty troops. The band often had to move to find better lighting and to somehow stay out of the way of the jostling, noisy formations and other passengers. Many of the passengers not affiliated with the returning troops were new to Berlin. They looked at the mob scene with some trepidation and carried crying children rubbing sleep out of their eyes as they looked to find their next mode of transportation or make return reservations inside the RTO.

Band Operations timed events best as possible to reduce waiting time before the first train arrived. However, because of processing through the various Soviet checkpoints and unpredictable delays, the band had to be on site if the train arrived a few moments early. The band waited alongside the tracks, dressed for the weather. Eventually, from the direction of Zehlendorf, the train engine's searchlight plainly visible, the train slowly arrived and stopped. Noise escalated due to the engine's big diesel and the brakes shrieking in protest. The atmosphere was cacophonous, because by then the band was cranking out tunes from music pouches, trying hard to be heard over the din.

One particular troop return at the RTO featured the presence of the Deputy Brigade Commander, Colonel Michael Collins, who sported a cast on a broken foot sustained while running, and Command Sergeant Major Gary Donaldson, CSM of the Berlin Brigade. A Berliner approached the entourage, clearly upset. After speaking to anybody who paid any attention to him, he finally directed his comments toward CSM Donaldson, who merely nodded at his comments. Colonel Collins looked on, but said nothing. After the man had spoken his piece, clearly complaining about something, CSM Donaldson informed Colonel Collins that the man was complaining about all the noise, particularly emanating from the band. Colonel Collins' only comment was, "Well, we've only got one more train to greet. We'll be done with all this by 0530 or so, then they can all go back to sleep while the rest of us get on with our day."

The 298th waited for the Bremerhaven train, which arrived about 20 minutes later. The entire scene replayed itself, though on a smaller scale. The Bremerhaven train invariably had fewer passengers on board, even though the train commanders and conductors endeavored to switch some cars from the Frankfurt train to the Bremerhaven train to even it out slightly, as both trains waited at the East German border for processing.

Once back in Berlin, the Open House at Tempelhof Central Airport provided more performance opportunity for the 298th. Situated directly on TCA's tarmac with various aircraft parked allowing tours inside, food stands providing the usual festival snacks, and throngs of people, the band played on a temporary bandstand while onlookers sampled the offerings. The TCA Open House in 1988 yielded an interesting twist on an otherwise predictable acoustic concert band gig working out of music pouches only. At about 50 minutes into the 1-hour performance, the conductor—a senior NCO on this occasion—looked around the audience and noted several large movie cameras wielded by men lassoed to sound men with microphones on booms. A person beckoned and approached the bandstand.

The man introduced himself as one of the producers for a Hollywood film being shot in Berlin. Entitled Judgment in Berlin, this film starred Martin Sheen, Sam Wanamaker, and a younger Sean Penn. He asked if the band would consider playing a little beyond the 1-hour limit, and the conductor readily agreed. Calling up a couple additional selections, the band continued to play while the cameramen and soundmen filmed from several angles. The band concluded its concert and packed its gear. Tubist Erik Percoski recalled that he'd forgotten his cigarettes. Martin Sheen offered him one.

The director of the film planned for and obtained crowd scenes from the Open House as part of the movie. The 298th's presence at the time of the film shooting was merely happenstance. While the director obtained the additional footage of the band, all of that wound up on the cutting room floor. None of it made it into the film.

The French command sponsored a 25-kilometer run, which started close to Olympic Stadium in the British sector, and ended in the stadium itself. For those 298th musicians not directly participating in the run, the rest of the band formed and played a quasi-marching show on the field itself. Berlin hosted the summer Olympic games in that stadium in 1936. Adolf Hitler was embarrassed that Jesse Owens, a black man, soundly beat his German and international opponents, winning four gold medals. Hitler had been sure that his German sprinters would dominate those events.

The British command's grand show of the year was the annual Queen's Birthday. This spectacle took place on the Maifeld, a large, manicured field adjacent to Olympic Stadium where, during the 1936 Olympics, competitions in polo and equestrian events took place. The Queen herself and her family occasionally attended this large and detailed ceremony, featuring honor salutes fired by the larger howitzers using blank ammunition and marching maneuvers by foot soldiers.

Operation Cheer; Fasching Anfang & Parades; Platz Concerts

Throughout the 1950s when refugees from the Eastern bloc began crossing the Iron Curtain, the 298th performed concerts at various refugee centers within the city. These concerts, provided as a part of Operation Cheer, allowed the Western Allies to extend a hand in welcome to those looking for a better life. One of the larger refugee centers was located in Marienfelde, in the southern part of the American sector. An especially effective technique employed by the conductor entailed finding a child at random and then inviting him or her to come forward to conduct the next piece. The child's reaction to suddenly being thrust in the limelight, either enthralled or terrified, brought smiles to the audience as they realized the 298th encouraged them as they sought their own type of freedom.

The pre-Lenten festivities customarily called Fasching begin on November 11th at 11:11 a.m. across Germany, though Fasching itself was more popular in the south and west of Germany. However, Berlin's Neukölln district, in the north and east of Germany, celebrated the opening of the Fasching season by holding a large Sitzung, or council, in which participants dress themselves in bright colored costumes and garish hats curiously reminiscent of the Army's overseas cap, though much larger and more colorful. Throughout the Sitzung, speakers poked fun at politicians or personalities of the day. Intermittent through these endless speeches, on cue, the house band played a loud, raucous chord to accent the point just made. The 298th performed several of these Sitzungen in Neukölln.

Fasching, also known as Karneval which translates to Mardi Gras in New Orleans and Carnival in Rio de Janiero, calms down through the Christmas season and mostly through the New Year until the week before Ash Wednesday and the beginning of Lent. Fasching, as a precursor to Lent, has more of a religious bent in southern Germany where the Roman Catholic presence is stronger, but the headlines of Fasching and the more popular parades are found in the Köln and Rhineland regions. Rosenmontag, or Rose Monday, occurs on the Monday before Ash Wednesday and is the capstone of Fasching's celebrations.

For the 298th, participating in Fasching events outside of Berlin meant another trip on the Frankfurt duty train. The duty train was more than a mode of transportation. It was part of the job itself, and therefore deserves some explanation.

Forming at about 6 p.m., the band packed up marching instruments, music pouches, and appropriate gear and loaded them and uniform bags on the bus for the short trip to the RTO. After collecting ID cards, the band was dismissed for a short time to allow for document processing. Many band members took the opportunity to convene in a neighborhood Kneipe located just across the street from the RTO for a little refreshment. After a beverage, the band formed again at the RTO for compartment assignments, which Band Operations staff had already finalized. After packing the instruments in the baggage car of the train, located just behind the train's engine, the band boarded the train at their assigned car and awaited departure.

The duty train traveled overnight and featured compartments in which the normal seating areas were already formed into beds. A narrow passageway ran along one side of the rail car. Restrooms, which featured toilets that emptied directly onto the tracks below, were located on the end of each car where a door connected one rail car from the next. Signs requested passengers not to use the facilities while the train was stopped, for obvious reasons. This sign was not always obeyed, particularly at stops in East Germany. After departure at 8:15 p.m., the 298th passengers settled in for the trip. Band members then encountered the ubiquitous Schaffner (porter) hawking refreshments on the train, who announced his presence by rapping on the compartment door with a coin intoning, "Coffee! Tea! Marblecake!" His cart was laden with instant coffee, tepid and not nearly up to German standards, and the tea wasn't much better.

The train traveled slowly out of the RTO and headed toward the various checkpoints, the first being in Potsdam where the West German engine was exchanged for an East German engine. The train commander and NCO conductor disembarked and presented flag orders and ID cards to the Soviets for processing. While the Soviets processed documents, the train commander and NCO executed a walk-around inspection of the train while halted. Soviet sentries observed this process from a discreet distance. Following this process, the train proceeded slowly through East Germany, a distance of about 110 miles, stopping at various places, before arriving at the Soviet checkpoint in Marienborn where the Potsdam process was repeated. Train engineers and workers then uncoupled the East German engine and attached a West German engine for the trip across the border and into West Germany. Once across the border in West Germany, the train picked up speed and stopped less frequently. The 298th, however, disembarked in Kassel at approximately 4 a.m., where it was imperative to do so quickly. The train schedule permitted only a 10-minute stop in Kassel.

After arguing with a train station employee who initially didn't allow the band the use of the platform elevator, a Band Operations NCO convinced the man to unlock it. The band grabbed its gear and moved to the exit of the Kassel train station and encountered the ubiquitous "green weenie" Army school bus. Outfitted with frosted windows and poorly functioning heat, this bus served as the transportation medium for the 298th from the Kassel train station to Bad Hersfeld, located about an hour away. An Army 5-ton truck provided the transportation for instruments, gear, and uniform bags.

Once in Bad Hersfeld, about 5:30 a.m., the 298th was dropped off at one of the Army dining facilities for breakfast. Paying the obligatory fee as the band members were all paid an additional sum of money each month to provide their own meals, a stipend known as "separate rations," the band sat down to eat. Following breakfast, the band boarded the bus again and headed to an Army gymnasium to change from civilian clothing into uniform and to prepare for the day's activities. Beginning with another Fasching Sitzung in the late morning, the band heard the non-stop speeches, awaiting the cue to play endless B-flat major chords. Following this encounter, the band moved over to the start point of the Fasching parade and waited.

Band Operations personnel provided a uniform and packing list as preparation for this job, decisions that required evaluation of not just the type of commitment but the weather as well. On one Fasching parade, the weather forecast included snow deep enough to require combat boots to be worn under the dress blues trousers instead of the normal low quarter shoes.

For this particular Fasching parade, weather conditions at noon were about 40° F., with a chance of rain forecast.

An hour after the scheduled start time during which the band often played music for those onlookers who were already in the festive spirit, the parade started. And then stopped, briefly, before starting again. Occasionally, a person dressed in a typical Fasching costume would meander through the formation, equipped with a tray, a dozen or more shot glasses, and a bottle of schnapps. The schnapps did a good job of fending off the cold and helped provide a bit of revelry for the band as well. As most of the onlookers had had a fair amount to imbibe, on occasion the celebrations got out of hand. Sousaphones were a prime target for those throwing hard candy, which resulted in the corresponding dents. Sousaphone players learned in subsequent years to place a fabric cover over the bell, thereby preventing tipsy onlookers from scoring a "goal." More seriously, a half-open can of beer was tossed, hitting a bandsman on the head. No injury resulted, but the band's formation tightened up and playing stopped. Parade officials moved in to escort the band through the area. One bandsman, marching on the right file of the band closest to the onlookers, experienced soccer of a different type. An onlooker dropped an ear of corn down the bell of his euphonium. This act could have resulted in a chipped tooth or worse, but apart from a jolt to the face, no permanent damage was done. Eventually, after a dozen or more stops during which the band played a pop tune for the crowd, the parade ended. Countless horse droppings, piles of slushy snow, and shouts of "Helau!", a Fasching greeting that is intended to keep evil spirits away and a throwback to Fasching's religious origin, were encountered. The band survived another Fasching parade.

Toward 3 p.m. or roughly two hours after the parade started, the band found its bus, truck and drivers, and packed away instruments. The weather worsened. Temperatures dropped 20° F. since the start of the parade and the rain began falling, converting into ice when it hit the pavement. After the parade, the band prepared to travel down to Giessen to pick up the Frankfurt-Berlin duty train on its way north and east toward home. Since the duty train left Frankfurt at about 7:30 p.m., the train normally arrived in Giessen at about

8:30 p.m. There should have been plenty of time to make the one-hour trip to Giessen, but for the worsening weather. CWO David M. Smith said, "We had driven approximately 10km of the 90km trip to Giessen, and at that rate we'd arrive Giessen about 7 hours after our train departed."

Mr. Smith ordered the bus and truck to return to Bad Hersfeld, arriving there two hours later. On the return trip, the road conditions had deteriorated to the point that only the bus's forward momentum kept it from sliding sideways from the crown of the road to the shoulder. Operations Sergeant Dave Olszyk recalled getting out of the bus at one point to test the road surface. He remarked on social media, "It was more appropriate for Katarina Witt [a noted German Olympian ice skater] than for motorized travel." Once back in Bad Hersfeld, Mr. Smith and the Operations staff got to work. Calling the Bad Hersfeld Officer of the Day to try to arrange for meals and billeting, the answer came back—no billeting available, dining facility closed. The best that could be done was to have the band get something to eat in the McPheeters Barracks bowling alley. After NCOs made sure their people got something to eat, the next task was to try and find a place to hole up for the night.

The answer came in the form of the courtroom. The Judge Advocate General (JAG) had a courtroom that could be pressed into service as a place for a bunch of tired soldier/musicians to spend the night. Dave Olszyk arranged for and obtained sleeping bags and foam mattresses from the Army's Central Issue Facility. The JAG and his staff of lawyers and German secretaries weren't notified of this arrangement, so when they arrived at 7 a.m. the next morning and encountered a pile of sleeping and grunting bodies scattered throughout their courtroom, they were startled.

Meanwhile the effort continued to coordinate with Berlin for Finance to release approximately DM 9,000 for normal German railroad tickets. As the band missed the duty train the previous evening and had not manifested on the next night's train, travel via duty train was impossible at this late time. The only option was to get the band on the German rail system out of Bad Hersfeld and north to Helmstedt. Helmstedt was the official crossover point for travelers driving to and from Berlin and located directly on the border between East and West Germany. In Helmstedt, buses would be waiting to make the transit to Berlin. Flag orders, the travel documents necessary to transit the East German corridor, were already prepared.

After much bureaucracy and back-and-forth, Berlin finance released the funds and purchased the necessary rail tickets. The band boarded the German train in Bad Hersfeld and encountered jammed train compartments as the ice storm had affected most of Germany, negating travel on the autobahn. The best the band could do was to muscle onto the cars wherever they could, perch on bass drum/sousaphone cases, and hook their garment bags onto whatever appendage could be found. Following this encounter, the entire area of Bad Hersfeld/Fulda became known as the "Fulda Triangle."

Fulda, a small town located about 45 minutes south of Bad Hersfeld, hosted other elements of the 11th ACR. Both towns, Bad Hersfeld and Fulda, became focal points for the 298th in the mid-1980s. While other Army bands, particularly in Würzburg and Frankfurt, were geographically closer than the 298th in Berlin, the 298th had developed a rapport with the 11th Armored Cavalry Regiment's commander and support staff, along with the town officials themselves. Consequently, the 298th supported the 11th ACR on many occasions during this time to the point that entering the "Fulda Triangle" was easier than leaving it.

Larry Hill, tubist with the 298th, recalled a hail storm in the middle of yet another Fulda/Bad Hersfeld parade. Pelted with pieces of ice, trumpeter Dave Slothower (1986-89) played a remarkably well-controlled trumpet solo to the tune "Brazil" through the most furious part of the hail storm as the band staggered up the street.

The 298th, along with all other Germany-based bands, performed Platz concerts frequently. Requiring little equipment other than instruments and no sound reinforcement and operating out of music pouches, these jobs provided entertainment on the fly. Easy to set up and tear down, platz concerts comprised the principal way in which the 298th entertained the German audience. These setups could and often were augmented with minimal additional equipment such as sound reinforcement for singers, instrumental soloists, and the announcer. With such setups, the 298th performed dozens of such events throughout Berlin and the rest of Europe, even in winter when freezing weather threatened to render trombone slides and trumpet/euphonium/tuba piston valves stuck.

One such event occurred just prior to Christmas. Known as the Alt Rixdorf Christmas Market ("Alt Rixdorf" being an earlier designation for the northern part of the Neukölln district), this annual affair took place close to Richardplatz, the heart of Neukölln. Vendors set up their individual stands, each offering various types of ornaments, Christmas objects, small gifts, and the traditional mulled wine known as "Glühwein." Entertainment was also offered at designated times. The 298th participated and provided entertainment for shoppers and onlookers who clutched their steaming cups of Glühwein and hot chocolate to combat the cold. Seizing an opportunity, CWO David Smith authorized old-fashioned "Turm-musick" by stationing small antiphonal brass quartets in the lofts of opposing buildings. The result was a glorious rendition of Baroque music in the spirit in which it was performed hundreds of years ago. Trumpeter Billy Weems (1985-88) led one of these antiphonal quartets by his consistent, excellent playing, which carried over into the other quartet from across Richardplatz.

Still other Platz concerts were performed throughout Berlin for various types of street festivals. Most such festivals occurred in the Spring-Summer-Fall seasons, but typically occurred regardless of weather conditions. They all featured a central small entertainment stage surrounded by a type of tent structure. The length of the street offered vendors selling their wares ranging from Bratwurst with French fries to Döner kebaps, to typical carnival food, to plastic cups of Schultheiss or Berliner Kindl beer. The 298th arrived at the designated time, set up, and played. Afterwards, the event organizers presented a number of tickets which the band could use to obtain snacks and drinks.

Other Berlin Performances

Beginning in the 1960s and carrying over until deactivation, all three Western Allied bands convened to perform "Gute Freunde Musizieren für Berlin." The event, organized as a charitable fund raiser for the victims of crime, initially began in the Berliner Sportpalast. The Sportpalast, located in Schöneberg and built in 1910 principally as an indoor ice hockey and skating rink facility, had other uses through the years as a concert hall, convention center, and indoor sports venue such as boxing. The facility closed in 1973 and was demolished. After the demolition of the Sportpalast, concert organizers moved the event to the Deutschlandhalle, another concert venue located in the Westend area of Charlottenburg. The Deutschlandhalle seated approximately 8,000 people and provided an ideal venue for this event that turned into a "battle of the bands."

This event demanded the full capability of the 298th and every aspect and talent of the band was used in preparation for it. This was no platz concert. The British Army rotated many of its battalions of varying regiments in and out of the city. Each battalion had a small band of about 20 musicians. For this event, the British massed their bands together to provide the physical size roughly equivalent to the other bands.

The French band historically did not provide much competition. Very much a training unit for young musicians, the 46th Infantry Regiment band of the French Army participated in the event and offered their special flair with the musicians in their kepis (headgear), drummers twirling their mallets, and the uniform ropes and cords that seemed to envelope all of them. When the 298th had an opportunity to visit Quartier Napoleon in Wedding where the French band was stationed, those visiting learned how little music the average French bandsman knew when he arrived in Berlin. The French NCOs then managed to teach and train the younger musicians the necessary instrumental and marching skills all within a matter of a few months. As the French Army largely consisted of conscripts, the turnover in personnel was high and the training workload never ceased. The level of performance the French band achieved was remarkable on that basis.

When it came to sheer entertainment, the battle usually came down to the affable, but intense competition between the Polizeiorchester Berlin and the 298th Army Band. Trumpeter Brian Benson (1980-83) who, following his Berlin tour became a bandmaster, wrote and arranged music in his head and generated the individual parts with astonishing speed. Capable of churning out lengthy, detailed medleys of popular tunes of the day including the themes to various Steven Spielberg blockbuster movies such as Star Wars, Raiders of the Lost Ark, E.T., The Extra-Terrestrial, and others, Brian expertly intertwined these melodies rhythmically and tonally to yield hugely popular tunes that never failed to bring the Berliners to their feet.

The Polizeiorchester, under the leadership of various conductors but perhaps most notably Michael Kern, formed a swinging big band augmented by traditional wind/concert band instruments. The result was a sound that brought Berliners what they wanted to hear—a mixture of both traditional marches, novelty tunes, and good old-fashioned American swing.

Competition for microphones characterized some of the rehearsals during the mid-1980s. As the number of microphones was limited, each bandleader determined to present his band in the best possible sound, and that meant placing microphones where they were needed. This competitive spirit showed itself between the leaders and the musicians. The audience never failed to demonstrate its appreciation for fine performances by whistling and stomping their feet, along with hearty applause, irrespective of who played. The entire concert brought not just badly needed funds for victims of crime, but also provided a rich musical experience for the audience.

All great gigs have an ending, and after the audience had filed out following the performance, the various bands had equipment to gather, pack, and load onto trucks. Bruce Gleason, euphoniumist with the 298th from 1989 to 1991, offers some insight from the 1989 performance:

November 2, 1989

Last night the band participated in a joint concert with the British Light Infantry Corunna Band, the Band of the 1st Battalion of the King's Regiment, the French La Musique du 46eme Regiment d'Infanterie and das Polizeiorchester Berlin (Berlin Police Band). The performance took place at the Deutschlandhalle, which is one of the larger auditoriums in Berlin. The proceeds from the annual concert, which draws some 5,000 people, sponsored by the Berlin Police, go to victims of crime. It is certainly a worthwhile cause, and the musicians of the different bands have an opportunity to perform together and hear what the other bands are doing.

After the concert, three of us from the U.S. Berlin Brigade were about ready to leave with the equipment truck, when the French equipment truck backed into ours. The dent was extremely minor, but since our driver was liable for any damage, it was necessary to report the "traffic accident." This normally wouldn't be much of an ordeal, but we are in Berlin, where pretty much nothing is normal. Since we are in Berlin, the Berlin Polizei had to be notified, and since we are U.S. military personnel, our MPs had to be notified, and since the other vehicle involved was French military, the French MPs had to be notified and since we were in the British Sector, the British MPs had to be notified. We had to wait until everyone had arrived before we could leave, and after filling out reports in numerous languages and dialects, and coming close to the dissolving of NATO, we went home.

Internationale Grüne Woche (Green Week) is the largest exhibition for the food, agricultural and horticultural industries in the world. This event, held in January every year, features vendors that display every imaginable food and beverage item from around the world. Sampling the wares (formerly free, but now there's a small charge) is part of the fun. Small groups, scattered throughout the huge convention complex, provide entertainment.

The 298th supported Green Week by sending various smaller ensembles. The full band didn't perform since floor space was at a premium due to the huge crowds. Playing everything from rock to funk to jazz to even putting forth a woodwind quintet, Green Week veterans played and sang. With vocal work from Robert Waldron and Teri Fleshman (trumpet and saxophone, respectively), they were joined by a long list of other hard working musicians such as guitarists Mike Kaufman, Charles W.T. (Frogg) Consaul, John Birch; pianists Mike Seals, John Hopkins, James Pinkerton, Jeff Barnes, Paul Salomone; trumpeters Joe Morgan, Dave Slothower, Dan Guth; saxophonists Herbie Hart, Willie (P.K.) Pollock, Paul Dickson, Jerry Larson (normally an oboe player), Michael Conwell (also on flute); trombonists Vic St. Clair and Rick Fleshman; drummers Monte Pursifull, Bobby McGuffin, Doug (Dallas) Millar, Darrell Fair; bassists Sully Frettoloso, Bruce Malone, Teal Warren, and many others.

Of the many musicians who supported Green Week, Charles W.T. (Frogg) Consaul (1987-94) distinguished himself as one of the very few musicians who played the gig all by himself. A guitarist by job title, but equally adept on piano, bass, banjo, drums, and various low brass instruments, not to mention voice, Frogg wrote his own music and lyrics, and occasionally—just to see who was paying attention—altered them while singing. He played hour after hour, just by himself, and entertained as if he were four or five.

Percussionist Monte Pursifull (1985-88) recalls the combo supporting a singer outside the 298th in the 1986 Green Week. This person made a name for herself by singing several of Whitney Houston's tunes. The remarkable thing about her wasn't her voice nearly as much as her feet. Monte wrote in social media, "The singer had feet so long that her toes extended 1/2-inch beyond the end of her open-toed shoes. The elevated platform put her submarines right at eye-level of the German audience. We had fun watching their reactions."

The gigs ran every day over the exhibition, with multiple shows per day being the norm.

Not known for playing Green Week, but nonetheless a small ensemble that performed at various venues in the city, Dan Hermann formed a German Polka Band in the mid-1980s. Featuring two clarinets, two trumpets, trombone, tuba, and drum kit, Dan's band was a hit at street festivals and beer tents.

Performances in West Germany

Chuck Ramsey (drummer and Operations NCO) recalled being invited on several occasions to the Hildesheim, Braunschweig, and Celle areas where a collection of former Berliners had, after World War II, relocated. Chuck referred to this organization as "Bunte Freunde, Berliner Freunde." This group sponsored several events in the 1970s. Consisting primarily of marching shows interspersed with a few concerts and combined often with the local British Army bands who were also stationed in the area, these shows provided another opportunity for military musicians of many nations to coalesce, observe each other, and socialize afterwards. One such encounter in the Hannover area brought the 298th and a battalion of the British Army Royal Green Jackets to the same venue. The Royal Green Jackets (RGJ) distinguished itself by marching at the pace of 140 beats per minute, instead of the normal 116-120. This tradition of the RGJ came as the result of their having been used as shock troops; their mission was to get to the battle as quickly as possible.

Northern Germany provided yet another mecca for the 298th and performances in various locations there included Cuxhaven, Wilhelmshaven, and Kiel. Mr. Smith remembers, "There was the Kiel Polizei Show when the announcer ad libbed something on the order of, 'And now, the best military band in Europe...from Berlin, The US Army Berlin Brigade Band!' and the north German audience leaned back in their stadium chairs, frowned and their body language said, 'Oh, yeah? Show me!' We stayed in the Olympic Village intended for the sailing/yachting athletes from the 1972 Munich Olympics (Editor, Sailing at the 1972 Summer Olympics)."[84]

The 298th enjoyed a partnership with the German Navy Band in Wilhelmshaven and traveled there in 1987 to welcome the U.S.S. John Hancock, a U.S. Navy destroyer anchored in the harbor, and to play a joint concert with the German Navy Band. Mr. Smith responded via social media, "We did a bunch of joint numbers in concert, but also some solo selections. We played the hell out of the Tchaikovsky Symphony 4 Finale and gained a bunch of musical respect from them. The LtCdr bandmaster and I each got these immense bouquets of flowers and, as we waved to the audience's applause, that's when the photo shutter snapped for the newspaper photographer. That's the picture that appeared in full color over the fold the next morning in the Wilhelmshavener Zeitung. The headline quoted a snippet of fluff from the Finale program note...in second-coming font, the words FIRE AND ICE screamed above the photo that, for all the world looked like the two of us were about to depart on our honeymoon just as soon as we could throw the bouquet." The captain of the U.S.S. John Hancock invited the band aboard ship whereupon he sponsored a tour of the ship's main areas, to include the engine room where the gas turbines pushed the vessel to speeds in excess of 35 knots. For many in the band, this was the first time on board a U.S. Navy warship. After the tour, the band ate lunch in the ship's galley, not necessarily a stellar experience. On yet another tour, several 298th members toured a German U-boat which lay alongside the pier and experienced the conditions, close quarters, and even stink of those mariners as they went out to sea time and again.

In association with a marching show in Hamburg, the band experienced a stubborn gate guard who refused to admit the band after arriving at its German Army Kaserne following a hard day of travel and performance. The guard, merely following orders, did so in an exemplary fashion. Untying that particular knot took a bit of time and effort.

Not all trips to West Germany were business-related, although very often pleasure was combined with performing. Quite often for personal reasons, band members would take their own transportation out to West Germany and meet the band at the job site. Trombonist Dan Hermann did one better.

Dan arrived in Berlin for his first 298th tour in 1977. Many people, American and German, asked him where his ancestors came from. Dan replied that he didn't know, but the questions ignited some genealogical curiosity in him about his family. At his next duty station in the Chicago area, Dan began doing some research of his family. He learned that his great-grandfather Ludwig Herrmann came from Stakendorf, located just east of Kiel directly on the Baltic Sea. Meanwhile, the German wife of a colleague, whose maiden name was also Hermann, asked her visiting parents if they would take a letter from Dan back with them to inquire officials in northern Germany about Dan's family. They readily agreed, and Dan's letter wound up with an older man named Hans-Detlev Spring. Hans did additional research on Dan's behalf, which prompted a correspondence between the two of them.

Dan arrived back in Berlin in 1985 for his second tour and after he and his family got settled, wrote Hans-Detlev again to let him know that he'd arrived back in Germany. Not much more was said and time passed, but when the 298th arrived in Kiel to do a marching show, Dan was told in the hotel that he had a visitor, who was his old friend Hans-Detlev. The two of them drove to Stakendorf the next morning and met a group of farmers. Dan introduced himself, which surprised them since none of them had ever seen

Dan before, but when Hans-Detlev explained who Dan was, they all turned out for handshakes and hugs as if Dan were a long-lost relative. They took Dan inside the house and showed photos of the farm from 100 years prior. It had not appreciably changed.

This meeting turned into a rekindled relationship that, once started, hasn't let up. Among other things, Dan learned that his great-grandfather Ludwig Herrmann was born in nearby Hansühn. The local church, which was founded in 1210, contained the family records that Dan sought. Ludwig had emigrated from Hamburg in 1886 and arrived in New York. He had a sponsor in Clinton, Iowa, learned to speak English and raised 16 children. Dan Hermann (his family dropped one of the "r's") would likely have never seen his ancestral home had he not gone to Kiel to play a marching show.

Traveling Through Europe

The 298th traveled infrequently during its early years through the 1950s and well into the 1960s. On rare occasions the band ventured beyond Berlin and some locations in West Germany. Sebby Papa still remembers the trip in 1947 that the 298th took to Antwerp, Belgium, in a somber ceremony to return many of America's war dead. Buried in various military cemeteries throughout France and Belgium, remains were exhumed and prepared for repatriation back to the United States, based on the wishes of next of kin. As Antwerp featured a major port, one or more ships had been loaded with steel coffins containing those honored dead. Before setting sail, these dead were afforded a proper sendoff.

While most travel anywhere for the 298th entailed taking the duty train from Berlin to either Frankfurt or Bremerhaven, other options were available, to include commercial and military flights. Bus travel through the East German corridor, processing through Checkpoints Bravo and Alpha, was also an option. But most of the time, the 298th traveled via duty train.

The terminus for the Berlin-Frankfurt duty train—the Hauptbahnhof (main train station) in Frankfurt—provided a traveling mecca of sorts for the 298th. The train out of Berlin, leaving at about 8:15 p.m., arrived in Frankfurt at about 6:30 a.m. Passengers traveling on the duty train found the Rail Transportation Office (RTO) upstairs in the train station. This area was restricted for authorized travelers and was not open to the German public. The RTO featured a waiting area and served as a processing center to check in and make return reservations. The Hauptbahnhof contained the usual amenities associated with any travel center—restaurants, bars, snack stands, souvenir shops. Travelers could find other items of interest outside the Hauptbahnhof, specifically on Kaiserstrasse, located just to the east of the station and across the main road Am Hauptbahnhof.

The 298th also traveled on the Bremerhaven duty train, but less frequently as the Frankfurt train. The Bremerhaven train traveled a shorter distance overall and thus arrived at its destination earlier. Most Bremerhaven trips were uneventful, but CWO David Smith remembers one occasion after the band arrived in Bremerhaven that the RTO staff refused to help the band unload its gear. That didn't present a huge problem by itself, but when the same staff refused to allow usage of a large cart on which the band could stack its gear to maneuver out to the band's bus, that created an opportunity for questions.

Not all trips began with a leg on the duty train. A commercial flight took the stage band to Stockholm, Sweden, in 1987, for several days. Flutist Michael Conwell (1984-86) became so enamored of his experience there he told his new wife all about the women that seemed to flock around the band during their time there. She found the story intriguing.

Saxophonist Cheryl Wason (1976-77) and the rest of the stage band flew to Edzel, Scotland, in October, 1977. The flight originated out of Tempelhof Central Airport and the aircraft was a C-130 transport plane. Complete with fold-down seats constructed out of webbing and requiring hearing protection while in flight, the aircraft posed special problems. Cheryl and the only other woman in the band at the time, saxophonist Debbie Boyd, had to figure out how to use the restroom facilities on board. The "facilities" are austere and consist of a separate urinal (that vented to the outside) and "honey pot" that did not. The urinal had a gray curtain that afforded a measure of privacy as did the honey pot, but the curtain on the honey pot was open toward the rear—with illumination. That meant the person on the throne's silhouette could be plainly seen while attending to the business at hand.

Clarinetist and principal Drum Major Sally Gerry (1992-94) recalled the band flying to Macedonia to support Task Force Able Sentry in 1993, not long before the band's deactivation. Departing with the Berlin Brigade Commander, the band traveled to the Balkans for one day to play a ceremony. Sally found it odd that the Reviewing Officer screamed at the top of his lungs while he pinned a medal on the ceremony's Commander of Troops and his staff. Sally found it odd and more than a little humorous that the medals fell off the award recipients during the Pass in Review. Sally was not able to find out why the ceremony was conducted in that way.

On occasion, the band traveled throughout Europe in a bus. Depending on the era, the transportation medium consisted of an Army bus or a very comfortable German motor coach, complete with a restroom and the accompanying admonition for all users of the facilities, regardless of sex, to please SIT DOWN, especially while the bus is under way. Cold drinks for DM 1,50 each were also available. A microphone situated just in front of the jump seat provided a tour guide the opportunity to entertain the passengers, but for the 298th, this feature permitted only the dissemination of vital information—

for example, a 10 minute break at the Autobahn's Rasthof. Hacky-sack, a curious game involving kicking a small beanbag from person to person, was popular in the 1980s and the occasion for this short exercise provided an opportunity to stretch one's legs.

On the lengthier trips, in particular to France, Belgium, Holland, and Luxembourg, the stops were welcome.

In 1985, 1986 and again in 1993, the 298th participated in the Doudou Festival in Mons, Belgium. This event brought in military bands all over Europe and the sheer amount of work was matched only by the intensity of the festivities. The interaction between all attending military bands provided ample opportunity to see just how other bands perform, but the main feature was simply the number of people attending this very popular festival. The Doudou Festival provided an atmosphere of fun, but it was also a dizzying, work-heavy weekend schedule that permitted very little downtime. It was literally one performance or rehearsal after another for most of each day. From parades during the day to platz concerts in the afternoon; to marching shows in the stadium to torchlight parades at night, Mons was mobbed by thousands of spectators and participants. Drinking Jupiler beer, a truly awful local brew, or the more exotic Belgian beers brewed elsewhere, to vin rouge/blanc, people partied. When it was all over, the 298th loaded up its assigned motorcoach and slept most of the way back to Frankfurt just in time to catch the duty train back to Berlin.

The town of Neumünster in northern Germany, a medium-sized town of about 70,000 inhabitants, featured an item not seen anywhere else in Germany. An all-girls band, named the Mädchen Musikzug Neumünster, invited the 298th to participate in a marching show in 1968. Lawrence (Fish) Brown still talks of giving trumpet lessons to one of the young ladies he encountered. The MMN, one of the few all-girl bands in Germany, formed in 1961. Numbering approximately 55 girls from ages 14-24, these girls perform throughout Europe and even toured the United States. Sponsored by the town of Neumünster and many former musicians, the band continues to play today, having recently celebrated their 50th anniversary.

The 298th traveled to Neumünster in 1985 to participate in one of their traditional concert settings, which, especially in northern Germany, entails inviting several international bands. Some of the guest bands, like the 298th, were military. Others were town bands from other countries and elsewhere in Germany. The resulting concert in the town's Holstenhalle featured marching maneuvers and entertainment that lasted up to three hours. Lengthy concerts such as this were normal for northern Germany; the audiences could not seem to get enough of each band. The Grand Finale, including all of the participating units, filled the large floor of the hall and the concluding music rendered an atmosphere of camaraderie.

The 298th's musicians stayed overnight with private families, in much the same fashion as in Einhausen. This was decidedly different than usual; typically, the 298th stayed in German Army or Air Force barracks on the weekends while the German soldiers went home for the weekend. The generosity shown by the people of Neumünster illustrated the genuine love the townspeople have for music and its creation. This is especially notable because, in Germany, instrumental or vocal music is not generally offered as options in public school. For those students interested in learning to play an instrument, this effort has to be learned separately from school.

Regardless where the 298th Army Band performed, each member of the band experienced more of the world than they would have otherwise seen and heard. Each opportunity to travel brought the opportunity for each musician to represent the United States in his own way. While each performance required work, skill and talent, each musician took away a personal impression and an experience that molded him and the band at large. Above all, the 298th Army Band encountered enthusiastic, appreciative audiences wherever it went and responded to that appreciation by delivering its very best.

REUNIFICATION AND DEACTIVATION

The events leading up to the Wall's demise occurred with dramatic speed. Like the small trickle in a leaky dam that becomes a torrent, GDR policies, miscommunication, and Soviet refusal to intervene resulted in more than 133,000 East German citizens moving to the West in 1989. More than anything, a persistent call for freedom to travel by hundreds of thousands of people eventually helped bring down the Wall.

November 1-10, 1989

Egon Krenz, the communist head of state of East Germany (GDR), visited Moscow on November 1st. He had been presented with unmistakable and irrefutable evidence, largely ignored by his predecessor Erich Honecker, of an economically dying nation. Honecker's blind denial of absolute fact led to his removal from his position the previous month, replaced by Krenz. Krenz appealed to Mikhail Gorbachev for Soviet economic assistance. Gorbachev explained quite firmly that the Soviet Union was not in a position to provide that assistance and the discussion turned to other matters. Gorbachev also demurred on any discussion concerning a possible reunification between the two Germanys as it was not an item on the Soviet Union's political agenda. This effectively shut the door on any Soviet interference to address the increasing numbers of East German citizens moving to the West and as a result of this meeting and popular pressure, the travel requirements by GDR citizens to Czechoslovakia were eased again. GDR citizens would no longer need a visa and a passport to travel there.[85]

On November 3, officials in Czechoslovakia (CSSR) informed the GDR ambassador that no effort to establish refugee camps for the flood of GDR citizens arriving in the CSSR would be taken. Officials told the ambassador that GDR had two choices: one, "introduce measures to end the influx of 'political refugees' [into the CSSR] or two, organise a clearance procedure so that 'as many former GDR citizens can leave the CSSR for West Germany (FRG) every day as arrive daily in the FRG embassy [in Prague].'".[86] Czech officials and the people had found it noteworthy that the GDR allowed the West German embassy in Prague handle the influx of East German citizens, some 6,000 at the time, rather than centrally control the process in East Berlin.

The East German SED Politburo, the seat of power in East Germany, met in an afternoon session on November 3 to allow those 6,000 GDR citizens staying on the West German embassy grounds in Prague to depart for West Germany without returning first to East Germany. This decision also guaranteed their citizenship status and allowed them unequivocal access back into the GDR. Krenz gave a television and radio broadcast that night that promised quick release of an accompanying draft new travel bill, but gave no specifics. In his speech he declared "no going back" for political reform and implored GDR citizens to remain in the country. Krenz then made preparations to handle the next day's massive demonstrations on East Berlin's Alexanderplatz at which up to 500,000 people were expected. Some 40 other towns and cities across the GDR also had protest rallies scheduled. In light of the increasing vocal and physical protests, up to and including booing Politburo member Günter Schabowski off the stage with shouts of "Abtreten!" (get off the stage!), the Volkspolizei was ordered to move to the background, but other "social forces" were made ready at the Brandenburg Gate to prevent any overt effort to break through to the border.[87] The GDR government hadn't quite given up on themselves.

On November 6, the GDR government released the new travel bill that Krenz had promised and a new storm of outrage erupted. The 30-day travel limit per year and the ill-defined reasons why application to travel could be denied were found unacceptable. A new round of protests occurred throughout the country. Meanwhile, in Bonn, one of Krenz's representatives secretly appealed to West German officials for new loan guarantees, ostensibly to help pay for the GDR citizens now appearing in West Germany through the CSSR. The West Germans used noncommittal delaying tactics to the point that Krenz now understood his options had run out.[88] West German Chancellor Helmut Kohl realized that his negotiating power had risen substantially and through discussions between officials, expressed the willingness of West Germany to provide financial and material help to the GDR in exchange for the GDR's guarantee "that the formation of opposition groups will be permitted and affirm that it will hold free elections within a period yet to be announced. It should be noted that this path is possible only if the SED gives up its claim to absolute power."[89]

On the next day, November 8, 1989, the entire GDR Politburo resigned in an effort to resolve the growing crisis of East Germans fleeing the country, which amounted to 350 per hour. Egon Krenz stayed in power, however, and continued working with the Central Committee of the SED.[90] Finally bowing to reality, the Interior Minister then made a public announcement to confirm and recognize that the opposition group "Neues Forum" was a recognized association. The CSSR then increased the pressure on the GDR by detailing complaints of CSSR citizens in Bohemia of their failure to understand why GDR citizens had been allowed to migrate to West Germany (BRD) through the BRD embassy. They then requested that the GDR allow their citizens to emigrate directly into West Germany without involving CSSR territory.

On Thursday, November 9, Gerhard Lauter, a colonel in the GDR's interior ministry and three of his colleagues met to discuss and write yet another new draft of travel regulations meant to address the torrent of opposition most recently voiced. Chronik der Mauer web site explains: "The

[Lauter] group soon agrees that, in future, all restrictions regarding applications to leave the GDR permanently should be dropped. The officers consider it irresponsible, however, to force all those wanting to leave the country to take on the status of emigrants. They want to preserve the GDR. For this reason, they include regulations regarding the right to 'private trips,' i.e. visits, in the Council [of Minister's] resolution, along with those concerning permanent departure. Applications are still to be made for permission to travel or leave the country. The State Security Service expects the general populace to react with a rush – but a rush on the relevant authorities (the *Volkspolizei* district offices), not a rush on the border."[91]

A key element in the document stipulated release of the information for the next day at 4:00 a.m. This was to allow for subordinate units and border control offices time to be notified. Lauter and his group had discussed the points expressed in the document heatedly during their session, but in the end, they discounted the guidance they had received from the Politburo's Central Committee. Lauter had a staff member type the document; he signed and stamped it, then released it for courier delivery to Krenz and the Central Committee.

Krenz received the document and read it verbatim to the Central Committee, which was in session. Günter Schabowski was absent, however. No one objected to the language in the document and no discussion ensued. After the Central Committee's meeting ended, Krenz located Schabowski and gave the document to him along with a press release. These papers were needed for the upcoming 6:00 p.m. press conference, which was only minutes away. Krenz failed to mention that the information within the document should not be released until the next day at 4 a.m.

While Schabowski had officially resigned from the Politburo, he was still appointed as SED (the East German communist party) spokesman. He would lead the upcoming press conference, accompanied by three of the Central Committee members. Some 200 international journalists, including NBC's Tom Brokaw and his camera and sound crew, were scheduled to attend.

In a video interview[92] after the news conference, Brokaw explained that he and his colleagues listened to the largely boring presentation and dozed somewhat in the process as they had just arrived from the U.S. that morning and were exhausted. Shortly before 7 p.m., however, an Italian journalist asked Schabowski about the newest travel regulations. Schabowski had completely forgotten about discussing the points contained in the document that Krenz had given him earlier and after he had shuffled through his papers looking for it, eventually locating it with the help of a staffer, he began reading it verbatim. Again, Schabowski did not know that the information was to be withheld (Youtube)).[93]

The fact that a senior SED member would actually field questions from the press and answer those questions live and unfiltered was itself a remarkable event never before seen (Hertle, 1999).[94]

The question from the Italian journalist queried Schabowski if the previous set of travel regulations so vociferously denounced a few days before was a mistake. In a matter of only a few days, several sets of regulations had been drafted and announced, the most recent angrily rejected by the populace. Schabowski responded to the contrary, but was interrupted by another journalist who asked specifically when the new regulation would take effect. Another journalist asked the same question. Brokaw noted in his video interview that immediately, the journalists and others in the room perked up at Schabowski's words and the resulting questions from the floor. In response to the questions and the newer intensity within the room, Schabowski looked through his papers, seemed to find the answer to the question, "When?" and answered, "Immediately, without delay."[95] This response had a stunning impact within the room. The journalists questioned themselves and each other if they had heard correctly, according to Brokaw. With that, the press conference ended at 7 p.m.

Brokaw said that he had previously scheduled an appointment with Schabowski, followed him upstairs, sat him down, and invited him to once again read from that piece of paper from which he had made that startling announcement. Schabowski confirmed what he had said, announced that the decision had been made, and assured that the borders, even to West Berlin, would be opened, responding to Brokaw's questions in English.[96]

Meanwhile, at 7:05 p.m., the news broke around the world first with the Associated Press: "GDR Opens Borders."

While the Wall did not open immediately, GDR citizens began gathering at the crossover points at Invalidenstrasse and Bornholmerstrasse, among others. The Stasi told the border guards to defer people and send them back until the next day, but the crowds continued to gather. The problem became acute and absent orders from higher authority, the GDR State Security Service opted to allow a "valve" solution. This stopgap measure meant to allow the most vocal and insistent people through the border gradually upon presentation of a passport. Unbeknownst to these people, their identity papers were stamped alongside their photo. This stamp effectively removed their citizenship and prevented their return to East Germany. Absent instruction from senior GDR officials, who remained silent through the night, confusion and drama continued to build at the Wall's crossover points. By 10:00 p.m., the situation at Bornholmerstrasse had become volatile as people continued to gather and press in toward the passport control officers; the "valve" solution proved to be an unworkable solution. Those who had gone through the border and returned were allowed back in.

The decisions made by the lieutenant colonel in charge of the Bornholmerstrasse control point had a cascading effect. At midnight, all Wall crossover points were opened. The border guards no longer told GDR citizens that they should go home and wait till the next day and for those that returned in short order, they were allowed back in. The press of humanity had become untenable.[97]

Finally, after 28 years, the Berlin Wall was gone. While it would be several years before the Wall's physical presence was removed, the barrier itself was now just a speed bump. The people of eastern Europe had spoken over the past year. Little by little, their voices were heard. Eventually, their expressed wishes were granted by a political system that permitted freedom only on the state's terms.

For all but the most informed and involved newshound, these events were unknown to the average 298th musician. The work schedule had remained predictable; physical training, rehearsals, performances, and military training occupied the day's activities. Evenings were spent with family or friends and off-duty time on the weekends saw band members traveling, shopping, or relaxing.

Bruce Gleason, euphoniumist (1989-91) wrote in a letter to friends back home that in the early evening of November 9th, he had been in the band building when a fellow band member announced the news about the East Germans opening their borders. Bruce then called trumpeter Dave Slothower (1986-89), who drove in from his off-post quarters. They then set out for Checkpoint Charlie. When they arrived, roughly 200 people had gathered and were observing the gathering crowds. Bruce and Dave stayed for a couple hours and then moved north to the checkpoint at Invalidenstrasse. The traffic had gotten worse. "By the time we got there, thousands of people were there welcoming the East Berliners that were beginning to trickle out. As each car drove into the West, the crowd cheered. People were crying. It was midnight and everyone in the city seemed to be out."

They then headed south for the Brandenburg Gate, just a few blocks away. They saw tens of thousands of people along with Tom Brokaw and his camera and sound crew, broadcasting live. They stayed there about 90 minutes and then returned to Invalidenstrasse where even more people had gathered to watch the East Berliners stream through the checkpoint.

Bruce had previously applied for and received an East Pass for the next day, Friday, November 10th. He arrived at Checkpoint Charlie at about 1:30 p.m. and saw thousands of people along Friedrichstrasse, cheering the oncoming East Berliners as they motored and walked through. Bruce processed through the MPs at Checkpoint Charlie and walked through the East Berlin control point.

Once in East Berlin, Bruce found it interesting that while many people had apparently crossed to West Berlin, many others were still in East Berlin going about their normal business. Bruce then attended a performance of Puccini's *La Boheme* at the Komische Opera House.

Checkpoint Charlie after the Fall of the Wall

Bruce arrived back at Checkpoint Charlie at 10:30 p.m. and noted a long line of traffic and pedestrians waiting to cross. Bruce wrote, "the West Berliners at the border had taken on a party attitude and were hitting the cars with their fists and rocking the cars as they crossed and made their way through the crowd. I felt sorry for the East Berliners, many of whom had never been to the West in their lives, and now upon entering were having their cars shaken apart."

Bruce realized the next day that his best vantage point to see the unfolding events was through AFN television or even CNN. He was disappointed that he hadn't been able to get any photographs up to that point so he recruited Dave Slothower to tour the area again. Bruce, Dave, and Dave's wife Linda along with their two sons returned to the Brandenburg Gate. Getting there took easily twice as long as normal due to the choked streets and flood of people. They then took the opportunity to take photographs and to allow Dave and Linda's sons to experience history in the making.

Reunification and War in the Persian Gulf

The West German government had a policy of paying *Begrüßungsgeld* (welcoming money) to East Germans upon their arrival in the West for visits. The policy had paid varying amounts since 1970. After the Wall's demise, the amount of payment increased to DM 200. The financial load on the West German populace was significant: approximately DM 3-4 billion was paid in November-December 1989 alone. The West Germans bearing the cost of this program complained bitterly, an act that seemed to foreshadow further resentments as the costs of building an entire country began to be realized. The *"Begrüßungsgeld"* program ended in July 1990 when the economic and currency reform occurred making the Deutsche mark the currency of both nations, paving the way for Reunification itself.

The official reunification of Germany– *Tag der deutschen Einheit* – occurred on October 3, 1990. This date represented the end of the Allies' occupation of Berlin and spelled an end to the role of the U.S. Commander of Berlin (USCOB). The last officer to serve in that position, Major General Raymond E. Haddock, had assumed command of the U.S. sector in Berlin on June 1, 1988. He therefore had seen virtually all the political changes that had enveloped Europe and Berlin. But while the simple honor guard ceremony at Clay Headquarters on October 1, 1990 provided Haddock a suitable but subdued ceremony to acknowledge the end of his tenure and of those who preceded him, this did not mean the end of the U.S. forces presence in Berlin.

At least not yet. The Two Plus Four talks that had begun in early 1990 between West and East Germany, along with the original victorious Allies of World War II – Great Britain, France, the Soviet Union and the United States – began the legal process to end the post- World War II agreements that addressed Germany. These talks also addressed a number of other issues, not the least of which was the guarantee of Poland's western border. Poland was fearful that the negotiations that would combine both East and West Germany would lead to German attempts to reclaim territory ceded to Poland after World War II. The issue was largely a legal one: while both East and West Germany identified the Oder and Neisse Rivers as comprising Poland's western border, no such agreement existed with the reunified Germany (Cawley, 1990).[98]

The Two Plus Four Treaty also stipulated that Soviet forces were to leave East Germany by the end of 1994. Similarly, the Western Allies were obligated to withdraw all combat forces from Berlin also by the end of 1994 following withdrawal by Soviet forces. Nothing, however, was stated in the agreement concerning American and NATO forces within the former West Germany. The Americans would stay in support of NATO. The Two Plus Four talks continued until they were signed by all parties on September 12, 1990. Ratification of the treaty was swift with the two Germanys and the three Western Allies but the Soviet Union delayed ratification until March 4, 1991. After the Soviet Union's collapse in December 1991, Russia honored the Soviet Union's provisions in the Two Plus Four Treaty, a matter of some concern due to the instability in Russia itself.

The speed of events taking place surprised everybody in the 298th. From the Wall's collapse in November 1989 to formal reunification 11 months later, and then final ratification of the treaty 6 months after that, the pace of change was nothing short of astounding. U.S. forces, including the 298th, would leave Berlin. The Army's senior leadership made no mention of the 298th's future other than it would depart. The idea of no Western Allied presence by 1994 seemed fantastic, even improbable.

The 298th continued its overall mission as always, but with the added twist of a new audience. Bruce Gleason again wrote home of a gig that was the same in many respects, but vastly different in others.

In May 1990, the 298th played another outdoor festival. The program was largely the same as in similar concerts: German polkas, big band favorites of the 1940s, and current pop tunes. Surrounding the concert venue, various vendors had set up their wurst and beer stands and even one type of stand that hadn't been seen before in and around Berlin. This one, and similar stands, offered fruit wines of various types.

This concert took place in Werder, in the former East Germany. This was the first occasion of a U.S. military band to have performed in the former East Germany outside of East Berlin.

Werder celebrated its 111th Tree Blooming Festival in 1990. A festival of 10 days in duration from late April till early May, this event unfolded on an island in the middle of the Havel River. Werder itself is located west of Potsdam directly alongside the Havel River. But Bruce found the atmosphere of the town and its people very different than he had previously encountered. Wherever the band had played, whether in Berlin or in West Germany, it was almost impossible to find people who have never seen a U.S. soldier. But in Werder, most townspeople had never encountered an American at all.

The band was well received and the people seemed to overcome their tentativeness, even to the point of asking for autographs, which was a great surprise to the band. Bruce wrote, "it seemed that they couldn't believe that we were actually in their town: a bunch of people in U.S. Army uniforms, with a huge military bus, accompanied by a four-ton truck to haul our equipment. The music seemed to be secondary, merely a vehicle to get us there. The point was we were a military group commonly looked on as enemies who had not only come in peace, but in goodwill to help them in celebration and enjoyment."

At this early stage of the Reunification process, making this event happen was no small feat. The State Department and various U.S. liaison offices were involved with the arrangements of obtaining special passports and visas, and all hoped that this cultural exchange would be the first of many to come.

Bruce noted in his letter that it was difficult for him to imagine a reunited Germany in this gathering of people in a small town southwest of Berlin. These people had lived under the watchful, unforgiving eye of communism for

45 years at that point to say nothing of contending with Nazism before and during World War II. Looking around at the general condition of the community, Bruce was hard-pressed to believe that East Germany had the highest standard of living of all of the Soviet bloc countries. Bruce noted that towns were almost totally devoid of advertising, billboards and posters and that the lack of basic construction supplies was evident due to crumbling buildings and their facades. Bruce saw no automobile dealerships, car insurance, or investment and brokerage firms. Bicycles were rare to see and fresh fruit and chocolate were uncommon as well. Bruce saw the vast differences in the two cultures, though they were one people.

General Haddock kept his farewell ceremony on October 3, 1990 brief but dignified. The 298th played Honors to him and to the Nation. His comments were short and to the point. It seemed as though Haddock had deliberately decided to keep the ceremony low-key. Or perhaps there were bigger concerns than simply closing the doors of an institution that had been in place for 45 years. Very much on everybody's mind was Iraq's invasion of neighboring Kuwait in August 1990 and President Bush's declaration, "This aggression will not stand." Operation Desert Shield, the buildup of forces in the Gulf region and primarily in Saudi Arabia, was well under way. While U.S. Army units in Berlin were not deployed, several soldiers within the command had individually deployed.

One of those soldiers was Sergeant Jeff Harper, tubist with the 298th. Desert Shield required deployment of the 1st Armored Division. The division band would deploy as well, and they needed a tuba player to fully complement the band. The 298th commander had surveyed his tuba players and concluded that Jeff would go.

While Jeff understood what he was ordered to do, leaving Berlin—even temporarily, as this assignment was—wasn't easy. He had recently become involved with his girlfriend and found the idea of leaving inconvenient. Despite these issues, Jeff packed his gear and departed for Ansbach, West Germany, where the 1st Armored Division Band prepared for deployment. Following Desert Storm and Jeff's return to Berlin, it was no surprise to learn that Jeff performed his duties in an exemplary manner and returned to Berlin a grizzled combat veteran. Those who saw Jeff go off to war saw him come back a new man. Confident and steadfast, Jeff made the 298th and the entire Berlin Brigade proud of him and his achievements under trying and uncertain conditions. Jeff took what he learned in Berlin and built an exceptional career for himself. Serving again in Afghanistan before he retired as a first sergeant, Jeff was destined to succeed.

In later years, unbeknownst to him initially, Jeff became somewhat famous. After Checkpoint Charlie was retired and removed from the center of Friedrichstrasse by crane and the former crossing-point and symbol of the dark Cold War returned to a more visitor-friendly and tourist-oriented site, two huge full-color photographs, perhaps 4' x 6', were erected. Facing north

The 298th's own Jeff Harper at Checkpoint Charlie

into the former East Berlin, a photograph of a typical Soviet soldier is to be seen. Facing south into the former West Berlin, a photograph of a typical U.S. soldier is to be seen. That U.S. soldier is none other than Jeff Harper.

Jeff to this day is rather light-hearted about it. He took no part in any decision to take a photo of himself and put it up in the center of a tourist mecca, and thus with a great deal of humor and completely tongue-in-cheek, Jeff accepts his role as Symbol of the Free World. Jeff's reaction to his photo runs in direct contrast to the serious business of waging war in Desert Storm and the final days of the conflict that saw the torched oil facilities and revealed the depth of depravity to which Saddam Hussein had sunk to extend his tyranny. Somehow, the impact of the war on life in West Berlin wasn't quite so dramatic.

Other than the aforementioned deployments of solitary soldiers to the Persian Gulf, operations continued in the Berlin Brigade as normal. Operation Desert Shield continued the buildup of coalition forces until January, 17, 1991 when the first air strikes over Baghdad occurred, signaling the start of Operation Desert Storm.

The 298th's normal operations effectively shut down. Band members entered into a tactical operational environment in which the band was assigned security of a portion of Andrews Barracks. Ordinarily, the 6941st Guard Battalion, the German-led and formed force responsible for security of U.S. forces facilities in West Berlin, performed the necessary security on a day-to-day basis. But with the war in the Gulf ongoing, senior military authority in Berlin opted to maximize the security presence. Other units on Andrews Barracks also had their sections of Andrews Barracks to patrol.

The Berlin Brigade's 42nd Engineer Company parked a Combat Engineer Vehicle (CEV), a tracked vehicle built on the same chassis as the M-60 main battle tank, just inside the Finkensteinallee front gate of Andrews Barracks. This vehicle featured a bulldozer blade on the front just under a short, stubby 165mm gun that pointed toward the gate area. The band sent a squad of soldiers over to the CEV to provide a presence. Band members knew nothing about the vehicle or its capabilities; they were simply ordered to enter the vehicle and maintain a presence. The side gate of Andrews Barracks led to Baselerstrasse; the band also patrolled this area, in addition to areas other than Andrews Barracks as well. Equipped with small 2-way radios, weapons, and normal field gear, the band pulled guard and little else for several weeks, particularly during the ground war.

Clarinetist Cindy (Gagnon) Raschke, (1989-90), remarked on social media that she and others had been issued live rounds to assume security positions in and near Clay Headquarters. She said it was the first and only time in her military career that she had been issued live ammunition other than at the rifle range. So while Desert Storm seemed at the other end of the world, the threat against U.S. military targets had not appreciably diminished since 1986 when

Libya's terrorist-sponsored organization struck the LaBelle Disco, killing two U.S. soldiers, a Berlin civilian, and wounding scores of others.

On March 15, 1991 the Treaty on the Final Settlement with Respect to Germany was made effective. Monetary reunion had already been completed on July 1, 1990 as a component of Two Plus Four and thus the expensive process of Reunification began. The Wall and its older cousin the Iron Curtain had hidden from view much of the physical condition of East Germany. When the Wall fell, the overall state of the country was exposed. Examination by government and private industry revealed a nation that had been severely neglected by the communists. Infrastructure including roads, bridges, tunnels, even communication and street light systems had crumbled and barely functioned. Environmental experts determined very quickly that the level of pollution of water, air and soil went far beyond acceptable levels. East Germany needed a lot of work and a lot of money.

Deactivation

Deactivation of units continued. Checkpoint Charlie had already been retired on June 22, 1990 in a dramatic ceremony during which the temporary structure, essentially a custom travel trailer that simply rested on the street's surface, was hoisted via a large crane from its position on Friedrichstrasse. The crane then deposited the trailer on a large flatbed truck. The 298th played appropriate music throughout this ceremony, which was attended by Secretary of State James Baker, his Soviet counterpart Eduard Shevardnadze, and U.K. Foreign Secretary Douglas Hurd, who intoned during his remarks, "At long last, we are bringing Charlie in from the Cold." ((Reuters), 1990)[99]

The United States Military Liaison Mission (USMLM) deactivation ceremony occurred on October 1, which coincided with the USCOB's final honor guard. Commensurate with German Reunification, the Three-Power Allied Kommandatura ceased to exist and the building in Dahlem in which the three Western Allies had worked since the Soviets walked out of the Kommandatura in 1948 was turned over to the Free University. The 4th Battalion, 502nd Infantry also deactivated in 1990, thereby leaving but two infantry battalions within the Berlin Brigade. Ancillary units also closed their doors throughout the Reunification process including the Helmstedt Support Detachment and the 6th Battalion, 40th Armored Regiment. The 7350th Air Base Group at Tempelhof Central Airport was inactivated on January 29, 1993, thereby turning over air operations to the Berlin Airport Authority. The 298th supported most of these deactivations where a formal ceremony was requested.

USMLM Deactivation

The Soviets abandoned their own checkpoints at Dreilinden/Drewitz in the southwest of Berlin, and in Marienborn, near Allied Checkpoint Bravo. Verbal reports had been received that the Soviets packed up and left without notifying anyone, somewhat of a surprise for the first person who encountered the empty checkpoint, expecting to be processed in the usual manner.

Bruce Gleason wrote home and described a remarkable day in which the 298th performed in East Germany for a contingent of Soviet soldiers. The 298th had not performed with or for Soviet troops since 1948, shortly before the Berlin Blockade started. On a Sunday in June 1991, the 298th loaded up full concert equipment and traveled by bus to a Soviet kaserne, located south of East Berlin in East Germany itself, an area off limits to Western Allies since the Wall went up in August 1961.

The band usually traveled in civilian clothes, and did so for this job. This set the band immediately apart from the Soviets greeting them. Bruce described the distinction in the Soviet military between conscripted soldiers and career military, one of these being that draftees have no civilian clothes and are not permitted any for their term of military service. All Soviet soldiers were in uniform for this performance. Before the concert the band was invited to tour the Soviet barracks, an austere setting consisting of a large bay with dozens of narrow, thin bunks with just a hint of personal space. Basic facilities, including an arms room, were provided and Bruce mentioned an open closet at one end of the room that held uniforms and helmets. Bruce compared this setting with his own in which the 298th soldiers living in the barracks, regardless of rank, had a private room with a small refrigerator and laundry facilities down the hall; most musicians had a fairly complete collection of stereos, VCRs, computers, TVs and for some, even a new car in the parking lot.

Cindy Raschke (Gagnon) and Soviet friend

A U.S. Marine major who also served as translator, told the band that each Soviet soldier was paid about $15 per month.

Bruce went on to describe the band's musical program, which went over wonderfully. They truly enjoyed the collection of pop, rock, big band and marches that the band had prepared; and especially enjoyed the Sixties rock tune *Louie, Louie* by the Kingsmen when three of the band's female musicians selected willing members of the audience to dance with them. During the break, many Soviet soldiers wanted to trade insignia, which produced quite a collection on both sides.

The band took photographs of anything and everything and all of that was permitted. The band had been told for years not to peer outside a duty train window while it was stopped somewhere in East Germany, or take photographs on the few excursions to the USMLM facility in Potsdam. Bruce also described the oddity of being surrounded by photos of Gorbachev and Lenin and seeing signs written in the Cyrillic alphabet.

The band ate dinner in the Soviets' mess hall. They offered their very best, but again Bruce silently wondered what the Soviet soldiers would have thought to the generous bounty and sheer variety offered by the American dining facility on Andrews Barracks. The Soviets offered a plate of cooked barley, a tiny sliver of meat, and bread. Surprisingly, the beverage was a semi-fermented sweet apple cider.

Before Bruce departed Berlin in August 1991, he had occasion to meet Manfred and Gisela, who had attended the same Berlin Philharmonic concert that he had. The three became fast friends and visited several cultural events in West Berlin together. With Checkpoint Charlie now a control point of the past, Bruce now had free rein to travel East Berlin and did so, with Manfred acting as tour guide.

Manfred had grown up in East Berlin during the war. He showed Bruce the street where the forty-six year old bombed out ruins of his boyhood apartment home were finally being removed and the windows from which he watched German and Russian soldiers fighting during the war's last days. Nearby, Manfred showed Bruce the alley where children had discovered a dead Royal Air Force pilot still strung up in his parachute after having bailed out of his plane.

They drove past the German State Museum on Unter den Linden, avenue of dictators, emperors and kings, where Frederick the Great had lived and where his statue still stands. Manfred's mother and other parents had brought their children to that site for shelter each morning during the heaviest period of Allied bombing. Manfred told Bruce how his mother had finally stopped doing that, deciding that it was better to keep them with her, so if one died the others would too. They visited the street where Manfred and other starving children had rummaged through trash cans searching for food. Manfred described how after the U.S. Army had finally arrived, he found a half-full container of Hershey's Chocolate Syrup and how after years of hard work and becoming a successful banker, he still has eaten nothing that tastes so good.

After the tour when they returned to Manfred and Gisela's home, they showed Bruce the forty-six year old can of lard that was among other food items in a package sent by an American family in the U.S. who had taken it upon themselves, like thousands of other U.S. citizens, to send food and clothing to needy Berliners. When Bruce asked him why they hadn't used it, Manfred explained that his mother said they should save it in case things got worse. They never did use it and when they began to rebuild their lives, they kept the lard to remind themselves of their gratitude.

As the 298th turned the corner into 1992 and 1993, the band received its last commander, CWO Larry Hyatt, and last first sergeant, 1SG Michael van Winkle, a trombonist. Musical training, physical training, and performances continued. The 298th participated in lengthy field training exercises in Hohenfels and Grafenwöhr, large U.S. Army training centers in northern Bavaria. These training exercises were lengthier than most the band had previously participated in, lasting approximately three weeks. However, in conjunction with the Hohenfels exercise, the band accepted a festival performance in Celle, several hours by bus north of the training area. They changed out of battle dress uniform, showered, and changed into a Class B uniform for the job. Sally Gerry remarked that, following this job, it was tough to go back to the field for more tactical training.

The band also made a return trip to Mons, Belgium, for the annual Doudou Festival. The band had not been there since 1986. Not much had changed insofar of the performance requirements. Marching shows, torchlight parades, concerts, and mountains of people, not to mention other military bands from other countries were on hand. The Doudou Festival was a lot of fun, but it was also exhausting.

The year 1994 would see the withdrawal of Soviet forces in East Germany and by December, removal of Western Allies combat forces from Berlin. For the 298th, this year would be one of the busiest yet, all while scaling itself down. One or two at a time, musicians began leaving Berlin for other assignments or for termination of service.

The bigger events of the final year began with the Berlin city government's request for a final Allied Forces Day parade. This parade traditionally brought out combat vehicles of all types and descriptions, cleaned and polished to a high gloss, from each of the Western Allies. Due to Reunification and political sensitivities, not the least of which was the collapse of the Soviet Union itself in December 1991, this parade had not been scheduled in 1990 through 1993. The parade was held on June 18, 1994 and ran the traditional course: beginning just west of the Soviet Memorial on the Strasse des. 17.Juni, marchers continued west, around the north side of the Victory Column, and on past the reviewing stand located just before the parade's end at S-Bahnhof Tiergarten. Berliners lined the streets to observe this last event and no doubt some of them waved a grateful goodbye as the soldiers of the three Western Allies completed this last parade for the city.

Other smaller parades in the separate districts followed. Sally Gerry performed as drum major alternating with Steve Ledbetter for a significantly smaller 298th throughout the summer as the band marched parades in various districts in the former U.S. sector, including Steglitz. She remarked that the citizens of these districts all wanted a last taste of the American Army band that had been in the city for so long.

By far, the biggest event of the year entailed deactivation of the Berlin Brigade itself in a ceremony attended by U.S. President Bill Clinton and international dignitaries. Planners working with the White House and others designated July 12 to deactivate the Brigade. The call went out to former 298th veterans still on active duty if there was interest and funds for temporary duty to return to Berlin to support this most prestigious of ceremonies. Many did, including trombonist Dan Hermann, euphoniumist Mike Herrmann, clarinetist Kim Todd, and euphoniumist Jamie Hillen, all of whom had served in the 298th during the 1980s. After the Berlin Brigade colors were cased for the final time, President Clinton said, "From Checkpoint Charlie to Doughboy City to Tempelhof Airport, more than 100,000 men and women have served in Berlin. More than anyone, they showed the patience it took to win the Cold War. More than anyone, they knew the dangers of a world on edge. They would have been the first casualties in the world's final war, yet they never flinched. In the long struggle to free Berlin, no one ever knew when the day of liberty would come—not when Harry Truman raised the flag in 1945, or when the first airlift planes landed in 1948, or when the hateful Wall went up on 1961. But in all those years, the defenders of Berlin never gave up. You stood your ground; you kept watch; you fortified an island of hope."

The president concluded, "Now we go forward to defend freedom and, strengthened by your devotion, we work for the day when we can say everywhere in the world what you made it possible for us to say here today in Berlin—mission accomplished (Markley, 1994)."[100]

While the Berlin Brigade as an entity was no more, the 298th stayed on. The band grew progressively smaller. Sally Gerry and those remaining referred to themselves as "First in, last out." This meme became a mantra. Photographs of the final events in the band's existence depict marching formations of less than twenty-five. The band's normal strength would have been 38 plus one warrant officer.

Not all of the year's activities were completely involved with shutting down Berlin. CWO David Ratliff, former trumpeter with the 298th (1974-77) and commander of the 298th (1980-84), had moved on in his career and commanded the 1st Army Band at Ft. Meade, Maryland in 1994. Mr. Ratliff's Operations NCO asked him if he'd like to take the 1st Army Band to Berlin to support an American exhibition football game between the San Diego Chargers and the New York Giants. The answer was an unequivocal, "Yes!"

The 1st Army Band flew to Berlin, played a few rehearsals (cramming 100 people inside the Bldg. 909 rehearsal hall was a bit of a challenge, Mr. Ratliff reported with a grin), and then played a marching show in Olympic Stadium in support of the football game. The combined bands (1st Army and 298th) accompanied a singer in the performance of U.S. National Anthem, and for the second time in the years in which Mr. Ratliff had served in Berlin, he conducted *Deutschland Über Alles*. Mr. Ratliff and his band took the opportunity to visit Berlin in the form of tours, Especially noteworthy was the moment during which Mr. Ratliff and others walked through the arches of the Brandenburg Gate, an event he thought he'd never be able to do.

As the summer slipped by and the 298th formed to play the final parades in the districts formerly occupied by American forces, the band took action to draw itself down. Charles W.T. (Frogg) Consaul said via social media that the Bonn government initiated a program through the Judge Advocate General's office whereby the 298th and others who were interested could purchase musical equipment for Pfennige on the Deutsche-mark.[101] Once the program had been properly vetted, many 298th members jumped at the chance to purchase some quality gear. Frogg said that he bought a King bass trombone, a Hirsbrunner BBb tuba, a King sousaphone, and an entire collection of electronic keyboards and sound gear. Frogg served the band through his long tenure in numerous musical ways on multiple instruments. The instruments he chose to purchase were carefully documented and receipts issued. Frogg said he did pass on buying the Latin Percussion marimba because colleague Steve Ledbetter either wanted it or didn't want anyone else to get it, but he did buy the glockenspiel that he marched with when he didn't march with either a bass trombone, sousaphone, or a banjo. That's correct—Frogg had on at least one occasion marched with a banjo.

Even uniform items were made available for purchase. During CWO David Smith's tenure (1984-88), the band had procured wool blues overcoats with ceremonial belts, normally not an item authorized for the 298th. These coats were also part of the "going-out-of-business" sale; Frogg was able to get one of these too. Frogg also made mention of a black jacket with the usual Berlin Brigade insignia on it was given to each band member. First in, last out.

Frogg recalled that hornist Deb Scharf (1992-94) initiated a project to have plaques prepared. Sally Gerry added that Deb went the extra mile by photographing all bandsmen while in performance, not an easy task. The photographs were prepared and individualized for each plaque. All band members signed them for one another as mementoes.

Sheet music was dutifully turned in using the normal Army supply turn-in process. Sally Gerry and Jeff Harper both confirmed that the sheet music was thrown in a dumpster as soon as it was turned in. This was a catastrophe in that many of the pieces that had been in the band's library since 1940 were permanently out of print and could not be replaced. Such was the push, though, to literally get rid of anything and everything as expeditiously as possible.

The 298th Army Band's deactivation orders were published on June 16, 1994. The effective date read September 15, 1994. The final flag lowering at Clay Headquarters on September 7, 1994 was to be the band's last official commitment as a unit, but not as a band.

Reinhard von Bronewski, retired Berlin police officer who worked side-by-side with American military policemen through his long career, explained via email that the remnants of the Berlin command had scheduled a Retreat ceremony on September 7. This ceremony intended to serve as the official flag-lowering ceremony with all the attendant film crews and Major General Walter H. Yates as reviewing officer. The band marched to its normal position on the south side of the flagpole area on Clay Headquarters, dressed in battle dress uniform with Kevlar helmets. The ceremony was conducted, unit guidons (flags) including the band's were cased, and the U.S. flag lowered and folded. The cameramen turned off their cameras and the remnants of U.S. forces in Berlin ceased to exist.

But this was not the case. The flag lowering on September 7 was for the cameras. The final flag lowering ceremony was to be held the next day on September 8, 1994.

Late in the afternoon on September 8, Reinhard heard a radio broadcast that in 30 minutes, the U.S. flag would be lowered at Clay Headquarters for the final time. Reinhard grabbed his video camera, raced to Clay HQ, talked his way onto the facility (he had no official business there), and taped the ceremony. He confirmed he was the only person there with a privately owned video camera, although he noted other foreign camera crews there.

Not without some emotion, Reinhard observed the band's march to their position, led by drum major Sally Gerry. The band was small at this point, numbering only about 20. Dressed in battle dress uniform with soft caps, the band played a traditional Retreat ceremony to lower the flag. Trumpeters played the bugle call "Retreat" and the flag was lowered and then folded by the honor guard.

Reinhard said that he specifically recalls the band laying its instruments at the foot of the flagpole following the ceremony. The symbolism was not lost on those who were there. After 49 years in the city and another 5 years before and during World War II, the 298th Army Band's mission was complete.

Following this ceremony, there was little else for the band to do other than finalize individual preparations to move to their next assignments. Those with sufficient time remaining on their overseas assignment were sent to the remaining bands in the former West Germany. Others received credit for their overseas assignment and were sent back to U.S.-based bands. Still others had reached the end of their enlistments and chose to leave the Army.

One small thing did happen before the band departed: Sally related that Major General Yates, the senior officer in charge of the remnants of the Berlin Brigade, brought baseball caps to the band hall and passed those out to those band members remaining. General Yates expressed his gratitude for the band's service and his personal touch was not lost on the band. It was another emotional moment.

At the end, there were only three bandsmen: percussionist Shawn

Mitchell, trumpeter Kyle Svoma, and First Sergeant Michael van Winkle. Shawn and Michael were headed for the 3rd Infantry Division in Bamberg; Kyle was assigned to the 1st Armored Division in Bad Kreuznach. Before they left, however, they had some final business to attend to.

At 8:00 a.m. on September 14, 1994, Shawn and Kyle left their hotel rooms near Johannaplatz in the Grunewald subdistrict and drove to Building 909 on Andrews. They met 1SG van Winkle there and awaited a local national, a woman, who was part of the team overseeing the turnover of the facilities back to the German government. The four of them toured Building 909 while the Americans pointed out the individual rooms in the building and the purpose for each. The woman also looked to ensure that all items had been removed from the building and that the building was in good condition. At the end of the tour, the woman appeared to be satisfied.

At the end of the walk-through, 1SG van Winkle said to Shawn and Kyle, "Good job in closing things up—see you [meaning Shawn] in Bamberg." With that, the first sergeant left the building and departed in his car, destination Bamberg. Shawn and Kyle remained long enough to turn the lights out, lock the door, and hand the keys over to the woman.

Shawn concluded, "I am proud to have been part of closing the final chapter on the 298th Army Band."

First in, last out.

AUTHOR'S NOTES

My tour in West Berlin lasted almost nine years. During that time I went to work, shined boots and brass, pressed uniforms, stood in formations, played

Marching guide file--Allied Forces Day, 1987

the euphonium, marched the 4-Ring, stared at communism, had a lot of fun, and finally began to appreciate what it was like to be an American and free. The presence of the Wall and its ugly scar across the city made it clear to me how fortunate we Americans truly are.

Berlin is much more than a city. It's an attitude. A way of life. The people show pluck, kindness, generosity, impatience. It's also a city that had come to terms with the Wall but hated its presence nonetheless. Some hated the presence of the Western Allies, but most remembered the dark days of the Airlift and being hungry.

Getting to Berlin wasn't easy. In March 1982, the Army assigned me to the 2nd Armored Division Band at Ft. Hood and shortly after arriving there I knew I couldn't stay. I loved Texas itself—the state offered opportunities for music (I studied the euphonium with Carlton Morris, whose methods I still use today) and traveling (I bought a motorcycle and rode 7,000 miles in six months), but the band's facilities were deplorable. The best the 2nd Armored Division could do for the its band was to assign a condemned, 1950s-era clapboard movie theater infested by aggressive, flying cockroaches and an occasional family of skunks that took up residence under the building. I knew

I wanted to get back to Germany, where I had just completed a three-year assignment at the 1st Armored Division Band in Ansbach, West Germany.

In Germany I had learned to appreciate performing in front of audiences who in turn appreciated what we were doing. A constant, steady diet of military ceremonies and parades characterized most gigs in Texas. I used a reenlistment option to leave Ft. Hood. When I talked to the reenlistment NCO I was surprised to hear that I could reenlist specifically for an assignment to Berlin, so I grabbed that opportunity. It still took six months for the paperwork to finalize before I could leave.

I flew out of JFK Airport after having dropped off my car earlier that day. The plane touched down at Frankfurt International and I took a connecting flight arriving at Tegel Airport in Berlin on January 11, 1983. SFC Jim Lindly picked me up at the airport, a gesture I appreciated. Jim was the brass group leader in the band; all brass section leaders in trumpet, trombone, horn, euphonium, and tuba reported to him. All incoming musicians arriving in the 298th were assigned a sponsor; Jim had agreed to be mine. Jim's presence at the airport was in marked contrast to my first assignment to Germany in which I processed through the 21st Replacement Detachment at Rhein Main Air Base outside of Frankfurt where the hospitality wasn't quite as pronounced or evident.

An assignment to Berlin was considered special. The close proximity to the Soviets and the reality of living and working 110 miles behind the Iron Curtain in an island of freedom were elements to consider. Everything I had heard about the assignment was positive—terrific facilities, adequate support, performing for appreciative audiences. I looked forward to this new beginning from several vantage points and determined to succeed at the assignment. I was still a young NCO with only a few years in grade as a staff sergeant and had just completed my eighth year in active service. Only 26 years old, I was ready for a new turn in life, as I was undergoing a divorce.

Jim and I shook hands and exchanged pleasantries. A 20-minute drive later, winding through the French and British sectors, we arrived at Andrews Barracks in the American sector and the band hall. I was struck at the sheer number of trees, bare at this time of year, in a large city. The band hall on Andrews, a brick structure three stories tall, lay cocooned in a quiet corner of the small kaserne. A professionally-prepared sign announced the 298th and the names of the commander and enlisted bandleader. I had an immediate favorable impression.

We entered the building, walked up a short flight of stairs and through a set of double doors into a long hallway. A normal office desk stood at this crossroads of the hallway and two entrances which formed the axis of the ground floor. The desk along with a couple of telephones, I was certain, formed the CQ's post. The CQ, dressed in his battle dress uniform (BDU) –

sat at the desk. A television, off for the moment, sat in the general area, along with an overstuffed chair.

I noted the spitshined boots and neat appearance of the CQ and I felt a little grimy by comparison.

Jim beckoned me to follow him and after I deposited my bags alongside the hallway wall, followed him into the enlisted bandleader's office.

Master Sergeant Lou Hurvitz got up from his chair, came around his desk, and shook my hand. He took a quick, but careful look at my appearance—I was dressed in civvies—and dryly noted, "Sergeant Lawless, you need a haircut."

I immediately remarked that I'd get one at my first opportunity. We talked for a few minutes, during which obligatory small talk and questions about traveling took place, and then I took my leave. Jim took me over to the supply room where I signed out bunk linen and other items. Grabbing one of my bags, he climbed the stairs up to the second floor with me to show me my room.

At the top of the second-floor stairs – a wide set of stairs – I turned left and headed down three doors. Opening the door, I found myself in a decent-sized room in which I would be the only occupant. I was happy about that. Three wall lockers, a bunk, a couch, a desk, a small refrigerator, and a couple of other furniture items including a carpet, comprised the room setup. The room was neat and clean, ready for someone—me—to move in. This was in stark contrast to my arrival at Ft. Hood – those people didn't even know I was coming much less prepare a barracks room for my arrival.

Jim made sure I was set up, then told me to look around and get comfortable, and then explained how to get to the barber shop on Andrews. I got my haircut and on the way back from the barber, I saw just how busy Andrews was. Brisk traffic, lots of pedestrians, cobblestones, the dining facility. This area of the kaserne adjacent to the main gate funneled most of the traffic, which made me appreciate the quiet northwest corner where the band hall stood.

About midway through unpacking, someone knocked on my door. I answered the door, and a guy I didn't know smiled and introduced himself. He said, "Hey! I'm Ralph Cuellar and it's just about time for you to come with me. We're going to Mom's."

I must have looked a little puzzled because he said, "Don't worry about it. Just finish putting that stuff away and when you're done, come next door."

As I had no clue what was next door, I followed him over there and encountered a large room that occupied the entire northeast corner of the 2nd floor. The room was lined with filing cabinets and I could tell this was the band library. Two other guys were in the room, both dressed in BDUs. They looked at me and smiled and said, "Mom's. You'll like it." With that, Ralph laughed and clapped me on the back and then crab-walked somewhat over to the coffee pot that was in the room and poured himself a half-cup. Taking a sip, Ralph said, "I have some problems with my back so I don't really move that well—but it doesn't stop me from marching. At least not yet."

With that we entered into some bandsman talk—previous assignments, people we might know, what we played. The other men in the room were Ray Martin, who played tuba, and Bob Frushour, who played horn and trumpet. Despite my jet lag, I was drawn into conversation for a time. At about 4 P.M. the duty day finished. We got into someone's car and headed over to "Mom's."

"Mom's" had another name. Also called "Kastanieneck" which, loosely translated meant "chestnut corner" it was just a local Kneipe. The guys explained that in Berlin, you didn't really see a Gasthaus like you would see in Bavaria. A Kneipe was simply a neighborhood bar that served all manner of beverages and provided a place for men and women to go and socialize while enjoying the local beer or soft drink. While Gasthäuse in other parts of Germany often had a menu, Kneipen usually did not.

"Mom," whose name was actually Waltraud, ran the bar. She didn't speak any English, but that didn't matter to Ralph. Ralph's German was almost as good as his Spanish and he ordered beers around. I noted with approval that Mom sold Löwenbräu, rather unusual in that Löwenbräu was a beer brewed in Munich—not in Berlin. I would later learn about the various Berliner beers and conclude that I liked the lighter Bavarian beers better than the beers brewed in the north of Germany—better water, perhaps, as the tap water in Berlin was full of minerals.

At any rate, the beer flowed, we talked and compared notes, and I thoroughly enjoyed myself in my first day in Berlin.

I learned very quickly that the 298th Army Band already had a full complement of euphonium players. Normally, only two are authorized per band. In this case, the band already had SSG Al Covin, SP5 Mike Herrmann, and SP4 Shawn Holtzapple. My boss, SFC Jim Lindly, was technically the brass group leader but he generally played euphonium when he wasn't performing as drum major. So for the second time in my 5-year military band career thus far, I was the fifth wheel.

I wondered about there being so many of us euphonium players and how specifically I was able to secure assignment with the 298th, so I asked MSG Hurvitz that question. He told me that they'd received positive reports on my playing skills and that two of the three players were scheduled to leave toward the fall of 1983. There would be an overlap of a few months and an overage in the euphonium section during that overlap period, but this was not a problem.

I settled into a routine of concert band rehearsal in the morning. We'd take a 15-minute break and head upstairs for the library where coffee was always on. Finishing up rehearsal at about 1130, the band had a lunch break and then convene again at 1300 for whatever else the day might bring.

The Brandenburg Express, a jazz-rock group, might rehearse. Or the full stage band. Frequently office work of various types were planned – administration, training, operations, transportation, supply, arms room, library all had to be done. After a day or two, I met guitarist SP5 Mitchel B. Kaufman. Most everybody called him "Mitch" but he prefers to be called Mike. The first words out of Mitch's mouth to me were, "You're going to PLDC."

I knew what PLDC was – the so-called "Primary Leadership Development Course." In a word, PLDC functioned as the lower rung in the Non-Commissioned Officer Education System (NCOES) and what it really entailed was another trip to basic training. I thought, "Lovely. After eight years active service, I get to go back to basic training."

But I wouldn't be going until the May-June time frame. When it was time, I packed my required gear, signed out my M16A1 rifle, and got on the duty train heading for Frankfurt.

Kransberg Schloss, located north of Frankfurt, had offered a few slots for Berlin soldiers to attend. This castle had an interesting history – initially built in 1170, it had stood for centuries to include having served as a headquarters for Nazi Germany's Luftwaffe during the early days of World War II, a rehabilitation center for German Army soldiers, and even as a personal retreat for Hermann Göring. Immediately after the war, the castle was used as a British-American detention center for former Nazis and during the Cold War, the U.S. V Corps used the facility as an NCO Academy.

Training at PLDC took me through basic leadership principles, field manual training in drill and ceremony, in particular holding formations and conducting movements, and running physical fitness training sessions. The training culminated with a series of field problems that required mastering basic infantry skills such as map reading and fire and maneuver. My stint at PLDC meant I'd miss the first of many Allied Forces Day rehearsals and then the parade, but I'd more than make up for that by marching in the runup to the Brigade Review and then capping off the Berlin marching season, the Independence Day performances.

In the meantime, I got settled in and discovered that Dave Young, a tubist who had served with me in Ansbach, was also in the band. He arrived an entire day before me, as had trombonist Kevin Entwistle (who is now a full Colonel).

Tubist Bob Brinkofski and bassoonist Dave Keller approached me one day not long after I arrived in the band and asked me if I'd consider working in the supply room. Bob explained that he was leaving Berlin in a few months and that they needed to find somebody to replace Dave, who would be moving up to the supply sergeant job from the assistant role. I declined at first, surprised at the invitation and not fully understanding the job. I'd never worked in an Army band supply room and had really only functioned as an operations assistant and various small roles, including truck driver. The supply job sounded foreign and, frankly, a little scary. Two staff sergeants, plus a third man, fellow euphoniumist Mike Herrmann, to run an Army band supply room? Seemed like overkill to me.

I chewed on the idea for a few days and asked a few questions. I observed both Brink and Keller and noted they worked well together. Mike Herrmann was a tall, affable man whose wit was razor sharp. I concluded that working with this group would probably be a good thing and therefore wound up spending most of my non-musical duty time in the supply room learning the job.

They told me that there were two property books – one for organizational equipment like rifles and trumpets, and another for installation equipment like bunks and wall lockers. Keeping track of all this gear while dealing with procuring additional equipment or sheet music or saxophone reeds or guitar effects boxes, along with getting uniforms cleaned and serviced, all of this kept us busy. Dave was a patient teacher and I quickly became immersed into the minutiae of maintaining a well-functioning supply room.

Before too long, Brink left Berlin which left Dave as supply sergeant, me as his assistant, and Mike as supply clerk.

Dave had a sense of humor. Typing out a formal Department of the Army (DA) Form 2765-1, which essentially looked like a computer card, he took one that requested procurement of an M-60A3 Main Battle Tank and took that to CW2 Dave Ratliff, along with a stack of other cards for various legitimate things.

An Army band is not authorized an M-60A3 Main Battle Tank. But that doesn't stop a band from requesting one. Mr. Ratliff got caught up in the big stack of documents and wound up signing off on the one that requisitioned the M-60 tank. Requisitions of all types were reviewed for accuracy and authorization by Supply and Services Division, in particular by Mr. Knopf, a retired chief warrant officer logistician serving in a civilian job. He was accustomed to finding all sorts of anomalies such as an Army band requesting an armored tank, but the number of questions and good-natured ribbing coming out of such a thing would have been the talk of the Berlin command for some time.

None the wiser of the pending storm, Mr. Ratliff returned the stack of endorsed cards to Keller, who couldn't hold it in any longer. Holding up the card in question, Keller laughed and said, "Something tells me I shouldn't turn this particular requisition in." Mr. Ratliff knew that something was awry, but patiently waited for the announcement. Keller admitted to the prank in setting up Mr. Ratliff for a potential problem, and then tore up the card. Everybody laughed at the good-natured joke, Mr. Ratliff included.

The band usually had four trombone players while marching a five-man front. This left one slot open in the front rank, which I usually filled. This was one of the easier positions in which to march because just about the only thing I had to do was to follow the drum major and make sure I kept up, even if he took off to the races. All bands aligned to the center file, which meant that I, and not necessarily the drum major, controlled the speed of the band. SFC Jim Lindly did most of the drum majoring and he was rather picky about his expectations and the way he did things.

We did a marching show in the Deutschlandhalle, a large auditorium in Berlin that featured a large central area rather than the usual stage. Participants marched in the central area with spotlights blazing. I failed to keep pace with Lindly and as a result, the band dropped back too far behind the drum major. This had the effect of putting the drum major out on the marching floor as an unwitting soloist. When he realized what had happened, he performed a maneuver to recover which put him back in the proper place in front of the band. We finished our segment without further incident.

I got royally chewed out for that, not surprisingly.

After I'd been in the city about a month, I received notification that my car had arrived in Bremerhaven. By this time I had obtained my US Army Europe driver's license, so all I had to do was travel on the duty train up to Bremerhaven, pick up the car, have it inspected, purchase auto insurance and registration, and travel back. The drive back to Berlin included my first solo drive through East Germany. First-time travelers had to undergo a briefing at Checkpoint Alpha (the entrance point into East Germany) conducted by the military police. My trip was uneventful, though I found the Soviet checkpoints through which Allied travelers also had to process dank and foreboding. I later learned about the various mild harassment techniques they used on the Western Allies, none of which were especially troubling.

My 1978 Chevy Nova had a factory-installed catalytic convertor. Germany, at this time, had not yet gone to lead-free gasoline. Knowing I had no plans to bring this car with me back to the U.S. after my tour in Berlin was complete, I set out to destroy my catalytic convertor by running leaded gas through it on the trip from Bremerhaven back to Berlin.

The result was one stinky situation. I stopped for a rest break and encountered a peculiar odor that most definitely meant that my catalytic convertor was destroyed. Lead-free gasoline came to Europe in about 1984.

My off-duty time included spending some time in discos. These gatherings of young people intent on listening and dancing to rhythm heavy music at extremely loud volumes sometimes provided opportunities for meeting at a later time. Conversing in a disco was almost impossible due to the volume, but after a few minutes of shouting to be overheard, I frequently asked for a phone number for a call and a more subdued conversation in a quieter place. I met Carola in one such place, in Zehlendorf. We became an item and through her coaching, my German improved considerably.

When the 1983 parade season came upon us, the deputy brigade commander, Colonel Frank Adams, decided to pay us a visit at the band hall. We all assembled in the rehearsal hall, somebody called "Attention!" when he entered the building whereupon we all leaped to our collective feet just to hear him graciously say, "As you were."

He wanted to give us a pep talk, as he knew the success of the upcoming season was going to largely depend on the performance of the 298th. His speech started with sincere accolades and assurances of how important our contributions were to the Western Allies. As several senior Soviet military officers attended the various ceremonies and parades in which the band was a central feature, he began talking about the Soviet Union and how no fewer than 25 combat divisions of the Soviet Western Force was poised to strike Berlin. Colonel Adams warmed to his subject. With his eyes flashing and his voice now starting to bellow, he proceeded to lambast and call the Soviets everything but human beings. He derided them, said they were as good as dead, and ranted and raved for a good 10 minutes.

The pep talk had a curious effect on most of us in the rehearsal hall. Stone silence. Colonel Adams was a rather imposing figure at well over six feet tall and whose BDUs were the original style, meaning the arms were too short. The resulting image reminded me of a fair-haired gorilla. He thumped his chest with his gorilla ham-like fists, bellowed and roared with his sleeves ending about where his elbows began. It would have been funny, but we weren't laughing.

Ceremonies were sometimes a showcase in competition between the Western Allies. The so-called "Queen Anne step" as done by one of the British bands in Berlin (there were a total of three) was seen by the commanding general and he thought it would be a great idea for the 298th to beat the British at their own game. Colonel Adams informed Mr. Ratliff that the band would do the Queen Anne step in time for the Brigade Review, which was the second of the three big marching events that comprised parade season.

We heard of this step as the "Queen Anne" or "glide step." But it would appear the proper term is "balance step" as executing it from quick time, or the regular march step, can very much lead to a loss of balance severe enough to appear as a total idiot.

In first practicing this glide step, we succeeded in looking like complete idiots. It took patience, drum taps for rhythm, and when we could do that without falling on our faces, we eventually moved up to playing and marching at the same time.

Mr. Ratliff selected Kenneth Alford's *The Standard of St. George* as the march to play for the portion of the ceremony known to us as "Sound Off" or "Trooping the Line." This maneuver was a popular one in Berlin as it involved only the band as we moved into position, played three chords, and stepped off to the march. The rule is, if the band is playing and marching, the band is compelled to repeat the piece from the top unless the band is cut off by the leader. At this point, the band would revert from quick time to balance step throughout the 32 bars of the opening, which is largely a fanfare. At the conclusion of the fanfare, the band would go back to quick time. We mentally used the phrase, "Now We're Fin-Ished" to denote that critical point where we all needed to go back to quick time together. Forgetting to resort to quick time was not an option. The effect was impressive, especially as the music lined up with the march step intricacies.

Playing a musical instrument at volume while marching is not for the weak. It's hard work and it's especially difficult when you're trying to concentrate on playing the music as well as keeping in alignment, keeping in phase, and otherwise not calling attention to yourself by making a mistake. So as not to fall victim to these types of embarrassing moments, I took it upon myself to memorize the euphonium part to all marches that customarily are played while on the march. I had little to no trouble in memorization, so this method kept me out of trouble.

Beginning in 1985, we had to vacate the band hall. Everything in the building had to be moved 100 yards to our south to building 904. Building 909, the band's home since 1951, was getting a much-needed makeover. The entire building was gutted. Plumbing, electrical, heating, all the interior walls were taken down, leaving only the exterior shell. The end result, costing DM 5 million, provided ample rehearsal space, practice sound modules (heretofore a problem with those who liked to practice late at night), ample storage for supply, and redesigned barracks rooms that were more consistent with respect to size. The elevator was placed back in service, a good thing when the 40-odd filing cabinets full of sheet music needed to be moved into the new library. Recording capability was improved, and the band took possession of the entire building except the basement. Telephone service was also greatly improved, with 8-9 lines rather than only three for the entire band.

In May 1985, I signed up for a supply course which was scheduled to be taught in Vilseck, Germany. This Army kaserne was strategically located just south of the U.S. military training center at Grafenwöhr, a training facility used heavily by many U.S. Army units. The supply course ran for two weeks in which I would learn how to do things the way I was already doing them. Nonetheless, I got in my car and drove through the East to the Zone and headed south. The trip was uneventful and I arrived, signed in, and got a room in the on-post facilities.

Days were spent in class and doing exercises, and little else. As this was not an official military training course (there were several civilians attending this particular course), there was no physical training, no cleaning details to do and, in general, no harassment. As I was once again in Bavaria, I reveled in the fundamental difference between rural Bavaria and urban Berlin. I encountered a slower pace in life, a decided contrast to Berlin's more tense and aggressive people. I encountered farm tractors on the roads with the warning triangles mounted on the back rather than the more common Opel seen in the city.

I recall going to a Bavarian Gasthaus, which was fairly empty and ordered a fairly standard meal of *Schnitzel mit pommes und Salat* and a beer and thoroughly enjoyed the lemon on the Schnitzel. The whole thing was like a two-week vacation and I was almost sorry to pack up and head back to Berlin. They gave me a certificate which was good for inclusion as a secondary MOS.

On average, the Deutsche-mark to U.S. Dollar conversion rate ranged from roughly 2.40 in 1983 to 2.76 in 1984. That trend continued to rise to a high of 3.17 in 1985, a rate that had not been seen in Germany since President Richard Nixon's administration in the early 1970s.

French hornist Ross Maser, a senior staff sergeant and Vietnam veteran, borrowed my car one day. While driving towards Andrews, a truck changed lanes without looking and hit my car. The car's left rear quarter-panel and half the trunk was caved in. The insurance company wrote it off as a loss and paid me roughly DM 2,500 for the privilege of junking out the car. I was able to collect the money and sell the carcass to a GI who repaired cars, evidently enjoying a challenge. I saw him some months later and asked him how the project had gone. He said he regretted buying the car and repairing it. Apparently the car's rust problem was severe.

The mid-1980s were filled by frequent trips on the duty train. It seemed like we were forever going to the Zone for a performance of one type or another. One series of gigs that simply found the band over several years took place in the Bad Hersfeld/Fulda military communities, particularly on Rosenmontag. The Rose Monday festivities basically aligned with the American equivalent known as "Fat Tuesday." The Germans were much more boisterous on this pre-Lenten holiday than most Americans, so after an overnight trip on the duty train, we arrived in Giessen at about 4 A.M. We'd then have to disembark in a hurry from the train as it didn't stop very long, grab our bags and our instruments and make our way through the Giessen Bahnhof to a waiting Army bus and a truck for the gear.

Climbing onto the bus, we'd bounce along for about 90 minutes before arriving in Bad Hersfeld, the home of the 7th Armored Cavalry Regiment. We'd line up to go eat chow and following that, prepared for a full day of parades and concerts. The weather was usually uncooperative. It being late February, we'd see snow and I distinctly remember one year we wore combat boots underneath our dress blues trousers since the snow was so deep.

Rosenmontag in Bad Hersfeld/Fulda provided no end to surprises and calamities. One year the weather stranded us. From that point, the area became known as "The Fulda Triangle." The band could get in, but getting out wasn't guaranteed. As the story in the "Performances" chapter indicates, I was the one who suffered the indignation of an ear of corn tossed down the bell of my euphonium. I was not happy about that. Fulda/Bad Hersfeld became such a problem that I made the decision to drive out to the Zone for the gig. I figured if I was going to get stranded, I could at least get stranded without having to babysit a bass drum.

My stay in the renovated Building 909 was relatively brief, as I had been selected for promotion to Sergeant First Class and simultaneously directed to attend the Advanced NCO Course (ANCOC). This meant after the promotion, which didn't occur until December 1986, I had to move out of the barracks and move into senior enlisted housing. My new home was a studio apartment in a leased building located some 3 miles from Andrews between Dahlem and Steglitz near U-Bahn Breitenbachplatz.

Schlangenbaderstrasse, the street on which this apartment building sat, featured a gathering of space-age looking structures. These were all apartments and all relatively high-rise. My apartment was located on the third floor of the third of three stairwells and consisted of a bedroom alcove, small kitchen with breakfast nook, bathroom, hallway, and room for an actual living room. I really enjoyed this. I could say good-bye to late-night rowdiness, entertain my own lady friend without signing her in at the front gate and in the CQ log, and otherwise start functioning like an adult.

Nevertheless, if I didn't want to go that far, but I wanted to go out and hobnob with a person or two, I would occasionally head just downstairs almost directly underneath my apartment. Betsy, the owner of this typical Berlin Kneipe, was an American ex-pat whose German was flawless and enjoyed the respect of her patrons for that reason. I'd go in and have a beer or two and share stories. One of my all-time favorite memories of Betsy wasn't one of her stories, though – it was her potato salad. She made hers by cooking the potatoes in their jackets, peeling them while hot, adding mayonnaise while hot, along with finely chopped leeks, bell peppers, celery, a bit of red wine vinegar, and salt and pepper. This is a recipe I still use today and is favored anywhere I've presented it.

Life in the BEQ was enjoyable, but not quite as convenient as living in the barracks. At first I jogged to work some three miles then jogged home after work. Later, I bought a car and most, not all, of the jogging went away. I was still an avid volksmarcher and regularly participated by running the lengthy courses.

Shortly after my promotion, I left the supply room and moved to Operations, where my language skills could be put to good use. I encountered bassoonist and drum major Dave Olszyk, who had things well under control. I learned to stay out of his way. After he departed Berlin in 1989, however, I became more involved.

In early 1988, my turn came up to go to ANCOC, so I packed my bags and headed back to the U.S. heading first to Michigan to visit for a few days and to borrow my Dad's ragtag van, and then drove down to Ft. Eustis, VA for the "common core" part of the training.

Common Core was followed by the "technical track" or the actual musical part of the training at the Army Element, School of Music at the Little Creek Amphibious Base just outside Norfolk, VA. I learned aspects of music that my earlier training never touched on—chord progression, arranging techniques, conducting. There wasn't much time to absorb all of what was offered, but I did well enough to pass the course, though I had a tricky moment. One pass/fail criterion of the course required the testee, while on the podium, identify, locate, and correct built-in errors in the music within a certain time limit. This sounds easier than it is. I did have to be retested when I couldn't find all the errors in rehearsing the concert band ensemble the first time. I passed the test the second time. I had had no trouble with the stage band portion of finding and fixing errors, oddly enough, especially for a euphonium player.

Once back in Berlin, I once again entered the band's schedule, though the housing office chose to end its lease with the building in which I lived. That and my marriage in June 1989 prompted two additional moves culminating in living in a German apartment rather than American housing. At this point, my German was vastly improved to the extent that I took, and passed, the Defense Language Institute's examination for German. This was sufficient to be awarded the Additional Skill Identifier "L GM" in my personnel records. I was very proud of that accomplishment as I had worked very hard in assimilating into the German culture. My wife and I moved into an apartment on Ostpreußendamm in Lichterfelde, only a 10-minute jog to Andrews.

On November 9, 1989 the Wall came down. The year 1989 saw great unrest in eastern Europe. Demonstrators protested in Hungary in late September. The frontier through Czechoslovakia opened for those in East Germany to leave through Austria. I read about that in the news, but never realized what it would bring. Instead, rehearsals, military training, gigs, occasionally some travel, home life occupied my mind.

The last person killed trying to cross the Wall didn't know, of course, that he was to be the last to die. In April 1989, the young man was machine-gunned while trying to escape to freedom. He should've waited. In little more than seven months, the Wall would come down and the Cold War would end.

November 9th was a Thursday, On that weekend, my wife and I had already planned to leave the city for a quiet weekend in Celle, near Braunschweig. The announcement came about the Wall's demise and my first reaction was to stay away from the downtown area. I knew pandemonium would be prevalent. The Wall's demise didn't alter our plans—we continued on, but I feared the crowds would make the various checkpoints impassable.

We were surprised to see only a bit more than the usual traffic at Checkpoint Bravo and the autobahn south and west of the city. We saw nothing noteworthy at the Soviet checkpoint either. Leaving Berlin, traffic was about normal. As we neared the border at Helmstedt, we saw the cheaply made, smelly Trabant and Wartburg East German cars out in force. They were all headed west. We waited about 45 minutes at the West German border, not bad considering the building traffic.

As Friday, November 10th continued, cars from eastern bloc countries poured across. The drivers of these vehicles from Poland, Hungary, Czechoslovakia, Rumania and mostly, East Germany, drove slowly, blocking traffic while rubber-necking at everything. It appeared that these people, most of them certainly seeing West Germany for the first time, were absolutely enthralled and probably a bit scared. They looked everywhere and anywhere. It was clear, though, that they felt strange, even a bit foreign, in a country that spoke the same language as they.

We noticed the people from the East did some grocery shopping. One of the items that was hugely popular was bananas. They bought all they could find, illustrating that bananas were a relatively rare commodity in their own country.

We enjoyed our weekend in Celle, so much so that we purchased a cockatiel from a downtown pet shop, and soon it was time to head back to Berlin. We packed up and left, fully expecting an absolutely jammed Checkpoint Alpha, just outside Helmstedt. We must've found a lull in the action, because we didn't have to wait long before processing through.

Monday saw a new round of craziness, however. The Wall was down and people were streaming over by the tens of thousands. An already crowded city was becoming absolutely choked with humanity. And people were chipping at the Wall. We bandsmen, along with all other soldiers, were told not to hammer at the Wall. It still belonged to the government of East Germany and if we were caught, it meant serious consequences. So we had to sneak at it. On Tuesday, bassoonist and drum major Leonard "Mac" Mutter and I drove to Zehlendorf and parked the car a discreet distance from the Wall. Armed with hammers and a cold chisel, we attempted to hide behind bushes while chipping away. Guards were still positioned in the towers, only 100 meters from us, but they did nothing but observe with binoculars. German civilians on the West side were openly hammering away. Mac and I got several nice samples each and headed back. We didn't want to overdo it.

What followed over the next two years was nothing short of a miracle. The political changes which were forthcoming would amaze us all—Berlin's status as an occupied city ended, Reunification of both Germanys took place, and the city that had a flavor all its own would change forever. As a bandsman

and Operations NCO, I was involved in many politically-flavored events. These ranged from providing musical support at a newly-created breach in the Wall, just down the street from my apartment in Lichterfelde, to performing at the ceremony which "gave away" Checkpoint Charlie to a German museum. Several years later I found out that an up-close video shot of me playing my instrument at the Checkpoint Charlie ceremony graced the opening scenes of a German documentary of Reunification. I distinctly recall the ceremony—as I stood in the front rank of the formation playing The Stars and Stripes Forever, I remember a person sticking a video camera directly into my face, no more than 2 inches away. This was a little disconcerting, but I continued playing. I was surprised to learn that the very footage wound up in the documentary.

As the Operations supervisor, I took part in Reunification activity planning insofar as the participation of the band was concerned. Band representation was frequently needed in meetings in which only German was spoken. I attended several of these meetings, occasionally with the band commander. Planning for Reunification and the eventual joining of a city long separated by the Wall were exhilarating and meaningful. Participating in these events brought it home to me how much the Wall's demise affected the life of

Berliners and the new arrivals from the East.

It was an exciting time to be in Berlin, yet also somewhat sad. Gone forever would be the city as many soldiers and airmen knew it. In time, the PX complex was razed, the duty train was stopped, and many of the housing areas were no longer flavored by American families.

Although German Reunification was a welcome sight for political as well as moral reasons, we all lost a little of something when The Wall came down on that November day in 1989. All the same, I am proud of my own service of almost nine years in that "unique" city and it will always remain in my heart as the cornerstone of my experience.

Desert Shield began in 1990 when Saddam sent his forces to annex Kuwait. My tour in Berlin, after several extensions, was finally going to end in February 1991 whereupon I had orders to report to the 3rd Armored Division Band in Frankfurt. The timing was serendipitous, however, as the 3rd Armored Division was deployed to Saudi Arabia and was preparing to wage the ground war against Saddam's forces in Iraq in that month. The Army, believing my assignment to the unit at this time would be disruptive, canceled my orders under an Army-wide program known as "Stop Loss." After eight years in the city, I was ready to move on, but the Army didn't agree with me. I remained in Berlin throughout Desert Storm.

The American Army was at war. While we in Berlin were not in the fight, we were obligated to ramp up security measures. The 298th patrolled the Andrews Barracks perimeter, accompanied a combat engineer vehicle while it was parked near the front gate, and provided a presence of watchfulness. We had no difficulties, though we knew our companions who were deployed were in harm's way. In March 1991, we stood down and returned to more normal duties.

During this time, I moved from Operations to Administration. I knew my time was winding down and I did not immerse myself into that job like I had my others. My mind was elsewhere.

I was ready to leave Berlin. I needed to leave Berlin to rejuvenate, to find myself again. I wanted and needed to finish my education and had but one more tour of three years to do that before retirement. After I finally got a green light to go, I packed my bags, climbed in my 1987 Ford Tempo and headed southwest through the unmanned Checkpoint Bravo, past the empty Soviet Checkpoint at Drewitz, and onto the Berliner Ring and points south and west.

Monday, September 16, 1991 was a bright sunny day. My disposition did not match the weather, however. I was relieved to have this long chapter in my military career over, yet I remained anxious. My next assignment was the 8th Infantry Division Band in Bad Kreuznach, Germany. This was my final assignment before retirement and I had a lot of work to do.

But I knew that even though I turned the key and shifted gears, I would be content to simply say, "Ich habe noch einen Koffer in Berlin." That suitcase is waiting on me and always will be there.

Appendix – 298th Army Band Leadership

The following is a chronological listing of the officers, commissioned and warrant, who commanded the 298th Army Band and its predecessors: the 108th Cavalry Band, the 156th Infantry Band, the London Base Command Band and the European Theater of Operations Band. The list also includes those senior noncommissioned officers who served as the band's enlisted bandleader. NOTE: Some dates of service may not be entirely accurate:

CWO Frank J. Rosato – original bandmaster of the 108th Cavalry Band/156th Infantry Band. Led band through pre-WWII National Guard call-up (November 1940 to active service in December 1941), then continued leadership throughout WWII. Led the band from various training assignments to England, then on to London, where the band became known as the ETO Band. Mr. Rosato led the band to Berlin where it remained following WWII. Departed Berlin in October, 1945.

WOJG James W. Abel – assisted Mr. Rosato initially. Commanded the 298th Army Band (as opposed to the 300th Infantry Band), which was largely a paper assignment. Mr. Rosato remained in operational charge of both the 298th and 300th Bands. 300th Infantry Band deactivated in late 1945; 298th Army Band remained. Mr. Abel departed Berlin in October 1945.

1LT Rosalyn Hershenson – has the distinction of being the only female officer to have commanded the band. She served following the departure of Rosato/Abel and endeared herself to the musicians with her sensitivity and positive personality. Commanded the 298th from 7 October 1945 to 12 April 1946.

1LT Harry A. Buzzett – An officer who served as commander of the 298th pending assignment of a warrant officer bandmaster. Commanded the 298th from 12 April 1946 to 15 June 1946.

CPT Gordon J. Hartzier - An officer who served as commander of the 298th pending assignment of a warrant officer bandmaster. Commanded the 298th from 15 June 1946 to 7 December 1946.

WOJG Peter Berg – Commanded the 298th from late 7 December 1946 to 7 January 1947.

2LT Lawrence J. Gallagher - An officer who served as commander of the 298th pending assignment of a warrant officer bandmaster. Commanded the 298th from 7 January 1947 to 5 March 1947.

CWO Louis Ferraro – A confirmed warrant officer bandmaster. Commanded the 298th from 5 March 1947 to 12 May 1947. During Mr. Ferraro's tenure, personnel strength climbed from a low of 21 enlisted men on 21 March to a high of 65 enlisted men on 10 May.

CWO Marion E. Durbin – A confirmed warrant officer bandmaster. Mr. Durbin took considerable effort in providing central leadership of the band after a lengthy series of commanders whose tenure was very brief. He had a fair eye to the history of the unit and provided much information on the 298th during his tenure via annual "Historical Reports." Commanded the 298th from 12 May 1947 to 14 February 1950. Mr. Durbin enjoyed approximately 65 musicians in the 298th at the beginning of his assignment. On 1 June 1947, the 298th Army Ground Forces Band was redesignated as the 298th Army Band. Actual strength of the 298th at the beginning of 1948 was 1 Warrant Officer and 31 enlisted men. However, an additional 1 Warrant Officer and 38 enlisted men were attached to the 298th from Headquarters and Headquarters Company, 7782 Special Troops Battalion for duty with the band. On 25 May 1948, 1 Warrant Officer and 22 enlisted men were relieved from their attachment and transferred to the 7753rd Augmentation Detachment (298th Army Band). Furthermore, on 29 July 1948, the 7868th Fife & Drum Unit (consisting of approximately 1 Warrant Officer and 30 enlisted men) was attached to the 298th as a Field Music Corps and served through the remainder of 1948.

CWO Carroll H. Grummish – A confirmed warrant officer bandmaster, designated initially as commander of the 7753rd Augmentation Detachment only. As commander of the 7753rd, also served as the supply officer for the 298th and had a reputation of denying ordinary supply-oriented requests and thus was dubbed "Mr. No." Mr. Grummish came from the Special Troops Battalion for the existence of the 7753rd Augmentation Detachment which was deactivated in 1949. Mr. Grummish and the extra musicians were then reassigned directly to the 298th following deactivation of the 7753rd. Mr. Grummish commanded the 298th very briefly from 15 February 1950 to 26 March 1950.

WOJG Gordon Booth – junior bandmaster working under Mr. Durbin's supervision.

CWO Wilmont N. Trumbull – commanded the 298th from 27 March 1950 to 1951.

CWO William J. Hershenow – Commanded the 298th from 1951 to April 1952. 298th History document confirmed.

WOJG Edward A. Matlack – served as Associate Bandmaster under Mr. Hershenow. On the 4 Jan 52 roster.

CWO Wilbur J. Moyer – Commanded the 298th from Apr 52 to 1953.

CWO Garreth Fabris – commanded the 7868th Fife & Drum Unit in 1952. The 7868th Fife and Drum Unit numbered as many as 30 men plus one CWO.

CWO Thomas Greening – served as a glider pilot in WWII. Commanded the 298th from 1953 to 1956

CWO Robert C. Lewis – served in 1st Combat Infantry Band during WWII as asst. bandmaster. Band later became Forces Command Band. Commanded the 298th from from 1956 to 1959.

CWO Edward J. Serafin – commanded the 298th from 1959 to 1962.

CWO Benjamin Cortese – commanded the 298th from 1963 to 1966.

CWO Owen Kirby – commanded the 298th from 1967 to 1969.

CWO Howard Vivian – commanded the 298th from 1970 to 1972.

CWO Al Tapia – commanded the 298th from 1972 to 1975.

CWO Richard Saddler – served as a trumpet player with the 298th in the early 1950s. Was one of the first African American soldiers to serve in a newly integrated Army. Served more than 40 years in uniform before retiring. Commanded the 298th from 1975 to 1977.

CWO Danny Jaynes – Commanded the band from 1977 to 1980. Mr. Jaynes is known to have recorded the only known record album of the 298th in 1980.

CWO David Ratliff – served as a trumpet player with the 298th in the mid-1970s. Served more than 30 years in uniform, achieving the status of senior warrant officer bandmaster in the Army. While commanding the 298th, Mr, Ratliff enjoyed the confidence of the command group and was able to rekindle the connection between Einhausen and the 298th. Mr. Ratliff commander of the band from 1980 to 1984. He and his wife Kay adopted a baby girl while in Berlin.

CWO David M. Smith – known as an exceptional musician and conductor. Able to artistically develop the band to very high levels. Commanded the band from 1984 to 1988.

CWO Ronald E. Bucher – commanded the 298th from 1988 to 1992.

CWO Larry Hyatt – commanded the 298th from 1992 to deactivation in September 1994.

Enlisted Bandleaders/First Sergeants (partial list)

Tech Sgt Henry Glaviano
MSG Richard Hawkins
MSG Edward A. Matlock (later appointed as WOJG)
MSG John E. McInturff, Jr. (1952)
1SG Warren "Bix" Bibey
MSG Bob Boden
Tech Sgt Gordon
MSG DiMartino
MSG Nathaniel Riddick
MSG Landon Hipkins
MSG Forest McGlasson
MSG Al Lewis
MSG Ed Green
MSG Juan Martinez del Carmen
MSG Thomas Easley
MSG George O. Pledger
SFC Jessie Wheeler
MSG William von Kamp
MSG Louis B. Hurvitz
1SG Joseph Bates
1SG Joseph Martin
1SG James (Dutch) Perry
1SG Michael van Winkle

About the Author

Allen Lawless retired from the U.S. Army as a euphoniumist in 1995 and returned to civilian life where he is a Quality Assurance Manager in regulated industry. He resides with his wife Margaret in north-central Missouri accompanied by three dogs and three parrots. He continues to perform on euphonium, bass trombone, tuba, tenor trombone, and is presently learning to play the upright bass viol.

Bibliography

(Reuters), E. (1990, June 22). *Checkpoint Charlie Comes In From Cold War Era*. Retrieved June 2, 2014, from LA Times: http://articles.latimes.com/1990-06-22/news/mn-436_1_checkpoint-charlie

Baker, C. (1997). *As Though I Had Wings*. New York: St. Martin's Press.

Cawley, J. (1990, March 22). *Economic Pact Okd By U.S., Poles*. Retrieved June 22, 2014, from Chicago Tribune: http://articles.chicagotribune.com/1990-03-22/news/9001230980_1_border-question-mazowiecki-poland

Connolly, K. (2001, November 13). *Libya Was Behind Berlin Bombing*. Retrieved from The Guardian: http://www.theguardian.com/world/2001/nov/14/kateconnolly

Dowty, A. (1989). *Closed Borders: The Contemporary Assault on Freedom of Movement*. New Haven, CT: Yale University Press.

Durbin, M. (1948). *Unit History, 298th Army Ground Forces Band, 1 Jan-31 Dec 47*. Berlin: Berlin Military Post.

Durbin, M. (1949). *Unit History, 298th Army Band, 1 Jan-31 Dec 48*. Berlin, Germany: Berlin Military Post.

Durbin, M. (1950). *298th Army Band Annual Report, 1949*. Berlin: Berlin Command.

Durbin, M. (1951). *298th Army Band Annual Report, 1950*. Berlin: Berlin Command.

Editor. (n.d.). *15 August 1961*. Retrieved June 14, 2014, from Chronik-der-Mauer: http://www.chronik-der-mauer.de/index.php/de/Start/Index/id/943798

Editor. (1996). *Ten Years After Chernobyl: What Do We Really Know?*

Vienna, Austria: International Atomic Energy Agency.

Editor. (2002). *The Armed Forces School of Music*. Retrieved February 22, 2014, from Willow Grove Park: http://www.wgpark.com/page.asp-pid=16.html

Editor. (2009, July 16). *AFN Berlin Celebrates 25th Anniversary*. Retrieved November 15, 2013, from AFN Berlin: http://www.oocities.org/eureka/Plaza/5246/afn_berlin/25years.htm

Editor. (2011). *30th anniversary of USAFE headquarters bombing*. Retrieved April 2, 2014, from Stars and Stripes: http://www.stripes.com/30th-anniversary-of-usafe-headquarters-bombing-1.153700

Editor. (2011). *Operation Downfall*. Retrieved November 3, 2013, from History Learning Site: http://www.historylearningsite.co.uk/operation_downfall.htm

Editor. (2014, June 24). *Chronology: RIAS-Berlin and the RIAS Berlin Commission*. Retrieved July 19, 2014, from RIAS-Berlin: http://www.riasberlin.de/

Editor. (n.d.). *A Brief History*. Retrieved March 15, 2014, from The Juilliard School: http://www.juilliard.edu/about/brief-history?destination=about/history.php

Editor. (n.d.). *Area History - Camp Crowder*. Retrieved March 22, 2014, from Welcome to Newton County, MO : http://newtoncountymotourism.org/camp-crowder-history.php

Editor. (n.d.). *Army Warrant Officer*. Retrieved May 25, 2014, from About.com US Military: http://usmilitary.about.com/library/milinfo/armyorank/blwo.htm

Editor. (n.d.). *Desegregation of the Armed Forces*. Retrieved July 19,

2014, from Harry S. Truman Library and Museum: http://www.trumanlibrary.org/whistlestop/study_collections/d esegregation/large/index.php

Editor. (n.d.). *Flughafen Berlin-Tempelhof*. Retrieved March 20, 2014, from Wikipedia: http://de.wikipedia.org/wiki/Flughafen_Berlin-Tempelhof

Editor. (January, 12 1989). *NY Times Archives*. Retrieved June 16, 2014, from NY Times: http://www.nytimes.com/1989/01/12/world/hungary-eases-dissent-curbs.html?scp=432&sq=Hungary&st=nyt

Editor. (n.d.). *Peaceful Revolution*. Retrieved June 2, 2014, from Wikipedia: http://en.wikipedia.org/wiki/Peaceful_Revolution

Editor. (n.d.). *Sailing at the 1972 Summer Olympics*. Retrieved June 14, 2014, from Wikipedia: http://en.wikipedia.org/wiki/Sailing_at_the_1972_Summer_Oly mpics

Editor. (n.d.). *Solidarity (Polish trade union)*. Retrieved May 24, 2014, from Wikipedia: http://en.wikipedia.org/wiki/Solidarity_(Polish_trade_union)

Editor. (n.d.). *The History of Fort Lee, Virginia*. Retrieved March 22, 2014, from Answers: http://military.answers.com/army/the-history-of-fort-lee-virginia

Ervin, B. (2005, August). BUSMVA Reunion. (A. Lawless, Interviewer)

Fairlie, I. P., & Sumner, DPhil, D. (2006). *The Other Report on Chernobyl (Torch)*. Berlin: IAEA and WHO.

Fleshman, J. (1986, May 30). Wounded Earn Medals. *Berlin Observer*, pp. 1, 12.

Foster, F. (2011). *United States Army Medals, Badges and Insignia.* Fountain Inn, SC: MOA Press.

Gallo, M. (1997). *The Night of Long Knives - June 29-30 1934.* New York: Da Capo Press.

Gerstenzang, J. (1986, March 28). *U.S. Navy Ends Maneuvers in Gulf of Sidra.* Retrieved from LA Times: http://articles.latimes.com/1986-03-28/news/mn-624_1_u-s-navy

Glaviano, H. P. (1992). *The 156th Infantry Band 1940-1945.* New Orleans, LA: 156, Inc.

Gleason, B. (1990, July 25). Independence Day 1990. *North Star Second Front.* Karstad, MN, USA.

Grummish, C. H. (1948). *History of the 7753rd Augmentation Detachment (298th Army Band).* Berlin: Berlin Military Post.

Harrison, H. M. (2003). *Driving the Soviets Up the Wall: Soviet-East German Relations, 1953-1961.* Princeton, NJ: Princeton University Press.

Heichler, L. (2002, May 30). *I Remember...How Berlin Mourned John F. Kennedy.* Retrieved May 18, 2014, from American Diplomacy: http://www.unc.edu/depts/diplomat/archives_roll/2002_04-06/heichler_berlin/heichler_berlin.html

Hertle, H.-H. (1999). *Chronik des Mauerfalls (Chronicle of the Fall of the Wall). Die dramatische Ereignisse um den 9. November 1989.* Berlin: Ch. Links Verlag.

Howley, F. (1950). *Berlin Command.* Cornwall, NY: Cornwall Press.

Huffman, R. (2011, October 28). *Frankfurt V Corps HQ Bombing Damage #1.* Retrieved April 2, 2014, from Baader-Meinhof.com: http://www.baader-meinhof.com/photo-frankfurt-corps-hq-bombing-damage-1/

Huffman, R. (October, 9 2011). *May 24, 1972 Heidelberg.* Retrieved April
2, 2014, from Baader-Meinhof.com: http://www.baader-
meinhof.com/may-24-1972-heidelberg/

Kempe, F. (2011). *Berlin 1961.* New York: G.P. Putnam's Sons.

Koefod, S. (2013, June 6). *"Dig In, Schneider!".* Retrieved March 22,
2014, from Susan Koefod:
http://susankoefod.com/tag/musicians/

Low, S. M. (1945, September 25). 82nd Opens Club with Big Shindig.
Berlin Sentinel, p. 3.

Markham, J. M. (1985, November 25). *Bombing at PX in Frankfurt
Wounds 34.* Retrieved April 2, 2014, from NY Times:
http://www.nytimes.com/1985/11/25/world/bombing-at-px-in-
frankfurt-wounds-34.html

Markley, G. (1994, July 15). Gone, But Never to be Forgotten. *Berlin
Observer*, pp. 1, 4.

Montgomery, N. (2005, August 5). *Baader-Meinhof Gang Attacked U.S.
Troops, Bases in 1970s-1980s.* Retrieved May 14, 2014, from
Stars and Stripes: http://www.stripes.com/news/baader-
meinhof-gang-attacked-u-s-troops-bases-in-1970s-1980s-
1.36617

Moore, W. (1949, June 22). Discontinuance of Unit. *General Orders #35.*
Berlin, Germany: Berlin Military Post.

Mullener, E. (1995, July 16). Playing at Potsdam. *New Orleans Times-
Picayune.*

Mynz, R. (1995). *Typology and Geography of European Mass Migration.*
Retrieved April 14, 2014, from United Nations Population

Information Network:
http://www.un.org/popin/confcon/milan/plen3/3rdplen.html

Nesbit, R. C., & van Acker, G. (2007). *The Flight of Rudolf Hess.*
Charleston, SC: The History Press.

Puddington, A. (n.d.). *How American Unions Helped Solidarity Win.*
Retrieved June 14, 2014, from Videofact.com:
http://www.videofact.com/help_for_solidarity.html

Reinert, E. a. (2008, April 14). *The Marshall Plan at 60: The General's
Successful War on Poverty.* Retrieved March 18, 2014, from UN
Chronicle:
http://web.archive.org/web/20080414103548/http://www.un.
org/Pubs/chronicle/2008/

Reinert, H. (2005). *Berlin Memories.* Vashon, WA.

Roberts, G. (1985, August 11). Boogie Woogie Bugle Boy. *Dixie
Magazine.*

RonaldV. (2013, April 26). *Berlin-Tempelhof.* Retrieved from Abandoned,
Forgotten, and Little-Known Airfields in Europe:
http://www.forgottenairfields.com/germany/berlin/berlin-
tempelhof-s434.html

Rosato, F. (1992). My Story. New Orleans, LA.

Smith, W. (1945, October 27). Currency Exchange Control. *Berlin
Sentinel*, pp. 3-4.

Stacey, W. E. (1988). *The Nicholson Incident.* Heidelberg, Germany: HQs,
US Army Europe and 7th Army.

Stivers, D. W. (2003). Victors and Vanquished: Americans as Occupiers in
Berlin, 1945-49. Ft. Leavenworth, KS: None - Discussion Paper.

Tagliabue, J. (1985, August 9). *CAR BOMB KILLS 2 ON A U.S. AIR BASE IN*

WEST GERMANY. Retrieved April 2, 2014, from NY Times: http://www.nytimes.com/1985/08/09/world/car-bomb-kills-2-on-a-us-air-base-in-west-germany.html

Tusa, A. (1997). *The Last Division - A History of Berlin 1945-1989.* Reading, MA: Addison-Wesley.

Unknown. (2004, July 21). *Victims in the Night of the Long Knives.* Retrieved September 19, 2005, from Axis History Factbook: http://www.axishistory.com/index.pho?id=4558

von Bronewski, R. (n.d.). *History of Clay Headquarters.* Retrieved July 5, 2014, from Berlin Brigade Memories: http://www.berlin-brigade.de/us-ins/clay-headquarters.html

Youtube), U. (. (Director). (n.d.). *Schabowski's Note* [Motion Picture].

End Notes

[1]Henry P. Glaviano, a veteran of the 298th and its precursor, the 156th Infantry Band, is the sole source of information for what follows in this and subsequent chapters that discuss the 156th Infantry Band, the London Base Command Band, and the ETO Band. His book entitled *The 156th Infantry Band 1940 – 1945*, published by 156, Inc. (a non-profit organization), and copyrighted on November 27, 1992, Library of Congress catalog number 95-92605, is a volume that documents this period of the 156th Infantry Band.

[2] Rosato, "My Story"

[3] Dixie Magazine (of the New Orleans Times-Picayune), cover story, August 11, 1985

[4] Mullener, the New Orleans Times-Picayune, July 16, 1995

[5] Tusa, pg. 11

[6] Tusa, pg. 13

[7] Tusa, pg. 13

[8] Tusa, pg. 13

[9] Tusa, pg. 13

[10] Howley, pg. 70-71

[11] Reinert, "Berlin Memories"

[12] Berlin *Sentinel*, October 27, 1945, pg. 3

[13] American military confiscated this building and used it for the "Office of Military Government – US" (OMGUS). It later became the central headquarters for the Berlin Command. The entire complex was renamed "Clay Headquarters" after General Lucius Clay. From the Berlin-Brigade.com web site: *"The Clay Headquarters compound was built for the German Air Force in the years 1936-38. Originally it was one os seven Luftwaffe district headquarters, Luftgaukommando III, reporting directly to the Air Minister (Goering). In 1943, the seven air-defense districts on German soil were consolidated into one Luftgaukommando-Mitte, headquartered on the same site. The new command was responsible for the air defense of the German homeland, including control of air defense artillery. Contrary to persistent belief, it was never Marshal Goering's headquarters."*

[14] http://www.historylearningsite.co.uk/operation_downfall.htm

[15] *Berlin Today*, August 1969

[16] RIAS website www.riasberlin.de/rcom-1/rcus-1-main.html

[17] Baker, pg. 7

[18] Howley, pg. 131

[19] Howley, pg. 156

[20] Howley, pg. 156

[21] http://web.archive.org/web/20080414103548/http://www.un.org/Pubs/chronicle/2008/webarticles/080103_marshallplan.html;
"The Marshall Plan at 60: The General's Successful War on Poverty" by Erik Reinert and Jomo K.S.

[22] Dietrich, pg. 106

[23] Durbin, *Unit History, 298th Army Ground Forces Band, 1 Jan-31 Dec 47*

[24] Durbin, *Unit History, 298th Army Band, 1 Jan-31 Dec 48*

[25] Kempe, pg. 244

[26] The 7753rd Augmentation Detachment was activated per General Order #5, HQ Berlin Military Post, dated 20 May 48, under Table of Distribution and Allowances 303-1344 at Berlin Military Post on 25 May 48. This information extracted from "History of the 7753rd Augmentation Detachment (298th Army Band)," written by Carroll H. Grummish.

[27] General Order #35, HQ Berlin Military Post, 22 Jun 49

[28] See Reinhard von Bronewski's website at www.berlin-brigade.de for more information.

[29] Gallo, pg. 267.

[30] http://www.axishistory.com/index.php?id-4558, obtained from this site on 9/19/05

[31] http://www.trumanlibrary.org/whistlestop/study_collections/desegregation/large/index.php

[32] http://www.juilliard.edu/about/brief-history?destination=about/history.php

[33] http://www.wgpark.com/page.asp-pid=16.html

[34] http://newtoncountymotourism.org/camp-crowder-history.php

[35] http://military.answers.com/army/the-history-of-fort-lee-virginia

[36] *http://susankoefod.com/tag/musicians/*. The European Band School mentioned by Schneider was located in Eastman Barracks, an Army facility neighboring the concentration camp in Dachau, near Munich. Eastman Barracks was an active U.S. Army facility from 1948 to 1973. The Music School itself was in place from the late 1940s until the mid-1950s.

[37] Durbin, *298th Army Band Annual Report, 1949*

[38] Durbin, *298th Army Band Annual Report, 1950*

[39] Foster, pg. 14

[40] Tusa, pg. 74

[41] Mynz, Rainer (1995), *Where Did They All Come From? Typology and Geography of European Mass Migration In the Twentieth Century*, EUROPEAN POPULATION CONFERENCE CONGRESS EUROPEAN DE DEMOGRAPHE, United Nations Population Division, pg. 2.2.1.

[42] Dowty, Alan (1989), Closed Borders: The Contemporary Assault on Freedom of Movement, Yale University Press, ISBN 0-300-04498-4, pg. 122

[43] Harrison, Hope Millard (2003), Driving the Soviets Up the Wall: Soviet-East German Relations, 1953–1961, Princeton University Press, ISBN 0-691-09678-3, pg. 100

[44] Kempe, pg. 4

[45] Dowty, pg. 122.

[46] Tusa, pg. 272.

[47] Tusa, pg. 271.

[48] Tusa, pg. 271.

[49] Tusa, pg. 278.

[50] Tusa, pg. 281.

[51] Tusa, pg. 282.

[52] http://www.chronik-der-mauer.de/index.php/de/Start/Index/id/943798

[53] Kempe, pg. 450.

[54] Kempe, pg. 449.

[55] Kempe, pg. 450.

[56] Kempe, pg. 454.

[57] Kempe, pg. 468.

[58] Kempe, pg. 473.

[59] Kempe, pg. 478.

[60] Heichler, "I Remember…How Berlin Mourned John F. Kennedy," published in American Diplomacy, http://www.unc.edu/depts/diplomat/archives_roll/2002_04-06/heichler_berlin/heichler_berlin.html

[61] Heichler, pg. 1.

[62] North Star *Second Front* newspaper, Karlstad, Minnesota, summer 1990. [Author's Note: Bruce is referring to the United States Military Liaison Mission (USMLM). Periodically, the 298th supported a garden party hosted by the USMLM commanders. Prior to Reunification, the 298th traveling to Potsdam, East Germany, required coordination through the U.S. State Department and the Soviets/East Germans.]

[63] http://www.stripes.com/news/baader-meinhof-gang-attacked-u-s-troops-bases-in-1970s-1980s-1.36617

[64] http://www.baader-meinhof.com/photo-frankfurt-corps-hq-bombing-damage-1/

[65] http://www.baader-meinhof.com/tag/campbell-barracks/

[66] http://www.stripes.com/30th-anniversary-of-usafe-headquarters-bombing-1.153700

[67] http://www.nytimes.com/1985/08/09/world/car-bomb-kills-2-on-a-us-air-base-in-west-germany.html

[68] http://www.nytimes.com/1985/11/25/world/bombing-at-px-in-frankfurt-wounds-34.html

[69] http://www.theberlinobserver.com/archive/1986V42/V42_N21_may_30.pdf

[70] http://articles.latimes.com/1986-03-25/news/mn-2_1_patrol-boat

[71] http://www.theguardian.com/world/2001/nov/14/kateconnolly

[72] Ibid

[73] William E. Stacy, "The Nicholson Incident –A Case Study of U.S.-Soviet Negotiations," HQ U.S. Army, Europe and 7th Army, Military History Office, June 1988, pg. 7 (declassified on 25 Oct 04)

[74] http://www.iaea.org/Publications/Booklets/Chernoten/facts.html

[75] http://www.chernobylreport.org/?p=summary

[76] http://www.forgottenairfields.com/germany/berlin/berlin-tempelhof-s434.html

[77] http://de.wikipedia.org/wiki/Flughafen_Berlin-Tempelhof

[78] http://www.ihr.org/jhr/v13/v13n1p24_Hess.html

[79] Nesbit and van Acker, 2011, pp. 95-97; 100.

[80] Aleksander Smolar, "'Self-limiting Revolution": Poland 1970-89', in Adam Roberts and Timothy Garton Ash (eds.), Civil Resistance and Power Politics: The Experience of Non-violent Action from Gandhi to the Present, Oxford University Press, 2009, ISBN 978-0-19-955201-6, pp. 127-43.

[81] http://www.videofact.com/help_for_solidarity.html

[82] http://www.nytimes.com/1989/01/12/world/hungary-eases-dissent-curbs.html?scp=432&sq=Hungary&st=nyt

[83] Cate, Curtis (1978). The Ides of August: The Berlin Wall Crisis—1961. New York City: M. Evans

[84] According to tradition, the Olympic yachting events must be held on the open sea. As Munich is land-locked, these events were held in Kiel Schilksee, in the north of Germany. http://en.wikipedia.org/wiki/Sailing_at_the_1972_Summer_Olympics

[85] http://www.chronik-der-mauer.de/index.php/de/Start/Index/id/754539

[86] http://www.chronik-der-mauer.de/index.php/de/Start/Index/id/754544

[87] http://www.chronik-der-mauer.de/index.php/de/Start/Index/id/754545

[88] http://www.chronik-der-mauer.de/index.php/de/Start/Index/id/652129

[89] http://www.chronik-der-mauer.de/index.php/de/Start/Index/id/652131

[90] http://articles.latimes.com/keyword/egon-krenz

[91] http://www.chronik-der-mauer.de/index.php/de/Start/Index/id/652138

[92] http://www.chronik-der-mauer.de/index.php/de/Media/VideoPopup/field/audio_video/id/40225/oldAction/Index/oldId/652138/oldModule/Start/page/0

[93] Documentary in Four parts, "Schabowski's Note," The History Channel. http://www.youtube.com/watch?v=bA14hAuQuLc

[94] Hertle, Hans-Hermann 9. November 1989, 18.00 Uhr: Schabowskis Auftritt; http://www.chronik-der-mauer.de/index.php/de/Start/Index/id/652138

[95] http://www.chronik-der-mauer.de/index.php/de/Start/Index/id/652138

[96] http://www.chronik-der-mauer.de/index.php/de/Media/VideoPopup/field/audio_video/id/40225/oldAction/Index/oldId/652138/oldModule/Start/page/0

[97] http://www.chronik-der-mauer.de/index.php/de/Start/Index/id/652138

[98] http://articles.chicagotribune.com/1990-03-22/news/9001230980_1_border-question-mazowiecki-poland

[99] http://articles.latimes.com/1990-06-22/news/mn-436_1_checkpoint-charlie

[100] Berlin Observer, 15 Jul 94

[101] As the Bonn government provided operational funding for all U.S. Army units in Berlin save for weaponry and tactical equipment, the value of musical equipment and related items was assessed in Deutsche-marks, not U.S. dollars.